Mastering Kong API Gateway
Strategic Management, Security Enhancements, and Performance Scaling

Nova Trex

Published by Wang Press

For permissions and other inquiries, write to:
P.O. Box 3132, Framingham, MA 01701, USA

Contents

4

10 Best Practices and Troubleshooting 265

Introduction

In the rapidly evolving landscape of modern software development, Application Programming Interfaces (APIs) hold a pivotal role, acting as the vital conduits through which disparate software components communicate effectively. APIs empower applications to harness functionalities across a multitude of services, transcending traditional boundaries and enabling seamless integration. As organizations increasingly depend on APIs to drive innovation and deliver value, the imperatives of strategic management, robust security, and scalable infrastructure for these interfaces become not just desirable but essential. This book, "Mastering Kong API Gateway: Strategic Management, Security Enhancements, and Performance Scaling," endeavors to address these imperatives comprehensively by delving into the powerful capabilities of the Kong API Gateway—a renowned leader in the arena of API management solutions.

Kong API Gateway offers an extensive toolkit designed for developing, managing, monitoring, and fortifying APIs. It efficiently facilitates the integration of microservices while ensuring that APIs are both protected from potential threats and capable of accommodating substantial traffic loads. Its lightweight architecture combined with a rich feature set makes Kong an optimal choice for developers and enterprises aiming to implement scalable and secure microservice environments.

The objective of this book is to furnish readers with an in-depth understanding of the Kong API Gateway, encompassing everything from foundational concepts to sophisticated functionalities. It spans detailed guidance on installation and configuration, an incisive exploration of its architecture, and insightful examination of its capabilities for routing and proxying requests. Central themes include API security enhancements, custom plugin development, efficient load balancing, and comprehensive monitoring, equipping you with the knowledge essential to refine and optimize your API management strategy.

Structured to unfold progressively from the fundamental principles of API gateways to the intricate workings of Kong, the book is replete with step-by-step tutorials, pragmatic real-world examples, and industry best practices that augment learning and provide real-world application value. Furthermore, it addresses prevalent challenges and techniques for troubleshooting, empowering you with the skills necessary to manage and resolve issues proficiently.

By the conclusion of this book, you will be proficient in the multifaceted functionalities of Kong API Gateway and poised to leverage its strategic capabilities for secure, efficient, and scalable API management in your projects. Whether your role is that of a software developer, a system architect, or an IT professional, this book aims to be an indispensable resource in your journey to master the strategic management of APIs.

Chapter 1

Introduction to API Gateways and Kong

API gateways have become essential components in the landscape of software architecture, serving as intermediaries that facilitate communication between clients and services. This chapter delves into the core concepts of APIs and their significance in the development ecosystem. It further explains the role of API gateways in enhancing API management by providing functionalities such as routing, security, and traffic management. The focus then shifts to Kong API Gateway, highlighting its capabilities and the advantages it offers in handling complex API interactions. By the end of this chapter, readers will gain a solid understanding of the foundational elements that make Kong an indispensable tool for modern API management.

1.1 Understanding APIs

APIs, or Application Programming Interfaces, are vital components in modern software development, acting as intermediaries that enable communication between different software applications. At their core,

APIs define the set of rules and protocols governing how one piece of software interacts with another. This interaction can occur between applications within a single system or across systems, potentially spanning global networks.

An API can be understood as an abstraction layer that exposes certain functionality of a system or service to the outside world in a structured manner. By providing a defined interface, APIs allow developers to leverage existing functionality and services without needing to comprehend the underlying complexities. This encapsulation of processes allows for greater modularity and scalability in software design.

The fundamental concept of an API revolves around its capacity to facilitate requests and responses between clients (requesters of services) and servers (providers of services). This interaction typically follows a client-server model, where the client sends a request to the server, and the server processes this request and returns the appropriate response. Here, an API dictates the nature of the requests allowed, the structure of data exchanged, and the response types expected.

In the context of web development, RESTful (Representational State Transfer) APIs and SOAP (Simple Object Access Protocol) APIs are two predominant paradigms. RESTful APIs use HTTP methods and HTTP status codes, and are known for their statelessness, scalability, and simplicity. They operate over HTTP and rely on JSON or XML to structure data. A RESTful API might use standard HTTP methods, such as GET, POST, PUT, DELETE, to perform operations on resources, which are identified through URIs (Uniform Resource Identifiers). Consider the following example, which illustrates a typical HTTP request to a RESTful API:

```
import requests

url = "https://api.example.com/resource/1"
response = requests.get(url)

if response.status_code == 200:
    data = response.json()
    print(data)
else:
    print("Request failed with status code:", response.status_code)
```

In the example above, a GET request is made to retrieve a resource from the API. The request is issued using the requests library in Python, which is a powerful tool for HTTP operations. The response is checked for a status code of 200, indicating a successful request, and the JSON payload is parsed and printed.

SOAP APIs, on the other hand, are more rigid, using XML exclusively for message formatting and providing a protocol for sending requests and responses. SOAP APIs require more overhead and are often chosen for their robustness and capability to handle complex operations.

Beyond the HTTP protocol, APIs can also facilitate communication through various protocols such as gRPC, AMQP, or custom protocols for specialized systems. In each case, the API functions as the defining interface that guides developers in integrating and leveraging different systems cohesively.

Another crucial aspect of APIs is their role in ensuring interoperability between disparate systems. By abstracting how data is exchanged and processes are initiated, APIs enable applications written in different programming languages or hosted on different platforms to function seamlessly together. This cross-platform operability is particularly essential in cloud computing environments, where diverse applications need to coordinate and exchange data efficiently.

The proliferation of APIs has ushered in an era termed the API economy, where businesses leverage APIs to achieve innovative integrations and new revenue streams. Companies such as Amazon, Google, and Facebook provide extensive APIs that allow developers to integrate their services into applications, expanding their reach and functionality while driving engagement and monetization.

Security is a paramount concern in the design and deployment of APIs. Authentication and authorization mechanisms, such as OAuth 2.0, JWT (JSON Web Tokens), and API keys, are commonly employed to safeguard API endpoints and ensure that only authorized entities can interact with the service. Consider the following example of implementing OAuth 2.0 in an API interaction:

```
import requests

token_url = "https://auth.example.com/oauth2/token"
client_id = "your_client_id"
client_secret = "your_client_secret"
auth_response = requests.post(token_url, data={
    'grant_type': 'client_credentials',
    'client_id': client_id,
```

```
    'client_secret': client_secret
})

access_token = auth_response.json().get("access_token")

api_url = "https://api.example.com/secure-data"
headers = {
    'Authorization': f'Bearer {access_token}'
}
secured_response = requests.get(api_url, headers=headers)

if secured_response.status_code == 200:
    secure_data = secured_response.json()
    print(secure_data)
else:
    print("Access failed with status code:", secured_response.status_code)
```

The mechanism demonstrated here involves obtaining an OAuth 2.0 token using client credentials, which serves as a secure means of accessing protected resources via APIs. This process is essential to maintain security standards and control access in a robust manner.

APIs also necessitate comprehensive documentation, which is critical for developers to understand their capabilities and intricacies. Tools like Swagger and Postman facilitate API documentation and testing, providing user-friendly interfaces for developers to explore and interact with APIs, ensuring they implement them correctly and efficiently.

In enterprise systems, APIs play a significant role in microservices architectures, where applications are decomposed into a suite of loosely coupled services that communicate through APIs. This architecture fosters agility, scalability, and resilience, supporting organizations in rapidly adapting to changing requirements and scaling their operations efficiently.

APIs also enable significant advancements in the realm of Internet of Things (IoT), where numerous devices communicate and coordinate tasks via APIs. This interconnected environment harnesses APIs to facilitate seamless interactions and data exchanges between sensors, devices, and backend systems, empowering functionalities such as smart homes, industrial automation, and predictive maintenance.

APIs are indispensable in modern software ecosystems, driving innovation, extensibility, and integration. By allowing diverse applications to communicate and work together efficiently, APIs underpin the agile, scalable, and interconnected world of computing today. Understanding their principles, operation, and implications is crucial for any developer engaged in contemporary software development practices. The next section will delve deeper into the concept of API gateways, a pivotal innovation that further enhances the management and utilization of APIs.

1.2   What is an API Gateway

An API Gateway is a crucial component in the architecture of modern distributed systems, serving as a single entry point for clients accessing APIs in a microservices architecture. By acting as an intermediary between clients and the backend services, an API Gateway simplifies the client-side architecture, reduces network latency, and provides enhanced control over API interactions.

The evolution of software architecture from monolithic systems to microservices necessitated a means to manage the complex web of service interactions efficiently. Microservices architectures involve several independent services that fulfill specific business capabilities and communicate with one another frequently. In such an environment, the role of the API Gateway becomes indispensable as it provides a streamlined, efficient, and secure way to interact with multiple services.

Functionally, an API Gateway handles several cross-cutting concerns, which allows backend services to focus solely on business logic. These responsibilities may include request routing, caching, authentication and authorization, load balancing, rate limiting, and monitoring. By consolidating these features within an API Gateway, it abstracts the complexities of interaction from the client-side code, allowing developers to maintain focus on the user experience aspects.

The concept of request routing is central to an API Gateway's functionality. When a client makes a request, the gateway inspects the request, determines the correct backend service or services that can fulfill the request, and then dispatches it accordingly. By doing so, it reduces the complexity for the client, obviating the need to manage multiple endpoints. Consider the following pseudocode illustrating simple request routing:

```
function routeRequest(request) {
```

```
if (request.path.startsWith("/users")) {
    forwardRequestTo("UserService", request);
} else if (request.path.startsWith("/orders")) {
    forwardRequestTo("OrderService", request);
} else {
    return "404 Not Found";
}
}
```

Here, the gateway determines the appropriate service based on the request path and forwards the request to the corresponding service endpoint, ensuring that client-side complexity is minimized.

Caching is another critical feature provided by an API Gateway. By caching frequently requested data, it reduces the need to call backend services repeatedly, lowering response times and improving performance. Strategies for caching can be defined based on cache-control headers, time-to-live (TTL) configurations, or customized application logic.

APIs are often exposed to public networks, hence security is a major concern that gateways manage predominantly through authentication and authorization mechanisms. API Gateways can enforce security protocols like OAuth 2.0, JWT, and API keys at a single choke point, thereby simplifying the security model across numerous services. For example, they might intercept incoming requests and verify JWT tokens as follows:

```
import jwt

secret_key = "your_secret_key"

def isAuthenticated(request):
    try:
        token = request.headers.get("Authorization").split(" ")[1]
        decoded = jwt.decode(token, secret_key, algorithms=["HS256"])
        return True if decoded else False
    except Exception as e:
        print("Authentication failed:", e)
        return False
```

In this context, the gateway parses and verifies JWT tokens supplied with client requests to ensure that only authenticated users are permitted access to sensitive resources. Such mechanisms play a vital role in maintaining the integrity and confidentiality of client interactions.

Load balancing is another essential capability of an API Gateway, directing traffic intelligently among instances of backend services to optimize resource utilization and improve application resilience. By distributing requests effectively, the API Gateway helps maintain service availability and performance, which is especially critical under conditions of varying loads.

Moreover, API Gateways enforce rate limiting and throttling policies, preventing abuse and ensuring equitable use of resources across multiple clients. By limiting the number of requests a client can make in a given period, the API Gateway can mitigate the risk of denial-of-service attacks and ensure fair resource distribution.

Observability is significantly enhanced by an API Gateway, which can log requests and responses, calculate metrics, and provide insights into API usage patterns. By doing so, it enables administrators to monitor application performance, detect anomalies, and gain insights that can inform scaling and optimization decisions.

API Gateways can also support transformations, allowing data to be formatted or enriched as it passes between client and service. These transformations may involve protocol translation, message enrichment, data conversion between JSON and XML, or other modifications required to ensure compliance with service and client expectations.

As systems scale, having a single cohesive management point like an API Gateway greatly simplifies deployment and development processes. They facilitate easier versioning of APIs, enabling developers to introduce new API versions while maintaining backward compatibility.

Selecting the right API Gateway involves evaluating factors such as ease of integration with existing systems, supported protocols, scalability options, security features, and community support. Widely used frameworks and tools such as Kong, AWS API Gateway, Apigee, and NGINX are popular choices, each providing unique advantages tailored to different use-case scenarios.

In distributed systems architecture, API Gateways function as facilitators of interaction and arbiters of policy. Their integration into microservices environments exemplifies a critical evolution in how modern software systems are constructed and operated. An effective API Gateway not only simplifies client-side architecture by providing a single point of access but also enhances performance, security, and management of the underlying services.

Through their numerous functionalities and capabilities, API Gateways contribute substantially to the success of service-oriented architectures by enabling agile, scalable, and resilient systems. Understanding and implementing them correctly are key aspects of leveraging microservices to deliver high-performance, secure, and maintainable applications that align with the needs of today's digital landscape. The following section will explore the specific implementation and benefits of using the Kong API Gateway in modern software environments.

1.3   Overview of Kong API Gateway

Kong API Gateway is a prominent open-source platform designed to manage and control APIs, focusing on scalability and flexibility. Originally developed at Mashape, Kong has rapidly emerged as a versatile and powerful tool in API management frameworks, underpinned by robust community support and enterprise backing. Its modular architecture, extensibility, and suite of functionalities have made it a popular choice for managing APIs in microservices environments.

Kong functions as a layer sitting between clients and backend services, subsuming the responsibilities typically associated with API Gateways, such as routing, load balancing, authentication, and monitoring. What distinguishes Kong is its flexibility to be employed in diverse use cases, ranging from simple API gateway configurations to complex API management solutions across hybrid and multi-cloud environments.

Central to Kong's architecture is its ability to natively integrate with various data stores, such as PostgreSQL and Cassandra, to persist configuration and state. This capability empowers Kong to operate in distributed setups, enabling high availability and horizontal scaling.

Built on top of NGINX, Kong leverages NGINX's high-performance, event-driven architecture to efficiently route requests and manage network traffic. The integration with NGINX also facilitates impressive throughput and low latency, vital for high-demand systems. Kong further enhances this base with LuaJIT, a just-in-time compiler that allows dynamic processing and customization of request and response cycles via plugins.

A crucial aspect of Kong's functionality is its support for an extensive range of plugins, which are instrumental in extending and tailoring its core capabilities. These plugins can be used for authentication, rate limiting, logging, and transformations. They can be either community-contributed or custom-developed, allowing enterprises to address specific needs and integrate proprietary solutions. Here is an example illustrating plugin configuration in Kong:

```
{
  "name": "rate-limiting",
  "config": {
    "minute": 20,
    "hour": 500,
    "policy": "local"
  }
}
```

The JSON configuration above demonstrates setting up a rate limiting plugin that constrains requests to 20 per minute and 500 per hour, applying the "local" policy. This showcases Kong's ability to handle complex rate limiting scenarios flexibly.

Kong equips engineers with an intuitive Admin API, presenting a RESTful interface to perform configuration and management tasks programmatically. This functionality is highly beneficial for automation, enabling DevOps teams to incorporate Kong configuration management into continuous integration/continuous deployment (CI/CD) pipelines effortlessly. Consider the following example of scripting API interactions using CURL:

```
curl -i -X POST http://localhost:8001/services/ \
--data "name=my_service" \
--data "url=http://my.upstream.service"

curl -i -X POST http://localhost:8001/services/my_service/routes \
--data "paths[]=/my-path"
```

The commands create a service in Kong and register a route pointing to the backend service at a specified URL. Leveraging Kong's Admin API in this manner allows rapid provisioning and alteration of API endpoints, consistent with agile development methodologies.

Kong offers a Developer Portal, geared towards enabling external developers to explore and utilize APIs effectively. This feature includes capabilities such as API documentation, testing tools, and self-service registration, facilitating developer onboarding and empowering API consumers to integrate with services seamlessly.

For enterprises with specific security and compliance requirements, Kong Enterprise Edition provides additional functionalities, such as fine-grained access controls, service-level agreements (SLAs), and analytics dashboards. These enhancements position Kong EE as a comprehensive API management solution for organizations aiming to align with industry regulations and corporate governance mandates.

Kong's ecosystem further includes support for service meshes through Kuma and its associated universal control plane, which extends API management capabilities into the service mesh realm. This effectively addresses the needs of organizations deploying decentralized applications requiring service-to-service communication security, observability, and traffic control.

Kong's flexibility extends to its deployment options. It can be installed on-premises, in cloud environments, or as part of container orchestrations using Docker and Kubernetes. This versatility ensures that Kong can accommodate the specific infrastructural peculiarities and deployment preferences of diverse organizations without altering its core functionality.

In Kubernetes environments, Kong can operate as an ingress controller, routing and managing traffic for Kubernetes-native applications effectively. This integration allows developers to apply robust API management policies at the ingress level, harnessing Kubernetes' orchestration capabilities and Kong's API management strengths seamlessly.

An intrinsic architectural advantage of Kong is its asynchronous event loop model, powered by NGINX and tuned via LuaJIT. This ensures Kong can handle massive concurrent requests with low latency and minimal resource footprint, which is critical in high-performance systems that demand rapid scale and adaptability.

Kong's commitment to open source and active contribution from a vibrant developer community promotes continuous improvement and innovation. This collaboration fosters a shared repository of plugins, tools, and documentation catering to diverse API management challenges, providing an ever-expanding suite of resources for enterprises deploying Kong.

Security is foundational to Kong's design, with built-in support for enforcing rigorous authentication and authorization mechanisms. It supports OAuth 2.0, LDAP, HMAC, and mTLS, among others, offering several avenues for safeguarding API endpoints. By acting as a security layer, Kong ensures data integrity and privacy, which is crucial for industries operating under strict data protection regulations.

Through detailed telemetry and logging features, Kong enables comprehensive monitoring and analytics, offering insights into API usage patterns, health, and performance. This data-driven approach allows DevOps teams to optimize API interaction strategies, forecast traffic patterns, and refine service delivery dynamics.

Kong's prowess in handling microservices use cases positions it as a strategic tool for digital transformation, where organizations transition to agile, cloud-native operational models. Its deployment accelerates the adoption of microservices, promoting modularity, scalability, and continuous delivery paradigms.

In summary, Kong API Gateway represents an articulate fusion of performance, extensibility, and community-driven innovation. Its attributes as a flexible, robust, and secure gateway make it a compelling option for enterprises pursuing excellence in API management. The subsequent section will address the key benefits of adopting Kong, elucidating why it remains an artifact of choice in modern API ecosystems.

1.4 Key Benefits of Using Kong

Kong API Gateway has become a leading choice for organizations looking to enhance their API management capabilities. The reasons for its widespread adoption are manifold, combining the layers of technical robustness, operational efficiency, and strategic enhancement that Kong provides to its users. Here, we delve into the key benefits conferred by implementing Kong as part of an API management strategy, unpacking each aspect with detailed examination.

The primary advantage of Kong lies in its high performance and scalability. Built on NGINX, Kong inherits the ability to manage vast quantities of requests with minimal latency. This performance optimization is central to its architecture, allowing it to efficiently process concurrent requests. Kong's lightweight, asynchronous event-loop model, powered by LuaJIT, contributes to its capability to scale dynamically alongside client demand, which is essential for mission-critical applications needing rapid adaptation to workload changes.

Scalability is further enhanced through Kong's native support for clustering. By deploying Kong nodes in a cluster configuration, organizations can achieve horizontal scaling, ensuring system reliability and resiliency. This setup accommodates growth by adding nodes seamlessly, distributing traffic efficiently without significant architectural changes. Here is an example of how Kong can be clustered using PostgreSQL as a database and announcing nodes over a shared local network:

```
kong start -c /etc/kong/kong.conf \
  --database=postgres \
  --db-url=postgres://user:password@host/dbname \
  --cluster-tls=off \
  --cluster-listen=0.0.0.0:8005
```

The configuration demonstrated above initiates a Kong node with PostgreSQL as its data store, alongside parameters necessary for clustering. This process epitomizes the ease with which Kong supports scale-oriented architectures.

Kong's extensibility is another significant merit. Through its plugin framework, Kong offers the ability to customize and enhance functionality across numerous domains such as security, logging, traffic control, and transformation. Kong plugins can be developed in Lua, allowing seamless integration into the core pipeline of API requests. This extensibility ensures that organizations can tailor Kong's behavior to align precisely with business requirements, adding proprietary logic where necessary.

One of the most compelling plugins is the JWT (JSON Web Token) authentication plugin, which solidifies security layers by enabling stateless token verification. This aligns with zero-trust models prevalent in modern security architectures, demanding validation for each access attempt. Below is a brief illustration of how to activate the JWT plugin:

```
curl -i -X POST http://localhost:8001/services/{service}/plugins \
  --data "name=jwt" \
  --data "config.claims_to_verify=exp"
```

In this case, a simple command attaches the JWT plugin to a service, stipulating the claims needing validation, which in this scenario includes expiration time. This approach reinforces security by integrating effortless token checking into the request cycle.

Kong's reinforcement of security extends beyond JWT, supporting a multitude of authentication methods including OAuth 2.0, Basic Authentication, mTLS, and HMAC. Each method provides a guardrail against unauthorized access, empowering developers to enforce stringent access control policies, tailored to their precise security postures.

By integrating with OpenTracing standards, Kong facilitates comprehensive monitoring and tracing of requests through systems. This visibility is pivotal in assisting teams with troubleshooting performance bottlenecks and producing insights to enhance operational efficiencies. Root cause analysis and system debugging are propelled by accessing detailed traces and metrics, captured and analyzed through platforms like Jaeger or Zipkin, seamlessly interfacing with Kong's tracing capabilities.

Another intrinsic benefit of using Kong is its robust traffic management capabilities. Kong can efficiently handle rate limiting, enabling the definition of policies that govern request quotas for specific users or applications. This feature is illustrated as follows:

```
curl -i -X POST http://localhost:8001/services/{service}/plugins \
  --data "name=rate-limiting" \
  --data "config.minute=10"
```

Invoking the rate limiting plugin allows administrators to restrict users to a fixed number of requests per minute, promoting fair use policies and protecting backend systems from overconsumption or denial-of-service attacks.

Moreover, Kong delivers granular observability and logging capabilities, seamlessly integrating with logging platforms like ELK Stack, Splunk, and DataDog. The access to real-time metrics and synthetic transactions empowers organizations to cultivate a data-driven approach to API performance management. Such insights provide a cornerstone for strategic decision-making and planning.

Kong also excels in enabling distributed tracing and monitoring. Aligning with tools such as Prometheus and Grafana, Kong offers capacities for real-time system health monitoring and diagnostics. This integration drives proactive infrastructure management, empowering DevOps practices that prioritize system reliability and availability.

Multi-datacenter resiliency can be harnessed through Kong's architectural support for geographically distributed deployments. This adds an extra layer of redundancy and disaster recovery capability, essential for business continuity in large enterprises operating across multiple locales.

Efficient API documentation is vital for any API ecosystem, and Kong complements this requirement by integrating with tools like Insomnia and Swagger. It allows developers and API consumers to explore and understand APIs through interactive documentation, test endpoints, and gain deeper insights into service capabilities.

Perhaps one of the more strategic benefits of Kong is its people-oriented open-source foundation, backed by a vibrant community and steered by active commercial sponsorship from Kong Inc. This blend ensures innovation continuity, access to a repository of best practices, and ongoing enhancements that keep Kong poised at the forefront of API management technology.

For organizations on Kubernetes, Kong's ability to function as an Ingress Controller provides seamless API management across containerized deployments. This benefits businesses by leveraging Kubernetes' container orchestration capabilities with Kong's API management controls, achieving a unified platform for hosting, exposing, and managing microservice APIs.

In summation, the breadth of Kong's advantages is deeply entrenched in its ability to deliver exceptional performance, enhanced security, managerial oversight, and strategic agility. The ecosystem it creates improves not only technical architectures but also provides a significant engineering edge that aligns with the current digital transformation trajectory many enterprises pursue. Understanding these benefits underscores why Kong continues to be an essential tool in the panorama of modern API ecosystems, driving efficiency and innovation. The upcoming section will delve deeper into how Kong fits into API management frameworks, underlining its capabilities in traffic, security, and analytics management.

1.5   Kong's Role in API Management

Kong API Gateway plays a pivotal role in the modern API management landscape, providing tools and frameworks necessary for efficient, secure, and scalable API operations. As organizations increasingly shift towards microservices and distributed systems, the necessity to effectively manage APIs has intensified. Kong stands out as a robust platform that addresses key facets of API management: traffic control, security enforcement, and analytics integration.

At the heart of API management is the capability to effectively control the flow of requests between clients and services, ensuring optimal utilization of resources while maintaining service quality and reliability. Kong addresses this through its sophisticated traffic management capabilities. By acting as the sole entry point for API requests, Kong actively manages how traffic is routed, balancing load across available service instances to enhance availability and performance. This is particularly beneficial in microservices architecture, where multiple instances of a service may exist.

Kong's load balancing features allow developers to distribute requests across different backend services based on factors like round-robin, least-connections, or through custom algorithms. This adaptability ensures that client requests are served from the most appropriate service instance, minimizing response time and optimizing service delivery. An example of configuring a load balancer in Kong is shown below:

```
curl -i -X POST http://localhost:8001/upstreams \
  --data "name=my_upstream" \
  --data "algorithm=round-robin"

curl -i -X POST http://localhost:8001/upstreams/my_upstream/targets \
  --data "target=ip1:port1"

curl -i -X POST http://localhost:8001/upstreams/my_upstream/targets \
  --data "target=ip2:port2"
```

Through such configurations, Kong nodes dynamically adjust traffic directions based on real-time conditions, enabling optimal energy to be exerted toward service delivery without unnecessary congestion or bottlenecks.

Security is another cornerstone of API management, ensuring data protection and access controls are consistently enforced. Kong enhances API security by offering a range of authentication mechanisms right out of the box, such as OAuth 2.0, LDAP, JWT, and Basic Auth plugins. These mechanisms provide a standardized way to authenticate and authorize requests, protecting backends from unauthorized access.

Moreover, the flexibility of Kong's plugin architecture enables the rapid onboarding of additional security measures, such as IP whitelisting, blacklisting, and bot detection. This modularity allows security policies to be tightly integrated into the API gateway layer, consistently protecting microservices from threats and maintaining regulatory compliance.

Kong also provides robust SSL/TLS termination capabilities to secure data in transit. This reduces the burden on backend services which no longer have to process SSL certificates themselves. Instead, SSL offloading occurs at the gateway, ensuring that all external communication adheres to secure protocols without performance degradation.

Here's a simple code illustration of how to configure SSL in Kong:

```
curl -i -X POST http://localhost:8001/certificates \
  --data "cert=@path_to_cert" \
  --data "key=@path_to_key"

curl -i -X PATCH http://localhost:8001/services/{service} \
  --data "client_certificate.id=<cert_id>"
```

In the given example, SSL certificates are uploaded to the Kong API Gateway and subsequently linked to a service, ensuring encrypted communication.

Analyzing and understanding API interactions are essential competencies in managing any ecosystem where APIs play a central role. Kong facilitates this by integrating with various analytical tools to provide comprehensive visibility into request patterns, latency, and usage metrics. This data allows operations teams to conduct performance tuning, detect anomalies, and respond to system events with informed insights.

24

Kong can natively integrate with solutions like Prometheus, Grafana, and ELK Stack, offering a detailed dashboard experience for monitoring real-time metrics. Additionally, logging plugins permit the capture of detailed transaction logs, which can be forwarded to centralized logging systems for aggregation and analysis.

Another key dimension of Kong's role in API management lies in its ability to support versioning strategies for APIs. As APIs evolve, introducing new versions without disruption is crucial. Kong provides mechanisms for API version control, enabling organizations to manage multiple API versions concurrently. This support aids in transitioning clients to new versions without breaking existing integrations.

For organization-wide API governance, Kong's declarative configuration and management via Kong Admin API and Kong Manager respectively, offer compelling benefits. These tools allow developers and administrators to define, deploy, and monitor APIs programmatically or via a user interface, ensuring consistency and repeatability in operations.

Kong also plays an instrumental role in service discovery within microservices environments. It can dynamically adjust its routing tables based on service availability, updating its paths to reflect changes in the service landscape. This capability is critical in containerized environments where services are frequently replaced or scaled up and down.

Furthermore, Kong's access control lists (ACLs) allow for precise control over who can access specific APIs. This is essential in regulated industries where data access needs to be managed according to strict policies. By encapsulating ACL configurations within Kong, organizations can control access at a very granular level, tailored to specific user groups or applications.

Service orchestration and transformation are other areas where Kong excels, with plugins capable of orchestrating complex workflows across services or transforming request and response data to meet client needs. This translates into efficiencies where client-side code complexity is reduced, with Kong handling intermediary data processing and manipulation steps.

The role of Kong in API management is transformative, presenting a versatile framework that addresses current needs while being adaptable to future directives. Its ability to integrate seamlessly with existing infrastructures, augmented by extensive community support and commercial offerings, positions Kong as an indispensable asset in any organization's API strategy. Its proficient management of traffic, versatile integration into security policies, comprehensive analytical capabilities, and support for modern development methodologies make it an ideal choice for enterprises looking to advance their API ecosystems.

Chapter 2

Installing and Configuring Kong API Gateway

This chapter provides a comprehensive guide to the installation and initial configuration of Kong API Gateway, detailing each step required to set up a robust API management system. Readers will be introduced to the system requirements and necessary prerequisites for deploying Kong in various environments such as Docker, Linux, and cloud platforms. The chapter further explains how to configure essential components like databases and run through basic command-line operations to verify and troubleshoot the installation process. By following this guide, users will be equipped with the knowledge needed to successfully install Kong and tailor its settings according to their specific use cases.

2.1 System Requirements for Kong

Kong API Gateway is a vital component in modern distributed systems, providing abstraction and management over RESTful APIs. Before embarking on the installation of Kong, it is critical to understand the underlying system requirements, which ensure a seamless deployment in development, testing, or production environments.

Kong is highly performant and versatile, supporting a wide range of environments. However, ensuring that your system complies with its prerequisites is mandatory for a smooth installation and optimal functioning.

The following sections delve into key aspects such as hardware requirements, software dependencies, network configurations, and environmental considerations required for deploying Kong effectively.

- **Hardware Requirements**

  Kong offers a lightweight and efficient footprint; however, its performance scales with the resources available. While minimal requirements ensure basic operation, scaling beyond these specifications is recommended for enhanced performance and reliability in extensive use.

  - **Processor:** A minimum of a dual-core CPU is required. For better performance under higher loads, a multi-core processor is recommended. Industry-standard CPUs from manufacturers such as Intel or AMD are suitable.

  - **Memory:** A minimum of 1 GB of RAM is necessary for initial deployment, although, in a production setting with anticipated high loads or numerous plugins, 4 GB or more is advised.

  - **Storage:** At least 2 GB of disk space is required for installation. Ensure additional storage capacity for logs, plugins, and other utilities as required by your configuration.

  Resource allocation should correspond to anticipated production loads, with additional consideration for expansion as demands evolve.

- **Software Dependencies**

  Kong requires specific software components to be installed on the host machine. These critical dependencies must be pre-configured to allow Kong to leverage its capabilities efficiently.

  - **Operating System:** Kong supports multiple operating systems. Common installations occur on Linux distributions such as Ubuntu (16.04 or later), CentOS (7 or later), and Debian (9 or later). Windows users may rely on Docker or Linux subsystem configurations.

  - **Nginx:** Though Kong bundles necessary dependencies, familiarity with Nginx is advantageous, as Kong is built atop it. Configuration files and optimizations can be tailored with a foundational understanding of Nginx.

  - **OpenSSL:** Secure communications necessitate the latest stable version of OpenSSL to support Transport Layer Security (TLS).

  - **PostgreSQL or Cassandra:** A choice between PostgreSQL (version 9.5 and higher) or Cassandra (version 3.x) is required since Kong utilizes these databases for configuration and state maintenance.

    ```
    -- Assuming a PostgreSQL installation, initiate database setup with:
    CREATE DATABASE kong;
    CREATE USER kong WITH PASSWORD 'kong';
    GRANT ALL PRIVILEGES ON DATABASE kong TO kong;
    ```

  Select PostgreSQL for ease of setup and maintenance in most instances, unless your design necessitates Cassandra's distributed database capabilities.

- **Network Configurations**

  Kong requires carefully configured network settings which include port configurations and secure communication pathways to function correctly in various scenarios.

  - **Ports:** Ensure that the following ports are open and available:

    * 8000: Default port for proxy using HTTP.

* 8443: Proxy L4 port for TLS [HTTPS].

* 8001: Administrative access via Kong Admin API.

* 8444: TLS-secured admin interface.

– **Firewall:** Adapt firewall rules to allow traffic on these ports, and implement least privilege principles to restrict access.

– **Load Balancing:** When deploying Kong in a clustered setup, correct load balancing between nodes ensures robust and responsive API management. Integration with load balancing solutions compatible with HTTP/HTTPS protocols is often preferred.

Macros and automation scripts can be used to maintain and verify these configurations across varied environments. For example:

```
#!/bin/bash
# Script to check and open Kong required ports if closed

declare -A ports=( [8000]="Proxy HTTP" [8443]="Proxy HTTPS" [8001]="
    Admin API" [8444]="Admin TLS" )

for port in "${!ports[@]}"; do
    if ! sudo lsof -i :$port -t > /dev/null; then
        echo "Opening port $port: ${ports[$port]}"
        sudo ufw allow $port
    else
        echo "Port $port: ${ports[$port]} already open"
    fi
done
```

• **Environmental Considerations**

Optimal deployment of Kong considers the physical or virtual environment in which it operates. This involves strategic decisions that affect longevity and compatibility with existing systems.

– **Virtualization and Containers:** Deploying Kong within a Docker container is advantageous for maintaining consistent environments across development and production. Docker can encapsulate all Kong dependencies, promoting a modular infrastructure approach.

30

- **Cloud Deployments:** When deploying in cloud environments such as AWS, GCP, or Azure, tailor your instance configuration to the expected workloads, adhering to aforementioned hardware specifications.

- **Scaling and High Availability:** For global deployments, configuring Kong in a cluster with multiple nodes distributed across regions ensures high availability and reduced latency. Employing a shared database across these nodes guarantees consistent API states.

- **Operational Tools:** Integration with CI/CD pipelines and monitoring solutions (e.g., Prometheus, Grafana) forms the backbone of a reliable and responsive Kong deployment. Automation scripts for launching, configuring, and monitoring Kong can significantly reduce operational overhead.

Here is an example Docker Compose file for quickly deploying Kong with PostgreSQL:

```
version: '3.7'

services:
  kong-database:
    image: postgres:13
    container_name: kong-database
    environment:
      POSTGRES_DB: kong
      POSTGRES_USER: kong
      POSTGRES_PASSWORD: kong
    ports:
    - 5432:5432

  kong:
    image: kong:latest
    container_name: kong
    environment:
      KONG_DATABASE: postgres
      KONG_PG_HOST: kong-database
      KONG_PG_USER: kong
      KONG_PG_PASSWORD: kong
      KONG_PROXY_ACCESS_LOG: /dev/stdout
      KONG_ADMIN_ACCESS_LOG: /dev/stdout
      KONG_PROXY_ERROR_LOG: /dev/stderr
      KONG_ADMIN_ERROR_LOG: /dev/stderr
    ports:
    - 8000:8000
    - 8443:8443
    - 8001:8001
    - 8444:8444
    depends_on:
```

```
    - kong-database
```

This setup showcases Kong's compatibility with containerized deployments, reducing environmental variability.

Adhering to these system and configuration requirements lays a solid foundation for a performant and reliable Kong API Gateway setup. This groundwork ensures that subsequent installation steps, including deployment and scaling, are built on a stable and informed infrastructure, seamlessly integrating Kong's capabilities into your broader system architecture.

2.2 Installing Kong on Various Platforms

The installation of Kong API Gateway across different platforms requires a clear understanding of platform-specific nuances and configurations to ensure a robust setup. Kong's flexible architecture allows for seamless installation on numerous environments, including Docker, Linux server configurations, and cloud-based platforms. This section provides an in-depth, comprehensive guide to installing Kong, tailored for each platform mentioned, complete with essential command sequences and configuration details.

Installing Kong on Docker   Docker provides an efficient, consistent environment for deploying Kong, isolating its dependencies and ensuring reproducibility across different hosts. It is especially useful for development environments or when integrating Kong into continuous integration/continuous delivery (CI/CD) pipelines.

Step 1: Pull the Official Kong Docker Image   Begin by pulling the latest Kong image from Docker Hub. This image contains Kong with all necessary dependencies bundled in.

```
docker pull kong:latest
```

Step 2: Set Up and Launch PostgreSQL Kong requires a database for state management, with PostgreSQL as a popular choice due to its simplicity and robustness.

```
docker run -d --name kong-database \
  -p 5432:5432 \
  -e "POSTGRES_USER=kong" \
  -e "POSTGRES_DB=kong" \
  -e "POSTGRES_PASSWORD=kong" \
  postgres:13
```

Step 3: Prepare Kong Configuration Kong must be configured to use the PostgreSQL instance. This is achieved by specifying relevant environment variables.

```
docker run --rm kong:latest kong migrations bootstrap -e KONG_DATABASE=
     postgres \
-e KONG_PG_HOST=kong-database \
-e KONG_PG_USER=kong \
-e KONG_PG_PASSWORD=kong
```

Step 4: Deploy Kong Container Finally, launch the Kong container, linking it with the PostgreSQL container.

```
docker run -d --name kong \
  --link kong-database:kong-database \
  -e "KONG_DATABASE=postgres" \
  -e "KONG_PG_HOST=kong-database" \
  -e "KONG_PG_USER=kong" \
  -e "KONG_PG_PASSWORD=kong" \
  -e "KONG_PROXY_ACCESS_LOG=/dev/stdout" \
  -e "KONG_ADMIN_ACCESS_LOG=/dev/stdout" \
  -e "KONG_PROXY_ERROR_LOG=/dev/stderr" \
  -e "KONG_ADMIN_ERROR_LOG=/dev/stderr" \
  -p 8000:8000 \
  -p 8443:8443 \
  -p 8001:8001 \
  -p 8444:8444 \
  kong:latest
```

Kong is now operational in a container. Traffic on predefined ports is managed, and the application logs can be accessed through Docker's standard output.

Installing Kong on Linux Linux environments provide a stable and efficient foundation for deploying Kong, suitable for both on-

33

premises servers and cloud-based virtual machines. Installation varies slightly across distributions, but generally follows a similar pattern.

Step 1: Add Kong Repository   First, include the Kong repository in your package manager. This example covers Ubuntu:

```
echo "deb http://apt.konghq.com/ $(lsb_release -sc) main" | sudo tee /etc/apt/sources
    .list.d/kong.list
sudo curl -o /usr/share/keyrings/kong-archive-keyring.gpg https://download.konghq.
    com/gateway-3.x-archive-keyring.gpg
```

Run the same step for other distributions by changing the repository link appropriately.

Step 2: Install Dependencies   Update package lists and install dependencies. Kong requires certain packages like OpenResty and OpenSSL.

```
sudo apt-get update
sudo apt-get install -y kong
```

Step 3: Initialize and Start Kong   After installation, Kong requires a database to store configuration data. Set up PostgreSQL or another supported database:

```
sudo kong migrations bootstrap
sudo kong start
```

Upon successful start, Kong listens on default ports, ready for API gateway tasks.

Step 4: Verify the Installation   Verification ensures that Kong is properly installed and running:

```
curl -i -X GET http://localhost:8001/
```

This query checks Kong's Admin API endpoint, expecting a response listing information about the Kong node. Any errors indicate configuration issues that need addressing.

Installing Kong on Cloud Platforms Cloud platforms simplify scalability and availability, allowing Kong to manage APIs in distributed environments. Each cloud provider may have unique nuances, but the general approach remains consistent.

Deployment on AWS Amazon Web Services (AWS) provides users with elastic compute services, ideal for deploying Kong in highly available architectures:

- **Select Amazon Machine Image (AMI):** Choose an AMI suited for your region, ensuring compatibility.

- **Configure Security Groups:** Open necessary ports using AWS security group settings, including the standard Kong ports.

- **Elastic Load Balancing (ELB):** For high availability across regions, configure ELB to manage routing requests to Kong instances.

Utilize cloud-init scripts during launch to automate installation tasks, such as:

```
#cloud-config
package_update: true
packages:
  - kong

runcmd:
  - [ "kong", "migrations", "bootstrap" ]
  - [ "kong", "start" ]
```

Deployment on Google Cloud Platform (GCP) GCP offers similar virtualized setups with integrations for CI/CD operations.

Steps include:

- **Create Instance:** Launch virtual machine instances and select an appropriate image.

- **Firewall Rules:** Configure firewall settings to allow traffic through Kong's ports.

- **Compute Engine Management:** Enable seamless integration with other GCP services like Stackdriver for monitoring and logging.

Use Google Compute Engine metadata scripts for dynamic configuration during startup:

```
#! /bin/bash

# Install Kong and dependencies
apt-get update
apt-get install -y kong

# Start services
kong migrations bootstrap
kong start
```

General Cloud Considerations   Across all platforms, ensure:

- **Persistence:** Use cloud-native solutions for persistent storage solutions, ensuring Kong data retention.

- **Authentication:** Implement strong authentication mechanisms for accessing Kong's services and admin APIs.

- **Monitoring:** Leverage cloud-native solutions (CloudWatch, Stackdriver) for monitoring health and performance metrics, crucial for diagnosing anomalies and maintaining operational stability.

Kong's deployment adaptability proves advantageous when working across such diverse environments, emphasizing consistent rolling updates and scalability enhancements.

Conclusion of Installation Aspects   This multi-platform installation guide for Kong API Gateway highlights its versatility and potential across various computational environments. As infrastructures evolve, Kong's infrastructure requirements are continually met, ensuring robust API management and operation. Whether employing Docker's containerized offerings, leveraging the stability of Linux servers, or harnessing the expansive capabilities of cloud solutions, Kong remains a critical asset in scalable, secure, and efficient API deployment.

2.3 Setting Up a Database for Kong

Databases underpin the functional backbone of Kong API Gateway's data management processes. Maintaining configurations, state information, and event logs necessitates a robust and scalable database solution. Primarily, Kong supports either PostgreSQL or Apache Cassandra as backend storage databases. Each database serves distinctive operational needs, influencing performance, scalability, and consistency within a given infrastructure.

This section encompasses detailed methodologies for setting up both PostgreSQL and Cassandra, considering varied deployment scenarios and performance tuning tips to optimize Kong's capabilities.

Role of Databases in Kong

Understanding the database's role within Kong is crucial for configuring efficient and effective data management. Databases in Kong primarily manage:

- **Configuration Data:** Routing rules, plugin configurations, and custom entities fashioned by the Kong Admin API.

- **State Information:** Session states and dynamic runtime data for managing API spans.

- **Cluster Coordination:** Synchronization of Kong nodes in a clustered environment using the database for state sharing.

Selection between PostgreSQL and Cassandra directly impacts these factors. PostgreSQL provides transactional integrity and ease of setup, whereas Cassandra offers horizontal scalability and high availability features optimal for distributed setups.

Setting Up PostgreSQL

PostgreSQL excels in environments requiring strong consistency and transactional capabilities. The following details the process of setting up PostgreSQL for Kong:

Step 1: Install PostgreSQL

37

Installation methods vary based on the operating system. The following Bash commands demonstrate a basic installation and setup on a Linux-based system:

```
# Update package lists
sudo apt-get update

# Install PostgreSQL package
sudo apt-get install -y postgresql
```

Step 2: Configure PostgreSQL

After installation, PostgreSQL requires configuration for optimizing performance and security:

```
# Switch to the PostgreSQL administrative shell
sudo -i -u postgres psql

# Create the kong database
CREATE DATABASE kong;

# Create a dedicated user for kong
CREATE USER kong WITH PASSWORD 'kong';

# Grant all privileges to the kong user
GRANT ALL PRIVILEGES ON DATABASE kong TO kong;
```

This foundational setup ensures Kong has the necessary privileges to create tables and manage schema updates within the database.

Step 3: Optimize PostgreSQL Performance

Performance tuning is critical for ensuring responsiveness under load:

- **Shared Buffers:** Allocate 25% of the system memory for PostgreSQL shared buffers.

  ```
  # Edit postgresql.conf (commonly located in /etc/postgresql/X.X/main/)
  shared_buffers = 4GB
  ```

- **Max Connections:** Allow sufficient connections to handle simultaneous operations from multiple Kong nodes.

  ```
  max_connections = 100
  ```

- **Work Mem:** Adjust memory size for complex queries.

  ```
  work_mem = 16MB
  ```

- **Vacuum settings:** Regular 'vacuuming' avoids table bloat and keeps indices effective.

```
autovacuum = on
```

Step 4: Initialize Kong's Database Schema

Ingest Kong-specific schemas and bootstrap the initial state:

```
# Run the Kong migration tool to set up the database schema
kong migrations bootstrap -e KONG_DATABASE=postgres -e KONG_PG_HOST=<
    host> -e KONG_PG_USER=kong -e KONG_PG_PASSWORD=kong
```

PostgreSQL's setup for use with Kong ensures strong consistency, catering to use-cases requiring immediate feedback on changes like transaction-heavy environments.

Setting Up Apache Cassandra

Apache Cassandra is preferred in environments necessitating a distributed, highly scalable, and fault-tolerant database. It uniquely supports Kong by enabling seamless horizontal scaling and accommodating rapid read/write operations at a global scale.

Step 1: Install Cassandra

Installation prerequisites include the Java Runtime Environment, assuring Cassandra's operational base.

```
# Install Java Development Kit
sudo apt-get install -y openjdk-8-jdk

# Add Cassandra repository and import the public key
echo "deb http://www.apache.org/dist/cassandra/debian 39x main" | sudo tee -a /etc/
    apt/sources.list.d/cassandra.list
curl https://www.apache.org/dist/cassandra/KEYS | sudo apt-key add -

# Install Cassandra package
sudo apt-get update
sudo apt-get install -y cassandra
```

Step 2: Configure Cassandra

Cassandra requires tuning configurations aligned with workload demands:

- **Commit log Directory:** Ensure sufficient disk I/O bandwidth and capacity.

```
commitlog_directory: /var/lib/cassandra/commitlog
```

- **Heap Size:** Tailor heap space dependent on node memory availability.

```
MAX_HEAP_SIZE="4G"
HEAP_NEWSIZE="800M"
```

- **Cluster Setup:** Manage replica consistency and token distribution via configuration files.

Step 3: Optimize Cassandra Performance

Performance tuning can be pivotal in large-scale setups:

- **Replication Factor:** Depending on your consistency requirements, adjust replication factors.

```
CREATE KEYSPACE kong WITH replication = {'class':'SimpleStrategy', '
   replication_factor' : 3};
```

- **Snitch Configuration:** Choose the snitch that best fits your network throughput and latencies.

```
endpoint_snitch: GossipingPropertyFileSnitch
```

Step 4: Initialize Kong's Data Schema on Cassandra

Prepare the Cassandra schema using Kong's built-in tools:

```
# Use 'Kongs migration tool to set up schema
kong migrations bootstrap -e KONG_DATABASE=cassandra -e
   KONG_CASSANDRA_CONTACT_POINTS=<ip> -e
   KONG_CASSANDRA_KEYSPACE=kong
```

Through deploying Cassandra, Kong's architecture benefits from automatic geographical distribution, and fault-tolerance, suitable for today's distributed systems environments requiring seamless data replication across multiple sites.

Database Management and Maintenance

For any deployment, ongoing database maintenance is pivotal for ensuring Kong's infrastructure remains resilient and responsive.

40

- **Backups:** Implement regular database backups, respecting the storage and recovery requirements of your organization.

- **Monitoring:** Utilize monitoring tools (e.g., Prometheus for PostgreSQL or OpsCenter for Cassandra) to keep track of performance metrics and trigger alerts for abnormal patterns.

- **Updates and Patches:** Regularly update database engines to benefit from optimizations and security patches.

Understanding the thorough nuances of PostgreSQL and Cassandra deployment and maintenance is central to optimizing their symbiotic operation with Kong, ultimately facilitating seamless API management deployments across varying operational scales. Each database's compatibility with Kong not only sustains these backend processes but ensures reliable and scalable API gateway functionalities.

2.4 Configuring Kong for the First Time

The initial configuration of Kong API Gateway is a critical phase in deploying a robust, scalable API management layer. This entails defining routes, services, consumers, and plugins integral to Kong's operation as an intermediary between API clients and services. A successful setup ensures seamless interactions, fostering efficient resource management and security controls right from the inception phase.

This section expounds upon the systematic steps for a first-time configuration of Kong, emphasizing critical aspects such as setting up core entities, integrating essential plugins, and ensuring security through tokens and access controls.

- **Ensure the Database is Properly Configured:** PostgreSQL or Cassandra should be set up appropriately, with migrations applied.

- **Verify Kong's Operational Status:** Ensure Kong is running; use the Admin API to verify its health.

- **Access Credentials:** Admin credentials or tokens (if any authentication is pre-enabled) should be available.

Verify Installation and Access Admin API

Confirm Kong is operational by accessing its root API:

```
curl -i http://localhost:8001
```

A successful response indicates a healthy Kong instance.

Configuring Services and Routes

Services and routes form the core entities within Kong. A *service* represents an upstream API to which Kong proxies client requests. A *route* defines the mapping of requests to specific services based on methods, hostnames, or paths.

Define a Service

Create a service representing your upstream application:

```
curl -i -X POST http://localhost:8001/services/ \
  --data name=my-service \
  --data url='http://httpbin.org'
```

Services leverage the 'url' parameter to specify the full URL of the upstream application, ensuring the endpoint is reachable and the schema (HTTP/HTTPS) is correctly identified.

Define a Route

Define a route, binding it to the service created. This ties specific client requests to corresponding services:

```
curl -i -X POST http://localhost:8001/routes \
  --data "service.name=my-service" \
  --data "paths[]=/my-path"
```

Routes support multiple criteria, such as paths, methods, and hostnames. Choosing the correct criterion is crucial for guiding requests effectively.

Configuring Consumers and Credentials

Consumers represent clients utilizing APIs managed by Kong. Assigning credentials such as API keys or OAuth tokens ensures security and access control.

Create a Consumer

Define a consumer, associating it with API access credentials:

```
curl -i -X POST http://localhost:8001/consumers \
  --data "username=example-user"
```

Consumers are integral in tracking API usage and implementing throttling measures.

Provision Credentials

Generate and associate API keys or other credentials with consumers:

```
curl -i -X POST http://localhost:8001/consumers/example-user/key-auth \
  --data "key=my-secret-key"
```

Equipping consumers with unique credentials aids in access logging, ensuring actors can be distinguished and audited efficiently.

Securing with Plugins

Plugins extend and secure API functionalities managed by Kong, including authentication, rate limiting, and transformation:

Authentication Plugin

Enable the key-auth plugin, necessitating valid API keys for route access:

```
curl -i -X POST http://localhost:8001/services/my-service/plugins \
  --data "name=key-auth"
```

This authentication method verifies client requests, preventing unauthorized access and ensuring secure communication channels.

Rate Limiting Plugin

Protect upstream services from abuse by enforcing rate limits on consumers:

```
curl -i -X POST http://localhost:8001/services/my-service/plugins \
  --data "name=rate-limiting" \
  --data "config.minute=100"
```

Specify limits based on time intervals (seconds, minutes, hours), and scope (consumer, service, route) to tailor protection levels to specific needs.

Leveraging Kong's Configuration Capabilities

Kong's rich configuration API extends beyond services, routes, consumers, and plugins, enabling advanced setups for logging, analytics, and more:

Distributed Tracing

Integrate tracing solutions like Zipkin or Jaeger to trace requests, diagnose latency issues, and gain system insights.

```
curl -i -X POST http://localhost:8001/plugins \
  --data "name=zipkin"
```

This plugin enables detailed request logging, providing vital insights into API performance metrics and network delays.

Logging and Monitoring

Define logging strategies to capture and archive request/response pairs, using plugins like 'loggly', 'datadog', or 'file-log'.

```
curl -i -X POST http://localhost:8001/services/my-service/plugins \
  --data "name=file-log" \
  --data "config.path=/var/log/kong_access.log"
```

Strategically choosing log paths and formats optimizes data indexing and analysis routines, allowing for effortless post-event investigation.

Scaling Configurations

Kong's configuration extends transparently across clustered setups, allowing shared consistency and high availability:

Node Synchronicity

Configure Kong nodes to maintain state synchronicity using database-backed or in-memory solutions, reducing downtime and enhancing failover capabilities.

Use the following configuration snippets for seamless clustering:

```
# Enabling clustering modes
database = postgres
pg_host = <shared-db-host>
cluster_listen = 0.0.0.0:8005
cluster_listen_rpc = 127.0.0.1:4500
```

Such configurations enable dynamic adjustments and routing of incoming client requests to the most efficient nodes, improving throughput and reliability.

Ensuring Security and Compliance

Securing Kong's configuration processes is pivotal for meeting regulatory standards and ensuring organizational security policies:

SSL/TLS Configuration

Configure SSL/TLS to encrypt communications, preserving data integrity:

```
# Enable SSL in the Kong configuration file
ssl_cert = path/to/ssl.crt
ssl_cert_key = path/to/ssl.key
```

Using strong ciphers and certificates ensures resistant protection against vulnerabilities and exploits.

Security Audits and Configurations

Assess and audit configurations periodically to mitigate risks, ensuring plugins and mechanisms evolve with emerging threats.

- Implement a JSON Web Token (JWT) for session handling and payload integrity.
- Use Web Application Firewall (WAF) plugins to defend against unauthorized access and attacks.

Package configurations and procedural scripts enhance compliance adherence and audit readiness, establishing a secure Kong deployment foundation.

Continuing Management and Refinement

The configuration process for Kong extends into ongoing management, involving retention policies, scaling strategies, and automated failover plans. Utilizing API-based endpoint frameworks, administrators can leverage scripts to invoke configuration changes dynamically, adaptationally responding to variable demands across environments.

Utilize tools like Kong Enterprise's GUI or vital third-party solutions providing comprehensive, visual configuration management interfaces and analytical dashboards, streamlining operational workflows and enhancing proactive measures.

Kong's extensive configuration potential, when harnessed optimally,

45

transforms API management into a cohesive, secure, and highly effective enterprise capability aligning organically with business objectives.

2.5 Basic Kong CLI Commands

The Kong Command Line Interface (CLI) is an essential tool for managing and administering the Kong API Gateway. It provides a robust set of commands for interacting with Kong's operational parameters and configurations directly from the terminal. Mastering the CLI commands is vital for efficiently deploying, managing, troubleshooting, and scaling Kong's capabilities in various environments.

This section delves into the foundational CLI commands that facilitate core administrative tasks and introduce more advanced operations for seasoned users seeking to leverage Kong's full potential.

Understanding the Role of Kong CLI

The Kong CLI is integral for:

- **Initial Setup and Configuration:** Setting up the database, configuring the service, and defining routing policies.

- **Maintenance Operations:** Starting and stopping the Kong service, reloading configurations, and running migrations.

- **Monitoring and Auditing:** Checking the current state of the Kong nodes, inspecting logs, and verifying system health.

- **Scaling and Performance Tuning:** Adjusting configurations dynamically to suit distributed environments and high-load situations.

These operations are executed using commands that are both comprehensive and intuitive.

Core CLI Commands

Starting Kong

Initializing Kong is one of the first commands you'll execute in deploying Kong instances:

```
kong start
```

Starting Kong initializes all specified configuration files and begins accepting traffic on defined proxy and admin ports. It's crucial to ensure that all dependencies, like databases, are accessible and correctly configured before issuing this command.

Stopping Kong

To gracefully halt Kong services:

```
kong stop
```

Executing this safely shuts down all Kong nodes, ensuring that open connections are neatly closed without abrupt termination, which is critical during planned maintenance phases.

Restarting Kong

Sometimes configuration changes require a Kong restart rather than a full reboot. This is particularly useful for minor adjustments that do not affect underlying dependencies or plugins:

```
kong restart
```

This command halts and subsequently reinitializes the Kong service, allowing for configuration updates to take effect while minimizing downtime.

Reloading Configurations

To apply minor configuration changes like new routes or services, a configuration reload is often more efficient:

```
kong reload
```

The reload command applies changes without fully restarting shards. It temporarily pauses traffic to update in-memory configurations but does not terminate active connections, maintaining service continuity.

Database Management Commands

Database interactions form the backbone of many administrative tasks within Kong, vital for schema adjustments and performance tuning.

Running Migrations

Kong's reliance on structured data necessitates occasional migrations, especially with upgrades or changes to API schema designs:

```
kong migrations up
```

The up command applies pending migrations to the database schema, updating tables and indices to the latest format as required by the version upgrades.

Rollback Migrations

Although rare, situations may arise that require rolling back a migration due to unexpected issues:

```
kong migrations rollback
```

This command reverts the database to its previous state. While powerful, it should be used cautiously and typically only in controlled environments to prevent data inconsistency.

Debugging and Logging Commands

Efficient troubleshooting is achievable with Kong's dedicated debugging and log management features.

Checking Kong's Status

Verify the current health and operational status of the Kong node:

```
kong health
```

This command provides detailed insight into running services and their statuses, enabling administrators to detect discrepancies between expected and actual operation.

Inspecting Logs

Examining Kong's logs provides transparency into runtime operations for performance analysis and error diagnostics:

```
tail -f /usr/local/kong/logs/error.log
```

Accessing logs directly or via syslog integration offers real-time monitoring capabilities, crucial for assessing system integrity and identifying bottlenecks or faults as they occur.

Advanced Configuration Commands

Furthering beyond basic operations, Kong's CLI enables intricate configuration management suitable for complex deployments.

Configuring Clusters

In a distributed setup, Kong nodes communicate using clustering protocols. Configuration commands enhance node scaling and state consistency:

```
kong cluster reachability
```

Ensuring nodes can correctly synchronize state information reduces latency and minimizes inconsistencies, a pivotal component of clustered architectures.

Environmental Variables Configuration

Kong allows runtime configurations via environment variables, a necessity for dynamic environments like container orchestration platforms:

```
export KONG_PROXY_LISTEN=0.0.0.0:8000
export KONG_ADMIN_LISTEN=0.0.0.0:8001
```

These configurations enable quick changes to network bindings, facilitating flexible deployments and rapid adaptation to network topology changes.

Creating Custom Plugins

Developing custom plugins or integrating third-party modules enhances Kong's extensibility. The CLI provides tools for plugin management:

```
kong start -v --vv --nginx-conf=/path/to/nginx.conf
```

This demonstrates how custom Nginx configurations are integrated into the Kong ecosystem, facilitating the addition of bespoke plugins tailored to specific traffic management or security requirements.

CI/CD Integration and Automation

For organizations employing continuous integration, the CLI serves as a conduit for script-based automation:

Automation Scripts

49

Leverage scripts for routine tasks, enabling robust CI/CD pipelines and reducing manual errors:

```
#!/bin/bash
# Automated Kong setup

kong start && \
echo "Kong started successfully." && \
kong migrations up && \
echo "Database migrations applied."
```

Efficient scripts are invaluable for automated deployment tasks, crucial for scalable, iterative development cycles.

Version Control Integration

Utilizing CLI within version control hooks ensures state management consistency:

```
# Git hook for Kong reconfiguration post-merge
post-merge:
  ./scripts/reload_kong.sh
```

These integrate seamlessly with tools like Git, ensuring infrastructure-as-code paradigms are maintained across development outfits, providing synchronization between code changes and infrastructure adjustments.

Ensuring Secure Practices

Even with powerful interfaces, ensuring security remains paramount, executed through careful control over Kong's exposure and access:

- **Access Controls:** Restrict CLI access with role-based policies to mitigate unauthorized changes.

- **Audit Trails:** Maintain logs of CLI operations, ensuring compliance and accountability.

- **Credential Management:** Secure environment variables and configurations during storage and transit using encryption.

Understanding and mastering the kong CLI establishes a foundation for effective, automated management of API gateways, bolstering structural integrity and operational efficiency. Leveraging these commands within continuous delivery pipelines translates to rapid, consistent deployments aligned with business strategies, driving modern digital transformation initiatives.

2.6   Verifying Kong Installation

Verification of Kong API Gateway installation is a fundamental step to ensure that the setup is operational and configured correctly. It encompasses a range of checks, validations, and tests that not only confirm the foundational installation but also test the readiness and accessibility of configured services and routes. This section provides a comprehensive exploration of the verification process, detailing techniques and tools that can facilitate a robust and thorough inspection of a Kong installation.

Initial Verification and Sanity Checks

Upon completing the installation, initial verifications are necessary to confirm that Kong is operational and that all essential services are up and running. Start with verifying the basic configurations and accessibility checks.

Checking Kong's Health via Admin API   The Kong Admin API serves as the primary interface for management operations and health checks. Accessing this endpoint verifies that Kong has started without critical errors:

```
curl -i http://localhost:8001
```

This response should include HTTP status code 200 OK and provide information about the Kong node such as its version, the configuration of databases, and enabled plugins.

Inspecting Running Processes   Confirm that the expected Kong-related processes are running using system utilities like ps or htop:

```
ps aux | grep kong
```

51

The results should list Kong's manage processes (Nginx worker processes among others), confirming that Kong's proxy and admin interfaces are actively managed.

Evaluating Configuration Files Review the key configuration files for correctness. Typically located in '/etc/kong/kong.conf', the configuration file should delineate database configurations, cluster settings, and network bindings accurately. Executing:

```
less /etc/kong/kong.conf
```

Ensures that configurations align with intended setups, checking for key entries:

```
database = postgres
pg_host = <IP Address>
pg_port = 5432
...
```

Network and Port Validation

Network configurations play a critical role in service accessibility and security. Verifying ports and firewall settings is essential.

Port Availability Checks Confirm expected ports for Kong's services are open and listening using netstat or ss:

```
sudo netstat -tuln | grep '8000\|8001\|8443\|8444'
```

The output should indicate listening states on proxy (8000, 8443 for HTTPS) and admin (8001, 8444 for HTTPS) ports. Matching configurations in the Kong setup file ensures network consistency.

Firewall and Security Group Verification Inspect firewall rules to validate open access on Kong's service ports:

```
sudo ufw status
```

For cloud deployments, confirming that security groups or equivalent cloud-based firewall solutions allow traffic on these ports ensures external reachability, without compromising security.

Functional Testing of the Kong Instance

Functional testing verifies not only the suitability of running services and configurations but also the logical operations within Kong's setup model, including routes and plugins.

Defining a Test Service and Route   Create a simple service and route to test API request handling. Using *httpbin* as a mock upstream service:

```
curl -i -X POST http://localhost:8001/services/ \
  --data name=test-service \
  --data url='http://httpbin.org'

curl -i -X POST http://localhost:8001/routes/ \
  --data "service.name=test-service" \
  --data "paths[]=/test"
```

This will act as a proxy path enabling straightforward testing of Kong's routing capabilities.

Testing API Reachability   Make a request through the Kong proxy to examine accessibility and response handling:

```
curl -i http://localhost:8000/test
```

The expected output will mirror a seamless passthrough via Kong, where headers and response metadata reflect successful packet forwarding and integrity preservation.

Plugin Verification and Assessment

Kong's extensibility heavily relies on plugins, which need thorough testing post-deployment to confirm they're functioning as desired.

Enabling and Testing a Simple Plugin   Enable a rate-limiting plugin on the test service for validation:

```
curl -i -X POST http://localhost:8001/services/test-service/plugins/ \
  --data "name=rate-limiting" \
  --data "config.minute=5"
```

Attempting more than five requests within a minute interval:

```
for i in {1..10}; do curl -I http://localhost:8000/test; done
```

Should produce rate-limited responses after five successful requests, confirming the plugin's operational integrity.

Performance and Load Testing

Beyond functional validation, simulate real-world conditions to rigorously test Kong's performance and reliability under load.

Utilizing Load Testing Tools   Apache *ab* or *wrk* can simulate HTTP request loads, replicating stress-inducing scenarios:

```
wrk -t2 -c100 -d30s http://localhost:8000/test
```

Key metrics gleaned, including average latency, request per second rates, and distribution of response statuses, provide insights into resilience and potential bottlenecks — foundational knowledge to tune systems for elastic scaling.

Benchmarking and Analysis   Regular benchmarks highlight trends and inform strategic investments in scaling resources. Leverage performance outputs for:

- **Throughput Maximization:** Identifying high-throughput load capacities ensures architectures are economically dimensioned.

- **Latency Reduction:** Minimizing response times enhances user experience; investigate latency sources like network transmission or server response processing.

Continuous Verification Practices

Implementation of continued verification strategies is prudent for maintaining operational standards and compliance within dynamic API ecosystems.

Monitoring and Alerting Systems Configure real-time monitoring tools like Grafana and Prometheus for seamless integration into Kong's operational matrix:

```
# Configure metrics endpoint and plugins
curl -i -X POST http://localhost:8001/plugins \
  --data "name=prometheus"
```

This enables comprehensive incidents visibility, automatically alerting upon deviations from defined metrics thresholds.

Automated Testing Frameworks Employ automated testing frameworks (such as *Postman*) for regression testing. Scripts automating endpoint testing ensure changes within the API or configurations do not introduce regressions or breakdowns.

By embedding automated test scripts into CI/CD pipelines, confidence in code deployments is solidified, with post-deployment tests verifying deployment integrity.

Verification processes secure Kong's status as an operational entity fully integrated and synchronized across any given infrastructure. Thorough verification practices ensure operability at scale, safeguarding against service degradation while emphasizing consistent availability and performance integrity. Comprehensive diligence in these areas paves the way for operational excellence in API management facilitated by the Kong API Gateway.

2.7 Troubleshooting Common Installation Issues

Installing Kong API Gateway shouldn't be a cumbersome task, yet complexities can emerge from diverse operational environments and configurations, giving rise to unexpected behavior or outright failures. Troubleshooting these installation issues is crucial for ensuring a swift deployment and harnessing Kong's robust capabilities confidently. This section outlines systematic approaches to diagnose and resolve common issues encountered during Kong's installation, ranging from dependency conflicts to misconfiguration errors, supplemented by command examples and best practices to streamline resolution.

Diagnosing and Resolving Dependency Conflicts

Compatibility between Kong and its dependencies forms the basis of a successful installation. Below are common dependency-related issues and their remediation techniques:

- **OpenResty and Nginx Conflicts**

  Kong's reliance on OpenResty, a Nginx distribution packaged with additional modules, can lead to conflicts with pre-installed Nginx versions:

  ```
  sudo systemctl stop nginx
  sudo systemctl disable nginx
  sudo apt-get remove nginx
  ```

  Ensuring that no legacy Nginx versions override OpenResty's configurations preserves Kong's operational environment.

- **PostgreSQL or Cassandra Issues**

  Database connection failures typically arise from incorrect database configurations or uninitiated services. Verify credentials and availability:

  ```
  psql -h <db_host> -U kong -d kong
  ```

  Ensure database connectivity is established and migrations reapplied if necessary:

```
kong migrations reset
kong migrations bootstrap
```

- **Missing Dependency Libraries**

  Installation errors may cite missing library files. Insufficient dependencies can usually be corrected by installing necessary packages:

  ```
  # General library dependencies
  sudo apt-get install gcc make openssl libpcre3 libpcre3-dev
  ```

  Maintaining an exhaustive list of required libraries in accordance with the Kong version releases guarantees smoother installations.

Configuration File Errors

Misconfigurations in Kong's main configuration file (kong.conf) often result in runtime errors, necessitating a review of settings:

- **Syntax Error Detected**

  YAML syntax errors or malformed entries within kong.conf may disrupt operations. Review the syntax meticulously for indents or typos:

  ```
  # Inspect configuration file with syntax checker
  sudo kong config parse /etc/kong/kong.conf
  ```

  Implementing syntax checkers prior to applying configurations averts minor errors from escalating into operational downtimes.

- **Networking Configuration Mismatches**

  Kong's ports should align with administrative and proxy needs without conflict. Validate connections using:

  ```
  nc -zv <IP_ADDRESS> 8001
  ```

  Network utilities help validate port exposure and ensure routes and binding directives are consistent with the intended policies.

Service Startup Failures

Errors during startup can mask deeper issues, from misconfigurations to incompatible system-level dependencies:

- **Service Log Review**

  Examining logs offers insights into service failures. Analyze error logs for common indications of faulty configurations:

  ```
  sudo tail -f /usr/local/kong/logs/error.log
  ```

  Consistently reviewing system and error logs post-execution assists in tracing recurring error patterns and honing in on root causes expeditiously.

- **Daemon and Process Monitoring**

  Issues around start-up failures necessitate daemon inspections and reboot protocols. Confirm process center stability with:

  ```
  sudo systemctl status kong
  ```

  Process monitoring through tools like *ps* or *htop* can provide snapshot insights into ongoing processes affecting Kong.

Database Connection and Access Issues

Connection failures to databases can stifle Kong's start-up, often stemming from authentication or network obstacles:

- **Database Access Validation**

  Ensure database access is consistent and credentials are valid:

  ```
  psql -U kong -h <db_host> -c '\l' # List databases
  ```

  For Cassandra, check node statuses:

  ```
  nodetool status
  ```

  Validating user roles and privileges can eliminate potential permission-denied scenarios.

- **Network Configuration Errors**

  Database hosts should be reachable via specified network interfaces:

```
ping <db_host>
```

Inaccessible hosts indicate potential IP misconfigurations or DNS issues that need resolution.

Checklist for Resolving Installation Issues

A comprehensive checklist ensures fundamental checks and measures are prioritized effectively.

- **Verify Dependencies:** Make certain that all Kong dependencies are correctly installed and no conflicts exist.

- **Cross-examine Configuration Files:** Analyze main configuration files and validate YAML/JSON entries for typographical correctness.

- **Check Logs for Errors:** Exhaustively review error logs to identify specific errors, taking notes on commonplace failure messages.

- **Confirm Network Connectivity:** Validate the accessibility of necessary network resources and correct any configuration discrepancies.

- **Review Security Group Settings:** Inspect firewall and security group settings to ensure API reachability aligns with policy requirements.

This meticulous checklist reinforces a structured approach towards managing and resolving the common issues encountered during installation.

Advanced Troubleshooting Techniques

If basic approaches do not resolve installation hurdles, dive into more advanced methodologies:

- **System Compatibility and Resource Profiling**

  Profiling system resources ensures that environment provisioning meets the prerequisites specified by Kong:

```
free -m && df -h && uptime
```

Resource scarcity can precipitate gradual reductions in performance, necessitating scaling initiatives.

- **Tracing and Diagnostic Tools**

  Implementing diagnostic tracing tools such as *strace* or *gdb* aids in pinpointing event interdependencies and identifying internal workflow impediments.

```
strace -p <Kong Master PID>
```

  Deciphering kernel call sequences grants visibility over internal errors, particularly where system-level interaction results in failures or bottlenecks.

- **Leveraging Community and Support Resources**

  Engage Kong's community forums, resources, and support portals, tapping communal solutions born from diversified experiential wisdom:

  - **GitHub Issues:** Browse issue logs to identify potential patches or community-driven solutions.
  - **Kong Nation Forums:** Leverage usage forums and knowledge bases for peer insights and shared expediencies.

  These engagements drastically widen troubleshooting perspectives and often uncover niche configurations or methods that may resolve entrenched issues.

Best Practices for a Smooth Installation Experience

Incorporate best practices to mitigate encountering common pitfalls from the outset.

- **Pre-Installation Planning:** Establish seamless integration scopes, comprehensively identifying all unique environment considerations.

60

- **Version Compatibility Checks:** Confirm compatibility between Kong, dependencies, and system specifications before installation.

- **Regular Backups and Snapshots:** Maintain configuration backups and database snapshots, enabling rollback recourse during calamities.

- **Continuous Testing and Monitoring:** Implement automated tests and constant monitoring to avert subtle misalignments and ensure high service delivery standards.

By systematically applying these methodologies, installations can be geometrically refined over time, establishing a team's or organization's proficient command over Kong Deployment and Management, promoting a culture of resilient and adaptive API operations.

Chapter 3

Understanding Kong Architecture

This chapter explores the architectural framework of Kong API Gateway, elucidating the roles and interactions of its core components. It examines how requests traverse through Kong, detailing the distinct functions of the control and data planes. The discussion includes the integration of nodes and clustering to enhance scalability and reliability. Furthermore, the chapter highlights the options for database configuration, including both structured and DB-less deployments, and explains the plugin system used to extend Kong's capabilities. Readers will gain a comprehensive understanding of how these architectural elements work in concert to provide a flexible and powerful platform for API management.

3.1 Core Components of Kong

Kong is an open-source API Gateway and microservices management layer that serves as a single entry point for managing and routing external and internal traffic. To understand the functional mechanics of

Kong, it is essential to dissect its core components: the Proxy, Plugins, and the Admin API. These components serve distinct roles that collectively enhance Kong's utility in service-oriented architectures.

The **Proxy** in Kong lies at the heart of API management, acting as an intermediary that manages API requests and responses between clients and upstream services. The Proxy is responsible for routing incoming requests based on predefined rules to the appropriate services, applying necessary transformations, logging access events, and providing metrics. This component ensures seamless communication and service exposure while maintaining an abstraction layer that shields backend systems from direct access by external clients.

Plugins are modular units of functionality that considerably extend Kong's capabilities by implementing additional features to requests or responses as they flow through the Proxy. These plugins can be both internal, bundled with Kong, or custom-developed to cater to specific business requirements. Their design is inherently flexible, enabling a wide array of enhancements, such as rate limiting, authentication mechanisms, logging, and request transformations. Plugins operate within the lifecycle of API requests, either at pre-defined phases or continuously during request and response processing.

The **Admin API** serves as the control interface for Kong, allowing users to manage and configure the API Gateway's behavior programmatically. It is architected to work via HTTP requests, making it highly accessible from various client tools and services. With the Admin API, administrators can define routes, manage services, configure plugins, and retrieve metrics, ensuring precise control and real-time adaptability of the Kong setup to meet the dynamically shifting demands of modern microservices architectures.

To establish a comprehensive understanding of these components, it is advantageous to delve into their operational intricacies and interrelationships. Consideration of their interaction within a broader architecture enables efficient deployment and configuration strategies.

The Proxy functions as the frontline interface, where its configuration determines the pathways through which traffic traverses the system. Central to its operation is the concept of **Routes and Services**. A *Service* in Kong defines the upstream target. Upstream services are essentially APIs to which Kong routes traffic. A typical definition includes properties such as 'host', 'port', and 'protocol'.

```
{
  "host": "example.com",
  "port": 80,
  "protocol": "http",
  "name": "example_service"
}
```

Correspondingly, a *Route* specifies the rules that trigger the routing of traffic to a particular service. Routes can encompass criteria such as HTTP methods, host names, paths, headers, and more.

```
{
  "hosts": ["example.com"],
  "paths": ["/api/v1"],
  "methods": ["GET", "POST"],
  "service": {
    "id": "example_service_id"
  }
}
```

In this configuration, any HTTP request with a host of 'example.com' and path '/api/v1' is proxied to 'example_service', which resolves to 'http://example.com:80'. Kong's flexibility in defining routes enables sophisticated request routing strategies suitable for diverse application environments.

Upon the arrival of a request at the specified route, Plugins come into play, enhancing Kong's capabilities by introducing new functionalities according to varying operational needs. Consider the common requirement to manage load through **Rate Limiting** plugins. These plugins mitigate the risk of overburdening backend services by setting request thresholds.

```
{
  "name": "rate-limiting",
  "config": {
    "minute": 100,
    "policy": "local"
  },
  "route": {
    "id": "example_route_id"
  }
}
```

In this configuration, the Rate Limiting Plugin is applied to requests directed by 'example_route_id', restricting to a maximum of 100 requests per minute. Plugins can be applied globally, or targeted at specific services and routes, which provides granular control over API traffic processing.

Kong supports an extensive array of default plugins, yet the platform's extensibility manifests prominently in its support for **custom plugins**. Written in Lua, custom plugins afford developers the flexibility to implement bespoke transformations and processing logic by tapping into Kong's ecosystem. Creating a plugin involves defining its phases (e.g., 'access', 'header_filter', 'body_filter', 'log') and implementing logic within these phases.

```
local responses = require "kong.plugins.responses"

local MyCustomPlugin = {
  PRIORITY = 1000,
  VERSION = "1.0"
}

function MyCustomPlugin:access(config)
  kong.log("Custom access logic")
  if not ngx.var.uri == "/allowed" then
    return kong.response.exit(403, "Access Forbidden")
  end
end

return MyCustomPlugin
```

This example demonstrates a simplistic plugin that allows requests solely to a specified URI, enhancing security measures contingent upon the logic defined within the plugin.

Interfacing through the **Admin API** adds another layer of configurability, facilitating automation and remote management. The Admin API adheres to RESTful principles, allowing CRUD operations on Entities such as 'services', 'routes', and 'plugins'. Consider a scenario of uploading a service definition via a cURL command to the Admin API:

```
curl -i -X POST http://localhost:8001/services/ \
--data name=example_service \
--data url=http://example.com
```

This POST request creates a new service entity named 'example_service', targeted to 'http://example.com'. The efficacy of the Admin API ensures streamlined interaction with Kong, providing asynchronous configuration capabilities that integrate seamlessly with CI/CD pipelines.

Effective utilization of these components demands an understanding of the interplay between the Proxy, Plugins, and the Admin API. Let us explore several concepts demonstrating this integration. Setting up Kong to handle secure communication involves configuring SSL certificates, a feature facilitated at the Proxy level. The ability to define certificates and pivotal security parameters through the Admin API fosters secure service exposure with minimal manual configuration.

For instance, configuring SSL certificates is achieved through the Admin API:

```
curl -i -X POST http://localhost:8001/certificates/ \
--data "cert=@/path/to/cert.pem" \
--data "key=@/path/to/key.pem" \
--data "snis=example.com"
```

The command uploads an SSL certificate with the specified SNIs (Server Name Indications), enabling SSL termination directly at the Kong Proxy layer. Such configurations contribute to an overarching strategy to secure API traffic through encrypting data in transit.

The conceptual architecture of Kong with its Proxy-Plugin-Admin API paradigm renders it a versatile tool. Its capacity to handle diverse architectural patterns, from simple load balancers to complex, multi-layer API management systems, catalyzes adoption in environments ranging from startups to large enterprises. Each core component, individually and collectively, bridges the gap between client requests and efficient, secure, and manageable API delivery, enabling robust service ecosystems.

3.2   Data Flow in Kong

The data flow in Kong is a fundamental aspect that encapsulates how requests are processed, routed, and managed within its architecture. Understanding this flow is crucial for effective deployment and optimization of Kong's capabilities in managing APIs. This section delves into the details of how data traverses through Kong, from the initial client request to the final upstream service interaction, while highlighting the various stages and components involved.

At the core of Kong's data flow is its capability as a Reverse Proxy. This mechanism ensures that client requests are forwarded to the appropriate upstream services based on predefined configuration, with Kong acting as the intermediary that maintains communication integrity, applies security policies, and handles processing logic as specified by plugins.

The sequence of processing a request in Kong generally involves the following steps: receiving the request, pre-processing with applicable plugins, routing determination, post-routing processing via additional plugins, forwarding to the upstream service, and returning the response to the client. Each step is integral to ensuring seamless and performant data handling.

When a **request** is initially received by Kong, it passes through the Gateway's listening interface, generally configured on a defined port such as 8000 or 8443 for TLS/SSL traffic. The versatility of the Gateway enables it to terminate SSL connections, providing the first layer of security and ensuring that sensitive data is encrypted in transit.

```
curl -i -X GET https://api.example.com/service-path
```

Upon receipt, Kong immediately begins evaluating the request through its configured **Routes**. The matching process involves analyzing HTTP attributes such as host, path, HTTP method, and headers against existing route definitions. If a match is not found, a default 404 Not Found is typically returned, signaling an unrecognized path or service.

Once a suitable route is identified, pre-configured **Plugins** are activated, providing the opportunity to enforce cross-cutting concerns such as authentication, rate-limiting, or logging. Plugin execution sequence is determined by their priority; plugins with higher priority values execute before others.

```
{
  "name": "key-auth",
  "config": {
    "key_names": ["apikey"]
  },
  "route": {
    "id": "authenticated_route_id"
  }
}
```

This sample constitutes a simple key-auth plugin applied to authenticate requests on a specific route by extracting the 'apikey' from a predetermined header, thus validating access against stored credentials.

With pre-plugins processed, Kong evaluates the **Service** associated with the route. Here, it resolves network location details, such as the upstream host and protocol, and is configured to optionally alter portions of the request as required by different services. Protocol translation, request transformation, and path modification are common operations at this stage.

To illustrate, consider a service defined in Kong that translates incoming HTTP requests to HTTPS for communication with secure backend systems:

```
{
  "host": "secure-backend.example.com",
  "protocol": "https",
  "port": 443,
  "name": "secure_service"
}
```

After routing to the correct service, Kong invokes post-processing **Plugins** configured for this route. These plugins often serve to enrich response attributes or add business logic that must be applied post-routing. Examples include injecting custom headers, transforming the payload response, or collecting metrics for monitoring purposes.

Kong's flexibility allows developers to adapt the sequence and nature of these plugins by defining custom logic through Lua-based scripting or by utilizing pre-built plugins. For instance, adding a response header post-processing can be achieved through a simple plugin configuration:

```
{
  "name": "response-transformer",
  "config": {
    "add": {
      "headers": [
        "X-Custom-Header: Kong"
      ]
    }
  }
}
```

Once pre- and post-plugins have been applied, Kong forwards the request to the **Upstream Service**. Here, it manages full-duplex communication, forwarding the request and awaiting the response from the service endpoint. Kong uses upstream keep-alive mechanisms by default to maintain efficient network connections and reduce latency in service communication.

Upon receiving the upstream response, Kong interacts again with any registered plugins that require post-response processing. These plugins offer the chance to log requests, modify response data, or add custom error handling measures before relaying the final output back to the client.

In understanding the full **request-response lifecycle** within Kong, it is essential to consider the concurrent execution of multiple requests. Kong's architecture is built atop NGINX and the LuaJIT language layer, providing synchronous and asynchronous request handling. By leveraging NGINX's event-driven architecture, coupled with LuaJIT's high-performance execution, Kong is capable of serving thousands of concurrent requests, benefiting from minimal I/O blocking and efficient context switching.

Internal optimizations, such as Kong's use of the plugin iterator pattern, ensure that the platform can dynamically load and execute configured plugins with low overhead, further enhancing throughput.

```
top -b -n 1 | grep 'nginx: worker'
```

This command illustrates how one might monitor Kong's performance under a load, revealing active worker processes and associated CPU/memory utilization—integral metrics for assessing operational efficiency.

Finally, **error handling** within the data flow serves as a critical element for robustness. Kong provides multiple methods for managing errors, including customizing error messages via the error-handler plugin, redirecting unsuccessful attempts, and alerting through log messages. This configurability empowers administrators to implement comprehensive error management, enhancing the resilience of services exposed through Kong.

The way data flows through Kong is distinguished by a clear sequence of processing steps supported by flexible configurations and robust plugin interaction. Together, these elements provide a powerful framework for managing APIs with precision, allowing complex routing and processing logic to be abstracted on top of simple configuration blocks.

70

The detailed understanding of this flow empowers administrators and developers to optimize their use of Kong, improving performance and reliability in distributed systems.

3.3   Role of Kong Nodes and Clustering

The deployment architecture of Kong often necessitates the consideration of nodes and clustering, especially as API traffic and management expand across increasingly complex and distributed systems. Understanding the role of Kong nodes and the benefits and methodologies of deploying a cluster of nodes is essential for designing scalable and robust API gateway solutions. This section discusses the anatomy of Kong nodes, the mechanics of clustering, and how these contribute to achieving resilience, high availability, and horizontal scalability within an enterprise setting.

A **Kong Node** is a distinct instance of Kong that executes the API gateway and manages routing, plugins, and data flow as defined by its configuration parameters. Each node runs autonomously with its own instance of NGINX enhanced by Kong's plugin capabilities. The distributed nature of microservices necessitates that these nodes should be stateless, able to handle requests independently without relying on any persistent state contained within any other node.

Nodes inherently support the scaling of API management capacity; however, operating in isolation does little to harness the full potential afforded by distributed architecture. An evolution towards **Clustering** Kong nodes offers compelling advantages including automatic load balancing, failover support, and consistent configuration management across nodes.

In essence, a **Kong Cluster** is an assemblage of multiple Kong nodes functioning in concert to serve the API gateway purpose for services. Clustering enables each node to be dynamically aware of the existence and state of other nodes within the system, ensuring synchronized configuration and deployment flexibility. This is achieved through the formulation of a shared data store, typically a database-like PostgreSQL or Cassandra, which maintains consistent state across all nodes.

To configure a basic Kong cluster, each node must be pointed to the same shared database. For instance, configuring Kong nodes to connect to a PostgreSQL instance involves specifying database details within the Kong configuration file, kong.conf.

```
database = postgres
pg_host = kong-database
pg_port = 5432
pg_user = kong
pg_password = kong
pg_database = kong
```

All nodes within the cluster use this collective database to retrieve and update configuration dynamically. As routes, services, and plugins change, such alterations are swiftly reflected across all nodes, thereby maintaining synchronization.

Performance bottlenecks can be mitigated through the flexible deployment of additional nodes. To add nodes seamlessly into a Kong cluster, one simply initiates a new Kong instance, pointing it to the shared database already employed by existing nodes. This rapid adjustability is central in responding to fluctuating demands without necessitating disruptive reconfiguration of individual nodes.

The mechanics of **load balancing** in Kong clusters further enhance scalability. By deploying a separate load balancer (e.g., NGINX or HAProxy) ahead of Kong nodes, incoming API traffic can be distributed evenly among the cluster, ensuring optimal utilization of resources and reducing latency. Modern infrastructure environments, like Kubernetes, automate this balance through the orchestration layer, mapping traffic to node pods efficiently.

A key advantage of clustering is **high availability** (HA). In a cluster, the failure of individual nodes does not precipitate system outages as traffic is simply rerouted to alternate nodes within the cluster. This resilience ensures continuity and robust service delivery, minimizing downtime and providing fault-tolerant operations.

In clustered modes, Kong must also address the challenge of service **discovery** and routing. While Kong itself routes based on pre-set configuration, clustering benefits from service discovery mechanisms that adapt dynamic service changes over time. Integrating systems like Consul or etcd can inform Kong's proxy layers of updated backend IP addresses without requiring reconfiguration of routes.

As Kong nodes within a cluster maintain coordinated state via a shared data store, managing **consistency** becomes indispensable. The CAP theorem posits inherent trade-offs between consistency, availability, and partition tolerance in distributed systems. Using a strong-consistency model, as facilitated by PostgreSQL, ensures that configuration changes propagate predictably, whereas options such as Cassandra may offer eventual consistency with inherent latency effects tolerated in highly asynchronous environments.

A pivotal aspect of managing mechanism in Kong is **health checking** and node status monitoring. Keeping track of node health ensures the smooth operation and automatic redirection of traffic away from faltering nodes. By default, Kong provides monitoring via Admin API endpoints, whereas more sophisticated setups might integrate external monitoring suites like Prometheus and Grafana to deliver comprehensive visibility across clusters.

```
curl http://localhost:8001/status
```

The command outputs vital statistics such as database connectivity and node health, aiding in proactive maintenance.

For organizations deploying multi-regional setups, **geo-distributed** clusters extend Kong's reach and performance by deploying nodes in datacenters across different geographic locations. This dispersion reduces latency by placing nodes closer to end users while maintaining a single global configuration set – critical for multinational enterprises delivering content to globally distributed clients.

The **security** implications of clustering nodes necessitate stringent adherence to best practices. Ensuring secure communication between nodes, configuring ingress points with proper encryption protocols (such as TLS), and guarding administrative access are all imperative measures to preserve data confidentiality and integrity.

```
sudo certbot --nginx -d api.example.com
```

This command configures an SSL certificate for a Kong node using Let's Encrypt with certbot, fortifying the communication channel against interception.

Version upgrades across the cluster must be meticulously managed to ensure **compatibility**. Kong nodes should be updated in succession, ensuring no single point of failure exists during the upgrade process. Blue/green deployments or canary releases may be suitable techniques in minimizing risks and ensuring seamless rollouts.

Overall, the establishment of a Kong cluster is foundational to unlocking the platform's full potential in demanding network environments. With nodes operating cohesively, backed by powerful load balancing, consistent and rapid state updates, high availability, and robust security, organizations are empowered to scale dynamically, handle spikes in API traffic, and deliver outstanding service reliability across large operational zones. Understanding and implementing the nuances of nodes and clustering allow for optimal performance and a competitive edge in API management efficacy.

3.4 Kong Control Plane vs Data Plane

In the context of Kong architecture, the concepts of control plane and data plane are pivotal in understanding how the platform manages and routes API traffic while maintaining overall configuration governance. These two planes serve distinct functions and principles, contributing to different aspects of API management—one concerning operational control and the other involving data flow and traffic handling. This section delves into a detailed exploration of Kong's control plane and data plane, elucidating their roles, interactions, and the strategic benefits they offer in highly scaled environments.

The **Control Plane** in Kong is primarily responsible for configuration, management, and policy enforcement. It oversees the administration of APIs, including defining routes, services, consumers, and plugins. The control plane acts as the brain of the Kong ecosystem, dictating how requests should be handled by every Kong node.

Key functionalities of the control plane include:

- **Configuration Management:** Through interfaces such as the Admin API, administrators define and update configuration that dictates API behavior. This includes routing rules, plugin activation and configuration, and security policies.

- **Policy Enforcement:** The control plane ensures that all config-

74

uration adheres to organization policies and regulatory requirements, acting as a gatekeeper to unauthorized changes.

- **Distributed Synchronization:** In environments with multiple data plane nodes, the control plane is tasked with synchronizing configuration changes consistently across the nodes to ensure
  uniform behavior.

- **Monitoring and Logging:** The control plane often interfaces
  with external systems for logging, monitoring, and analytics to
  provide insights into API usage and system health.

A typical interaction with the control plane involves utilizing the Admin
API to make changes to the configuration. Consider a scenario where
new rate limiting policies need to be applied to an existing service:

```
curl -i -X POST http://localhost:8001/services/example_service/plugins \
  --data "name=rate-limiting" \
  --data "config.minute=100"
```

This simple request initiates a rate limiting plugin on the specified service, dictating new consumption rules enforceable across all data plane
nodes.

The **Data Plane**, conversely, is closely linked with the execution of API
request management. It is focused on handling runtime traffic, processing requests, and executing the logic defined by the control plane.
The data plane serves as the muscle of Kong, implementing the rules
and configurations outlined by the control plane.

The primary duties of the data plane involve:

- **Traffic Routing:** The data plane executes routing policies dictated by configuration settings, determining the path each request should follow to reach its intended destination.

- **Plugin Execution:** As requests traverse through the data plane,
  applicable plugins are executed based on configured settings,
  providing functionalities like authentication, logging, and transformations.

- **Load Balancing and Failover:** Data planes may implement
  load balancing strategies to distribute traffic among upstream

services effectively, ensuring resiliency and continuity of service despite node failures.

- **Request and Response Handling:** The data plane is responsible for managing the lifecycle of requests, including translating the traffic as per protocol requirements and modifying headers or payloads if necessary.

A data plane environment typically constitutes multiple Kong nodes, each acting independently to process incoming requests. Consider the process of a simple HTTP request flowing through the Kong data plane nodes:

```
HTTP GET /api/v1/resource HTTP/1.1
Host: api.example.com
Authorization: Bearer <token>
```

This request reaches a Kong node within the data plane, which authenticates using an OAuth 2.0 plugin, checks rate limits, and then routes the request to an upstream service based on the predefined configuration.

```
{
  "name": "oauth2",
  "config": {
    "scopes": ["read", "write"],
    "token_expiration": 7200
  }
}
```

The configuration deploys an OAuth 2.0 plugin, integrating access token validation within the gateway's processing workflow, ensuring that only properly authenticated requests are handled.

The division of these roles into separate planes provides several strategic benefits, including:

- **Operational Efficiency:** By separating the management of configuration (control plane) from the actual data processing (data plane), Kong enables more efficient operations. This separation avoids the bottleneck of routing decisions being made continuously, allowing data plane processes to focus purely on traffic processing and rule execution. The dual-plane structure also facilitates improved scalability as the data plane nodes can be expanded horizontally without the need for scaling out the control plane.

- **Improved Security and Governance:** Security is reinforced through the convention that sensitive management and configuration tasks are centralized within the control plane. This centralization means fewer access points for potentially disruptive configuration changes, supporting stronger governance and compliance with regulatory requirements.

- **Fault Tolerance and Robustness:** Decoupling configuration from execution results in greater system robustness. If the control plane becomes temporarily unavailable, the data plane can continue functioning using the last-known configuration. This separation ensures continued traffic processing even during management plane disturbances.

- **Scalability and Flexibility:** Having dedicated control and data planes provides agility in scaling operations: the data plane can scale based on traffic demands, while the control plane can remain stable with minimum instances. This ensures that administrators can swiftly adapt to dynamic changes in load and operations without overhauling infrastructure configurations.

- **Monitoring and Observability:** Increased observability can also be a characteristic of having isolated planes. The control plane actively monitors configuration aspects and nodes' health, facilitating quicker detection and correction of anomalies within the data flow.

Kong Enterprise builds upon this dual-plane model with additional layers of management interfaces and service mesh integration. It presents a more granular set of tools ranging from automated certificate management to advanced analytics dashboards, enhancing the administrative control exercised over the broader architecture.

Practical Considerations and Deployment Strategies: Implementing a dual-plane architecture requires recognizing network latency and synchronization impacts. While the data plane should respond to real-time requests with immediacy, control plane activities, such as configuration updates, must propagate evenly despite inherent latency. Automated deployment tools and orchestration frameworks like Kubernetes can facilitate an optimized and managed process of configuration changes across clusters, ensuring minimal performance degradation.

Overall, understanding the dichotomy between the control plane and data plane allows architects and developers to harness Kong's capabilities effectively, achieving optimal performance and governance. The strategic separation optimizes both traffic management and configuration governance, rendering Kong a more robust, scalable, and secure solution for managing enterprise-level API traffic.

3.5   Database Options in Kong

In Kong's architecture, selecting appropriate database options is critical as it determines how configuration data and runtime metrics are stored, accessed, and synchronized across a distributed environment. Kong operates through flexible database systems, supporting both traditional database deployments and a novel DB-less mode. Each database strategy offers specific advantages and complements different operational requirements. This section provides an extensive exploration of the database options available in Kong, their configurations, practical implications, and scenarios where each is preferable.

Kong's architecture predominantly supports two types of databases: PostgreSQL and Cassandra. Both options serve different use cases based on the operational needs of scalability, consistency, and resilience.

PostgreSQL

PostgreSQL is a robust relational database known for its strong consistency model and support for complex queries. In Kong, PostgreSQL is often favored for deployments where transactional integrity and data consistency are prioritizations. It is particularly useful in environments where read and write operations require immediate consistency.

PostgreSQL in Kong operates under a synchronization model where all nodes of a Kong cluster access a centralized PostgreSQL instance for reading and writing configuration states. This setup provides consistent, reliable operation without the eventual consistency considerations associated with distributed databases.

Configuring Kong to use PostgreSQL involves specifying database connection parameters in the kong.conf file:

```
database = postgres
pg_host = kong-db-host
pg_port = 5432
pg_user = kong
pg_password = password
pg_database = kong_database
```

Advantages of using PostgreSQL with Kong:

- **Strong Consistency:** PostgreSQL guarantees ACID transactions, ensuring that all nodes see the current state of data simultaneously.

- **Robust Query Capability:** The SQL capabilities of PostgreSQL allow complex queries and reporting, which can assist in analytics and diagnostics.

- **Reliable Transactions:** PostgreSQL's transaction management ensures that all configuration changes either complete as intended or not at all, preventing corruption or intermediate states.

Considerations:

- **Single Point of Read/Write:** All nodes perform read/write operations through the centralized database, which may introduce performance bottlenecks if not properly managed or scaled.

- **High Availability Setup Required:** To guarantee uninterrupted service, database replication and failover mechanisms (like pgpool-II or patroni) need to be established.

Cassandra

Conversely, Cassandra is a NoSQL, distributed database designed for high availability and horizontal scalability. Cassandra's eventual-consistency model makes it ideal for scenarios where read/write scalability and partition tolerance are more critical than immediate consistency.

In a Kong environment with Cassandra, each node can handle part of the data set, offering impressive throughput for large-scale deployments. Configuring it in Kong requires specifying the cluster nodes and other parameters necessary for connectivity:

```
database = cassandra
cassandra_contact_points = 127.0.0.1
cassandra_port = 9042
cassandra_keyspace = kong_keyspace
```

Advantages of using Cassandra with Kong:

- **Scalability and High Availability:** Cassandra provides excellent horizontal scalability, allowing seamless scaling by adding additional nodes to the cluster.

- **Fault Tolerance:** Its distributed nature ensures that data remains available even if some nodes fail.

- **Geographical Distribution:** Supports multi-datacenter replication, making it suitable for geographically distributed clusters.

Considerations:

- **Eventual Consistency:** Applications need to handle temporary inconsistencies due to Cassandra's eventual consistency model, which might reflect as small time windows where data does not synchronize instantly.

- **Complexity in Management:** Cassandra's setup, tuning, and management are generally perceived as more complex compared to traditional RDBMS.

DB-less Mode

An innovative addition to Kong, the DB-less mode allows Kong to operate without a connected database, relying instead on declarative configuration files. This mode is highly appropriate for environments emphasizing infrastructure as code and scenarios where rapid deployments or lightweight operational footprints are beneficial.

In DB-less mode, configuration is provided directly to Kong through a YAML configuration file, which is read into memory upon startup:

```
_format_version: "1.1"
services:
- name: example_service
  url: http://example.com
  routes:
  - name: example_route
    paths:
    - /example
```

Advantages of DB-less Mode:

- **Simplicity and Speed:** Without a database dependency, Kong can be spun up rapidly, making it excellent for ephemeral environments like CI/CD pipelines or testing setups.

- **Reduce Operational Overhead:** By eliminating the need for database maintenance and orchestration, operational complexity is significantly decreased.

- **Infrastructure as Code:** Promotes static configuration management practices where configuration is versioned and managed within source control systems.

Considerations:

- **Config File Limitation:** As configurations are loaded into memory, extremely large configurations may impact performance and startup times.

- **Static Configuration Only:** Requires a restart to apply any configuration changes, making dynamic runtime changes impractical.

Choosing the Right Database Option

The decision to use PostgreSQL, Cassandra, or DB-less mode largely depends on the specific requirements of the operation environment and the goals of the deployment.

Use PostgreSQL when:

- Strong consistency and data integrity are paramount.

- Operations rely on complex queries and analytical reporting.

- The system benefits from clear transaction management practices.

Use Cassandra when:

- The environment requires large scale-out capabilities without sacrificing availability.

- Partition tolerance is preferable, potentially across multiple geographic regions.

- Achieving reliability through distributed architecture takes precedence.

Use DB-less mode when:

- Operations favor static configuration management with minimal operational overhead.

- Environments are highly dynamic and require rapid spin-up and teardown such as integration tests.

- Configuration sizes are manageable within memory constraints.

Managing and Monitoring

Regardless of choice, managing databases effectively is crucial. Proper monitoring for PostgreSQL involves tracking key performance metrics such as query execution times, connection counts, and I/O statistics using tools like pgAdmin or custom setups with Prometheus/Grafana.

For Cassandra, specialists often deploy tools like Cassandra OpsCenter or DataStax to monitor node statuses, read/write delays, and replication lag, ensuring optimal performance.

```
nodetool status
```

This command checks the ring status, providing insight into the load distribution across nodes and identifying potential bottlenecks.

Conclusion

The database options in Kong significantly shape the architecture and performance characteristics of the deployment. Whether leveraging the transaction consistency of PostgreSQL, the distributed resilience of Cassandra, or the operational efficiency of DB-less mode, understanding these options allows architects to tailor systems precisely to meet enterprise needs, traffic demands, and operational contexts. Selecting and configuring the appropriate database strategy is fundamental to harnessing Kong's full potential in robust API management.

3.6 Extending Kong with Plugins

One of the most powerful features of Kong is its plugin architecture, which allows for significant extensibility and customization to meet the specific needs of diverse applications. Plugins in Kong serve as modular units that implement additional behaviors and policies as requests flow through the API Gateway. This section delves into the details of how plugins extend Kong's capabilities, explores the lifecycle of plugins, and discusses both bundled and custom plugins. Moreover, the section provides insights into best practices for developing and maintaining plugins within the Kong ecosystem.

The Purpose and Power of Plugins

Plugins in Kong operate as individual scripts or modules that can handle request and response transformation, enforce security policies, perform logging operations, and more. They allow developers and administrators to customize how Kong processes traffic without altering the underlying core of Kong's operations.

Plugins integrate into Kong's request lifecycle at different phases and are triggered during specific events in request handling, such as before reaching an upstream service or when sending a response back to the client. By doing so, they modularly enhance Kong's functionality and facilitate extensions without disrupting the primary API processing logic.

Plugin Architecture and Lifecycle

Kong plugins are built using Lua, leveraging the powerful LuaJIT, which allows them to operate at high performance on top of NGINX. Each plugin encompasses one or more phases within the request lifecycle:

- **Access Phase:** Executed right after routing and before sending a request upstream. It's often used for authentication or modifying the request headers and parameters.

- **Header Filter Phase:** After receiving the response from upstream, plugins can modify response headers before they are sent back to the client.

- **Body Filter Phase:** Allows modifications of the response body stream.

- **Log Phase:** Typically used for logging requests and responses after completion of a transaction.

Plugin Configuration

Configuring a plugin involves adding it to Kong's configuration via the Admin API. For instance, to add a rate limiting plugin:

```
curl -X POST http://localhost:8001/services/{service_id}/plugins \
    --data "name=rate-limiting" \
    --data "config.minute=20" \
    --data "config.policy=local"
```

This command attaches a rate limiting plugin to a specified service, enforcing a threshold of 20 requests per minute.

Plugins can be applied globally across all requests, or bound specifically to services, routes, or consumers, allowing granular control over their application.

Bundled Plugins

Kong comes with a variety of bundled plugins that cover a wide range of common use cases:

- **Authentication Plugins:** Such as key-auth and OAuth 2.0, which handle validating user requests and managing session tokens.

- **Security Plugins:** Like IP-restriction, which limits requests based on client IP addresses, enhancing security.

- **Traffic Control Plugins:** Including rate limiting and request size limiting, which protect against misuse and overload scenarios.

- **Transformation Plugins:** Capable of modifying request and response data formats, making Kong versatile in handling different systems' interactions.

```
{
  "name": "ip-restriction",
  "config": {
    "allow": ["192.168.1.0/24"],
    "deny": ["0.0.0.0/0"]
  }
}
```

This IP restriction config allows requests from within the local subnet while blocking access from all other addresses, enhancing security with minimal configuration effort.

Developing Custom Plugins

While bundled plugins cover many scenarios, Kong's full potential is realized through custom plugins. These allow developers to address unique requirements or integrate with third-party systems in ways not feasible with generalized solutions.

Creating a Custom Plugin

To create a custom plugin, a developer must define the functionality in Lua, employing Kong's Lua plugin API. Custom plugins typically include the following components:

- **handler.lua:** Implements the core logic for the plugin, defining methods such as 'access', 'header_filter', etc.

- **schema.lua:** Outlines the configuration parameters accepted by the plugin, specifying data types and validation rules.

- **daos.lua** (optional): Manages persistence settings if the plugin requires database interactions.

Example of a basic custom plugin that logs request paths:

Simple custom plugin handler

```
local BasePlugin = require "kong.plugins.base_plugin"
local MyCustomPlugin = BasePlugin:extend()

function MyCustomPlugin:new()
  MyCustomPlugin.super.new(self, "my-custom-plugin")
end

function MyCustomPlugin:access(config)
  MyCustomPlugin.super.access(self)
  kong.log("Request path: ", kong.request.get_path())
end

return MyCustomPlugin
```

This snippet represents a foundational plugin engaging in the access phase to log the request path, demonstrating the simplicity yet power of custom plugin formulation.

Loading Custom Plugins

Once developed, plugins are loaded into Kong by modifying the 'kong.conf' file to include the plugin's module name in the 'custom_plugins' variable:

```
custom_plugins = my-custom-plugin
```

Restarting Kong or reloading configurations then activates the new plugin within the ecosystem.

Best Practices for Plugin Management

86

Managing plugins effectively requires attention to best practices to ensure smooth and efficient deployment:

- **Testing and Validation:** Rigorous testing of plugins in a staging environment prevents potential disruptions in production systems.

- **Documentation:** Adequately document plugin behavior, configuration parameters, and intended usage to facilitate future maintenance and team collaboration.

- **Version Control:** Maintain versioning of both custom and configuration files. This ensures a rollback path and tracks evolutionary changes over time.

- **Performance Monitoring:** Regularly assess the performance impacts of plugins, especially custom implementations that may introduce overhead if inefficiently coded.

Plugin Performance and Optimization

Not every plugin is suitable to be executed under minimal resource constraints; therefore, optimizing plugins is essential to avoid adverse performance impacts.

Profiling and Optimization

Profiling tools like luajit -jp can assist in analyzing the performance layers of Lua scripts, aiding developers in pinpointing bottlenecks within their plugin code.

Strategies such as caching heavy computations, reducing calls to disk or databases, and minimizing complex operations while operating within the plugin's lifecycle will enhance throughput and responsiveness.

Conclusion

Kong plugins stand as a versatile mechanism to expand the capabilities of the API Gateway. From built-in options providing immediate solutions to tailor-made extensions aligning with specific requirements, plugins empower Kong to adapt to various operational paradigms. By mastering the development and deployment of plugins, organizations

can maximize the utility of Kong, ensuring it fulfills both current demands and accommodates emerging technological landscapes effectively.

Chapter 4

Routing and Proxying with Kong

This chapter delves into the intricacies of routing and proxying capabilities within Kong API Gateway, laying out the processes for effectively managing incoming requests. It covers the creation and configuration of routes, service objects, and upstreams, establishing the pathways for interactions between clients and backend services. The chapter highlights advanced routing techniques, such as host-based and path-based routing, as well as strategies for implementing traffic control features like traffic splitting and canary releases. Through this exploration, readers will acquire the skills necessary to leverage Kong's routing features for optimized API traffic management.

4.1 Defining Routes in Kong

In the Kong API Gateway, the concept of routing serves as a fundamental mechanism that directs incoming client requests to the appropriate backend services based on specified criteria. This section provides a comprehensive exploration of how routes are defined and managed within Kong, focusing on the configuration components such as paths and methods. This is crucial for ensuring that client requests are processed and fulfilled by the correct service endpoints, thereby facilitating efficient API operations.

A route in Kong is essentially a rule that determines how client requests are matched and proxied to service objects. Each route is associated with a service, which in turn points to an upstream server. The configuration of routes can involve specifying parameters such as URL paths, HTTP methods, hostnames, headers, and others. The flexibility offered by Kong in route configuration allows developers to tailor their routing strategies to align with specific application requirements.

Routes are configured via the Kong Admin API. To create a route, one typically links it to an existing service, thus forming the crucial link between the incoming requests and the upstream service that will ultimately process them. The following illustrates a basic example of creating a route in Kong using HTTP methods, paths, and hostnames.

```
curl -i -X POST http://localhost:8001/routes \
  --data "hosts[]=example.com" \
  --data "paths[]=/myservice" \
  --data "methods[]=GET" \
  --data "service.id=<service-id>"
```

In this example, a new route is created with the criteria including the host 'example.com', the path '/myservice', and the HTTP method 'GET'. The request is linked to a service object identified by '<service-id>'. The route ensures that only GET requests targeting the specified host and path are proxied to the associated service.

Kong routes support various matching criteria, allowing developers to set up rules that fulfill dynamic and complex routing needs. These criteria include:

- **Hosts:** Matches any HTTP request that contains a specified hostname. Useful in cases where the same API gateway serves multiple domains or subdomains.

- **Paths:** Matches requests based on the URL path prefix. Supports both static and dynamic path segments.

- **Methods:** Limits the route to specific HTTP methods like GET, POST, PUT, etc.

- **Headers:** Allows for route matching based on HTTP headers. This can provide rich routing rules by inspecting custom headers transmitted with requests.

- **SNI (Server Name Indication):** Pertains to TLS-enabled services and allows matching based on a client's SNI (useful for HTTPS traffic).

When configuring routes, the choice of matching criteria significantly influences the routing logic within Kong. Developers must carefully consider which attributes of incoming requests are relevant for their use case, typically optimizing for performance and manageability.

Kong evaluates routes based on a precise order of attributes. This order is critical as it defines how Kong selects a route when multiple routes could match a given request. The evaluation order is as follows:

1. **Exact match of the host, method, and path:** An exact match on all three implies the highest priority.

2. **Exact match of host and method, with path wildcard:** When no exact path is provided, the wildcard (*) can act as a catch-all.

3. **Exact match of method and path, with wildcard host:** This is slightly less restrictive but still effective.

4. **Exact match of host, with wildcard method and path:** Using only hosts for broad matching scenarios.

5. **Wildcard matches across one or more criteria:** These are typically the most general rules, and thus, have the lowest precedence.

Understanding the evaluation order is essential to prevent unintended routing behavior that could arise from overlapping conditions in routes. This is particularly important during the management of large APIs or when dealing with multi-tenant systems.

Routes can be managed dynamically using Kong's Admin API. Admin API allows for creating, reading, updating, and deleting (CRUD) routes programmatically. The JSON payloads used in these requests specify the desired routing configuration. Below are some examples of the CRUD operations for routes.

Creating a Route   Similar to the earlier 'POST /routes' example, creation involves sending parameters that define the desired matching conditions and associating the route with a service object. For example:

```
curl -i -X POST http://localhost:8001/routes \
  --data "hosts[]=example.com" \
  --data "paths[]=/v1/*" \
  --data "methods[]=GET" \
  --data "methods[]=POST" \
  --data "service.id=<service-id>"
```

Here, the route accepts GET and POST requests directed to any URL beginning with '/v1/' on the host 'example.com'.

Retrieving a Route   Retrieving route details involves a simple GET request to the Admin API:

```
curl -i -X GET http://localhost:8001/routes/<route-id>
```

This retrieves the details for a route specified by '<route-id>'. The output consists of data such as the associated host, path, method, and service association.

```
{
  "id": "dcac7faf-81e2-4db7-ae8c-c61c1e33e99c",
  "path": "/v1/*",
  "hosts": ["example.com"],
  "methods": ["GET", "POST"]
  // Additional attributes
}
```

Updating a Route   To modify an existing route, an update request can be issued:

```
curl -i -X PATCH http://localhost:8001/routes/<route-id> \
  --data "paths[]=/v2/*"
```

This changes the path matching from '/v1/*' to '/v2/*', thereby directing traffic destined for the updated path pattern to the specified service.

Deleting a Route   Removing a route from Kong involves executing a DELETE request, which will cease all matched traffic routing through it:

```
curl -i -X DELETE http://localhost:8001/routes/<route-id>
```

Effective route management through the Admin API provides a powerful, flexible way to refine how traffic is handled, control access based on various conditions, and seamlessly integrate with orchestration and automation tools.

When implementing route configurations, several best practices should be taken into account. These entail:

- **Minimize Route Complexity:** Aim for routes that follow a clear and understandable logic. Complex rules can lead to maintenance challenges, especially in rapidly evolving API environments.

- **Efficient Ordering:** Leverage the evaluation order to preempt conflicts by designing routes starting with the most specific match criteria, descending towards more general rules.

- **Concurrency and Consistency:** When applying updates or changes to routes, account for potential race conditions in distributed systems or during rapid deployment workflows.

- **Logging and Monitoring:** Implement comprehensive logging mechanisms to capture route success and failure, enabling diagnosis and improvements based on traffic patterns.

With a careful approach to route configuration and management, Kong can effectively handle extensive API requirements while providing the fine-grained control needed in contemporary application landscapes.

This ability to define precise routes ensures efficient and reliable API Gateway operations, benefiting both developers and end-users by maximizing accessibility and performance of the services delivered through Kong.

4.2   Service Objects and Configuration

Service objects in Kong play a critical role in how requests are proxied and handled by the API Gateway. They represent the abstraction layer connecting routes to upstream services, effectively serving as the bridge between client requests and their designated backend services. This section elaborates on the importance of service objects, their configuration parameters, and best practices to manage them efficiently within Kong.

In Kong, a service object encapsulates the concept of an individual API service. It encapsulates a set of fields including the URL, protocol, host, port, and path that define the target upstream service. Configuring service objects correctly ensures that requests routed by Kong are forwarded to the appropriate backend services without discrepancies.

Creating Service Objects

Service objects are typically created and managed via Kong's Admin API. When a service object is created, it needs to be associated with at least one route to enable traffic routing. Below is a basic example of creating a service object using the POST method of the Admin API.

```
curl -i -X POST http://localhost:8001/services \
  --data "name=my-service" \
  --data "url=http://httpbin.org"
```

In this example, a service object named my-service is defined, targeting the upstream service located at http://httpbin.org. The URL is a required field, specifying the protocol, host, and optional path to the upstream service. Alternatively, each component can be specified individually by providing the protocol, host, port, and path.

Service objects can also be defined with additional configuration parameters to enable more sophisticated upstream interactions, such as timeouts and retries.

```
curl -i -X POST http://localhost:8001/services \
  --data "name=extended-service" \
  --data "url=http://example-service:80" \
  --data "read_timeout=60000" \
  --data "write_timeout=30000" \
  --data "retries=5"
```

Here, the extended-service object specifies:

- read_timeout: Maximum idle time in milliseconds for a read operation from the upstream service (default is 60000 ms).

- write_timeout: Maximum time in milliseconds for a write operation to the upstream service (default is 60000 ms).

- retries: Number of retry attempts upon failure to connect to an upstream service (default is 5).

Service Binding and Integration

For services to operate in tandem with routes, they need to be bound through route-service associations. Routes direct traffic based on specified hostnames, paths, etc., while services outline where these requests are sent. Binding involves linking a route specification to the service object. This binding is achieved when a route is created with a reference to the designated service object.

```
curl -i -X POST http://localhost:8001/routes \
  --data "hosts[]=example.com" \
  --data "paths[]=/apis" \
  --data "service.name=extended-service"
```

In the example above, a route is created which binds requests targeting example.com/apis to the previously configured extended-service.

Managing Service Lifecycle

Service objects in Kong undergo a typical lifecycle that includes creation, retrieval, updating, and deletion, effectively managed through the Kong Admin API.

Retrieving a Service

Service details can be retrieved using a GET request, allowing administrators to inspect current configurations.

```
curl -i -X GET http://localhost:8001/services/<service-id>
```

This command fetches the configuration of the specified service. The response might look as follows:

{

95

```
"id": "25fa7c57-7e98-4d12-b316-020672b2288f",
"name": "extended-service",
"url": "http://example-service:80",
"retries": 5,
"read_timeout": 60000,
"write_timeout": 30000
}
```

Updating a Service

Updating a service allows altering its properties to adapt to evolving backend needs.

```
curl -i -X PATCH http://localhost:8001/services/<service-id> \
  --data "retries=3"
```

This command reduces the retry count, streamlining the upstream request strategy when failures occur.

Deleting a Service

A service is removed by making a DELETE request, ensuring that the associated traffic paths are redirected or halted appropriately.

```
curl -i -X DELETE http://localhost:8001/services/<service-id>
```

Deleting a service necessitates consideration of the impact on associated routes and downstream functionality. Proper coordination ensures no loss of service availability.

Service Configuration Best Practices

Proper configuration and deployment of services in Kong require adopting best practices that bolster maintainability, performance, and scalability.

- **Consistent Naming Conventions:** Employing clear and consistent naming conventions for services aids in understanding and managing objects, especially in environments with numerous microservices.

- **Timeout Optimization:** Tailor timeout settings to reflect real-world expectations of service responsiveness. Adjustments ensure that resources are effectively released, preventing bottlenecks.

- **Retry Strategy:** Configure retry strategies based on the criticality and typical failure modes of the upstream service. A balance
  should be struck between persistence and performance.

- **Versioning Services:** When services undergo version changes
  or substantial modifications, versioning service objects helps
  manage gradual rollouts or phased deployments.

- **Monitoring and Analytics:** Enable monitoring plugins or
  Kong's internal telemetry to gather data on service performance,
  aiding in proactive adjustments or enhancements.

Advanced Service Configuration

In scenarios requiring advanced configurations, Kong's service objects
support complex and diverse use cases. For example, to route traffic
to a microservices architecture within a Kubernetes cluster, Kong can
directly interface with pods as upstream services:

```
curl -i -X POST http://localhost:8001/services \
  --data "name=k8s-pod-service" \
  --data "host=my-service.my-namespace.svc.cluster.local" \
  --data "port=8080" \
  --data "protocol=http"
```

This command registers a service targeting a Kubernetes service within
a specified namespace. Further, Kong's pluggable architecture allows
for integrating custom plugins which extend service functionality at the
gateway layer:

```
curl -i -X POST http://localhost:8001/services/<service-id>/plugins \
  --data "name=my-custom-plugin" \
  --data "config.key=value"
```

With such capabilities, service objects can not only route traffic but also
transform request and response payloads, authenticate users, and implement rate limiting. These integrations enrich the service definition
beyond fundamental routing.

Service objects serve as a cornerstone of Kong's routing architecture,
enhancing modular interaction patterns with upstream services.
Through meticulous configuration and adherence to best practices,
service objects bolster API gateway operations, facilitating
robust, secure, and efficient API traffic management. Implementing

advanced configurations further unlocks potential within microservice architectures, streamlining development and deployment workflows in dynamic environments. Each service object in Kong inherently empowers the gateway to scale its capacities, serving as a testament to the power and flexibility ingrained in Kong's API management philosophy.

4.3 Upstream Services and Load Balancing

Upstream services in Kong refer to the backend servers that process requests forwarded by the API Gateway after routing through defined service objects. This section covers the management of upstream services, including the configuration of load balancing strategies which distribute client requests across multiple upstream instances effectively. Proper management of upstream services is pivotal in maintaining reliable, scalable, and high-performance application infrastructures.

The concept of load balancing serves to distribute incoming network traffic evenly across available server instances to ensure no single server is overwhelmed. This prevents resource overload, optimizes resource utilization, and stabilizes response times, leading to a more robust service delivery.

In Kong, upstream services and load balancing are handled through a combination of entities such as upstream objects and targets. The upstream object represents one or more targets that comprise individual members of the underlying system, which are then collectively subject to load balancing.

Defining Upstream Entities

An upstream entity in Kong is a logical representation of a set of targets (e.g., server instances) that are load balanced. To utilize the load balancing capabilities of Kong, an upstream entity is created:

```
curl -i -X POST http://localhost:8001/upstreams \
  --data "name=my-upstream"
```

The command establishes an upstream object called 'my-upstream'. This object does not specify any backend servers yet but serves as the defining construct for a group of targets.

Once an upstream entity is set, targets are added to the upstream. Each target represents an individual address or node that the upstream service will communicate with.

```
curl -i -X POST http://localhost:8001/upstreams/my-upstream/targets \
  --data "target=192.168.1.101:80" \
  --data "weight=100"

curl -i -X POST http://localhost:8001/upstreams/my-upstream/targets \
  --data "target=192.168.1.102:80" \
  --data "weight=100"
```

Here, two targets at IPs '192.168.1.101' and '192.168.1.102' are added with a default weight of '100'. This weight influences the share of the load each target receives, relative to other targets in the upstream set. Adjusting weights directs more requests to more powerful instances or reduces load on constrained resources.

Load Balancing Strategies

Kong supports several load balancing algorithms that can be configured for upstream objects. The choice of algorithm influences how traffic is distributed across targets and can drastically improve service performance when matched to specific application requirements.

Round Robin

Round robin is the default load balancing strategy in Kong. It sequentially distributes requests across all available targets in a circular manner, maintaining request order and fairness. Each server receives approximately an equal number of requests, well-suited for homogeneous environments where backend server capabilities are uniform.

Least Connections

The least connections strategy assigns requests to the target with the fewest active connections. This approach is effective when targets handle requests of varying length, balancing loads dynamically based on server usage rather than static distribution models.

```
curl -i -X PATCH http://localhost:8001/upstreams/my-upstream \
  --data "algorithm=least-connections"
```

The command updates the upstream configuration to utilize the least connections algorithm, optimizing request handling for uneven workload distribution.

IP Hash

IP hash ensures that requests from a single IP address are consistently routed to the same target, useful for maintaining session stickiness. This strategy is crucial in scenarios where client state needs to be preserved without centralized session management.

```
curl -i -X PATCH http://localhost:8001/upstreams/my-upstream \
  --data "algorithm=ip-hash"
```

The IP hash method provides reliable connection consistency, enhancing the user experience through predictable routing.

Managing the Health of Upstream Targets

Effective load balancing not only distributes traffic but must ensure that only healthy targets receive requests. Health checks form a vital component of Kong's upstream management, automatically probing targets at regular intervals to ascertain availability.

Configuring Health Checks

Health checks in Kong are configured as active or passive, with distinct settings for managing target states.

- **Active Health Checks**: Periodic probes sent from Kong to the target, with configurable probes frequency, timeout, and HTTP status expectations.

```
curl -i -X PUT http://localhost:8001/upstreams/my-upstream/healthchecks \
  --data "active.type=http" \
  --data "active.timeout=1" \
  --data "active.http_path=/status" \
  --data "active.healthy.http_statuses[1]=200" \
  --data "active.healthy.interval=5"
```

This configuration establishes an active HTTP health check, probing the '/status' path every 5 seconds, allowing for target states to adapt dynamically.

- **Passive Health Checks**: Evaluation based on real traffic, rather than synthetic probes. Reactive to failures occurring under load, they adjust routing based on response status codes and thresholds for marking targets unhealthy.

```
curl -i -X PUT http://localhost:8001/upstreams/my-upstream/healthchecks \
  --data "passive.unhealthy.timeout=5" \
  --data "passive.unhealthy.http_failures=3" \
  --data "passive.unhealthy.tcp_failures=3"
```

The passive check is configured to dynamically mark targets as unhealthy upon reaching failure thresholds, thus avoiding routing to problematic instances.

Health checks enhance the robustness and reliability of upstream services by ensuring traffic is routed only to healthy, performing targets. Integrating both active and passive checks within upstream configuration offers comprehensive coverage and reduces service outage risks.

Load Balancing in Dynamic Environments

Modern application architectures are dynamic, often employing containers, serverless technologies, or elastic infrastructure. Kong's upstream services and load balancing approach allows for smooth adaptation to such environments, supporting rapid scaling and reconfiguration.

Kubernetes Integration

For Kubernetes-based deployments, leveraging the service discovery and scaling capabilities of the platform, Kong can directly interface with Kubernetes services as targets. This provides native support for automatic service registration and scaling.

```
curl -i -X POST http://localhost:8001/upstreams \
  --data "name=k8s-my-service"

curl -i -X POST http://localhost:8001/upstreams/k8s-my-service/targets \
  --data "target=my-service.my-namespace.svc.cluster.local:80"
```

These commands register a Kubernetes service as a target, maintaining synchronization between Kong's load balancing mechanisms and Kubernetes' inherent scaling capabilities.

Microservices and Serverless Architectures

Kong upstream management effectively supports decentralized, cloud-native traffic patterns. Service latencies from serverless function calls or disparate microservice interactions can be smoothed via intelligent load balancing strategies, removing bottlenecks, and enhancing application responsiveness.

For instance, in event-driven architectures, where upstream targets can be dynamically instantiated, Kong's load balancing accommodates asynchronous task processing and queues to handle traffic bursts even in highly volatile scenarios.

Through advanced upstream management and load balancing capabilities, Kong ensures resilient and scalable API Gateway operations. By facilitating dynamic distribution models and strategically incorporating health checks, it optimizes application performance irrespective of deployed environment complexity. The strategic application of load balancing facilitates improved resource use, stabilized response times, and minimized downtime, critically contributing to high-quality, consistent service delivery. Kong's integration within contemporary ecosystems like Kubernetes further solidifies its position as a powerful, adaptable API management solution.

4.4   Path and Host-based Routing

In API Gateway operations, efficient routing is achieved through precise mechanisms such as path-based and host-based routing. Kong allows for these types of routing configurations enabling refined control over how incoming requests are directed to appropriate services. This section dives into the development and deployment of path and host-based routing strategies, exploring their nuanced applications and the practical aspects of their configuration within the Kong API Gateway.

Path-based and host-based routing are indispensable techniques for any API strategy aiming to scale across varied clients and endpoints. These techniques ensure client requests are succinctly matched and forwarded to backend services configured to process them. This not only aids in traffic management but also assists in maintaining orderly and scalable deployments.

Understanding Path-based Routing

Path-based routing enables request distribution based on the request

URI. It routes incoming API calls to different services based on the URL path of the request itself. This granularity empowers developers to partition services logically, allowing for the separation of feature-based deployments or accommodating different application modules.

For example, an API Gateway might direct '/user' requests to a user management service and '/product' requests to a product catalog service. This delineation allows for specific application logic and resources to operate independently, optimizing organizational goals and enhancing maintainability.

```
curl -i -X POST http://localhost:8001/routes \
  --data "methods[]=GET" \
  --data "paths[]=/users" \
  --data "service.id=<user-service-id>"

curl -i -X POST http://localhost:8001/routes \
  --data "methods[]=GET" \
  --data "paths[]=/products" \
  --data "service.id=<product-service-id>"
```

Two routing rules are established here. Requests with paths containing '/users' are directed to the 'user-service'. Similarly, requests with '/products' are routed to the 'product-service'.

Static vs. Dynamic Paths

- Static Paths: Define exact matches. An HTTP request exactly matching '/static-path' would be directed as configured. Precision is its strength, ensuring requests flow predictably.

- Dynamic Paths: Use parametric or wildcard routes like '/dynamic/*', capturing a broader range of paths. These allow dynamic handling, useful in scenarios like RESTful services handling CRUD operations across resources.

```
curl -i -X POST http://localhost:8001/routes \
  --data "paths[]=/v1/*" \
  --data "service.id=<v1-service-id>"
```

Here, all incoming requests prefixed with '/v1/' are routed to 'v1-service', facilitating version-based handling for APIs undergoing iterative development.

Exploring Host-based Routing

103

Host-based routing deals with directing traffic based on the domain name provided in the request header. This is particularly useful when the API Gateway needs to serve multiple domains, acting as a reverse proxy that channels requests as per the origin specified in HTTP headers. It aligns seamlessly with multi-tenant architectures where one gateway serves varied clientele distinguished by domain.

```
curl -i -X POST http://localhost:8001/routes \
  --data "hosts[]=api.example.com" \
  --data "service.id=<example-service-id>"

curl -i -X POST http://localhost:8001/routes \
  --data "hosts[]=shop.example.com" \
  --data "service.id=<shop-service-id>"
```

In this setup, requests targeting 'api.example.com' are routed to 'example-service', while 'shop.example.com' requests find their way to 'shop-service'.

Combining Path and Host-based Routing

The true power of routing lies in combining path and host conditions, offering unparalleled flexibility. This hybrid approach is advantageous when serving complex applications with distinct subdomains and resources.

```
curl -i -X POST http://localhost:8001/routes \
  --data "hosts[]=api.example.com" \
  --data "paths[]=/v1/users" \
  --data "service.id=<user-v1-service-id>"

curl -i -X POST http://localhost:8001/routes \
  --data "hosts[]=shop.example.com" \
  --data "paths[]=/v1/orders" \
  --data "service.id=<order-v1-service-id>"
```

This enables configurations where routing logic is adapted to serve requests such as 'api.example.com/v1/users' through 'user-v1-service'.

Overcoming Routing Challenges

While path and host-based routing form the backbone of many Kong deployments, certain challenges can surface, requiring strategic solutions:

- **Scalability Concerns**: As applications grow, routing tables can become excessively complex. Leveraging dynamic routes and systematic naming conventions helps in managing growth without sacrifice in performance.

- **Route Overlap**: Similar or generic routes can introduce conflicts, necessitating route order tuning and evaluation of specificity to prioritize routes accurately.

- **Protocol Considerations**: Ensuring compatibility across HTTP and HTTPS is essential. Secure context mandates SNI (Server Name Indication) use for host-based routing, thereby optimizing SSL handshakes and reducing latency.

Routing with Regular Expressions

Advanced routing needs might require the utilization of regex patterns for capturing non-trivial matching logic. Kong supports regex pattern matching, a powerful tool for scenarios such as conditional routing based on complex URL structures.

```
curl -i -X POST http://localhost:8001/routes \
  --data "paths[]~=/api/v\d+/resources/\d+/items" \
  --data "service.id=<complex-routing-service-id>"
```

This example directs any path following '/api/vX/resources/Y/items' (where X and Y are numerical) to a predefined service.

Routing Optimization and Best Practices

Optimizing routing strategies involves more than just technical configurations—prioritizing clarity, maintainability, and future scalability is paramount. Some best practices include:

- **Route Segmentation**: Segment routes into manageable categories, potentially aligned with service ownership, functional areas, or API versions.

- **Predefined Patterns**: Utilize consistent path patterns and domain rules to simplify understanding and deployment, minimizing errors or compatibility issues in route handling.

- **Logging and Analytics**: Implement comprehensive logging for analysis of incoming requests' routes. This provides insights into peak address loads, misconfigurations, or potential rerouting benefits.

- **Security Alignment**: Ensure routing complements security practices, preventing exposure of sensitive endpoints and sustaining service privacy through disciplined allocation of routes and domains.

- **Evolutionary Strategies**: Routinely audit and adapt routing logic as services evolve. Applying an evolutionary approach helps align gateway configurations with emerging business or technical requirements robustly.

By deploying structured path and host-based routing, Kong not only manages client requests with precision but also enables the API Gateway to scale seamlessly with organizational ambitions. As Kong continues evolving, routing strategies must adapt synchronous with architectural patterns, technological advancements, and operational Commandments to keep performance and reliability at their zenith. The strategic execution of routing, supported by measured deployment of configurations and automation, fosters a harmonious ecosystem where API management leads directly to tangible business outcomes.

4.5   Advanced Routing Options

Routing within an API Gateway like Kong is a multifaceted process that can move beyond the traditional hostname and path-based methodologies. Advanced routing options provide nuanced and flexible approaches for directing requests in a way that aligns with specialized operational requirements. These sophisticated strategies include regex pattern matching, header-based routing, query parameter routing, and the implementation of custom logic to meet complex needs. Mastery of these advanced techniques enables system architects and developers to streamline traffic flow, optimize service interoperation, and enhance user experiences even within the most challenging and dynamic environments.

Regex Pattern Matching

Regex (regular expression) pattern matching allows for high flexibility in managing paths and other request attributes within routing rules. This pattern-based approach is particularly powerful when attempting to match a wide range of inputs that follow certain textual rules or patterns rather than exact strings.

Regex routing in Kong allows matching complex URL paths using regex patterns rather than strict strings or known patterns. This enables dynamic routing, linking disparate request forms to the appropriate upstream services without elaborate configurations.

```
curl -i -X POST http://localhost:8001/routes \
  --data "paths[]~=/store/(?<category>[a-zA-Z]+)/(?<id>[0-9]+)" \
  --data "service.id=<dynamic-service-id>"
```

In this scenario, all requests targeting '/store/<category>/<id>' are routed to a service defined by the pattern. Regex captures group categories (alphabets) and IDs (numerical), facilitating path-pattern based service lookups.

Header-based Routing

Header-based routing mechanisms enable decision-making based on specific HTTP headers included in the client request. HTTP headers convey metadata critical for routing scenarios including user-agent-based redirection, language negotiation, custom authentication tokens, and more.

Kong excels in incorporating header-based routing within its versatile routing framework. It allows for the customization of behavior whereby requests containing certain header attributes trigger specific paths or service rules.

```
curl -i -X POST http://localhost:8001/routes \
  --data "hosts[]=api.example.com" \
  --data "headers.x-consumer=gold" \
  --data "service.id=<premium-service-id>"
```

The above command ensures 'gold' tier requests (as identified by the 'x-consumer' header) reach 'premium-service', leveraging header intelligence for differentiated service management.

Multi-attribute Header Routing

Complex scenarios might demand multiple header conditions be met for determining the correct route. Kong's configuration capabilities support logical combinations of header attributes, allowing for versatile and targeted routing.

```
curl -i -X POST http://localhost:8001/routes \
  --data "hosts[]=mobile.api.example.com" \
  --data "headers.accept-language[]=en-US" \
  --data "headers.device[]=Android" \
  --data "service.id=<mobile-service-id>"
```

In this example, only requests associated with the 'en-US' language preference and from 'Android' devices are forwarded to 'mobile-service'. This allows for precise routing policies attuned with device-specific experiences or regional requirements.

Query Parameter Routing

Extending the analytical depth to incorporate query parameters into routing logic empowers developers to act on request-level intricacies, enriching API responsiveness with parameter-specific conditions. While traditional systems route based on paths or headers, query parameters bring the minutiae of requests to the forefront.

A well-known use case involves content negotiation or feature flag operation based on client-supplied query parameters. For example, activating beta features or service levels through query inputs.

```
curl -i -X POST http://localhost:8001/routes \
  --data "paths[]=/api" \
  --data "service.id=<feature-toggle-service-id>" \
  --data "querystring.beta=true"
```

In this configuration, requests where the query parameter 'beta=true' are directed specifically to a service equipped to handle experimental features, navigating users to enhanced application states as per query input directives.

Custom Logic and Plugins

For requirements irreconcilable via predefined routing options, Kong's extensibility through custom plugins comes to the fore. These plugins can intercept and dynamically rewrite requests using the rich plugin SDK, transforming inputs to ensure their compatibility or enhancement aligns with the anticipated service functionality.

Developers can craft Lua or JavaScript plugins to extend or adapt behavior beyond inbuilt capabilities, scripting complex operations like geolocation routing, user authentication redirection, or service-level transformations.

```
curl -i -X POST http://localhost:8001/plugins/ \
  --data "name=my-custom-transform-plugin" \
  --data "service.id=<service-id>" \
  --data "config.string=<transformation-logic>"
```

A Lua or JS plugin bound to a service can operationalize arbitrary business logic, offering a high degree of flexibility to enhance or steer routing decisions beyond the reach of core settings.

Combining Advanced Options for Routing Sophistication

Real-world applications typically require blending advanced routing methodologies, relying on a balanced application of path, host, header, and custom logic to meet the escalating demands of modern traffic management.

For instance, a content provider might need to serve different versions of an application based on device, language, versioning via paths, or query strings, realizing a configuration resembling:

```
curl -i -X POST http://localhost:8001/routes \
  --data "hosts[]=cdn.example.com" \
  --data "paths[]=/v2/assets/*" \
  --data "headers.Device[]=iOS" \
  --data "querystring.format=hd" \
  --data "service.id=<highdef-content-service-id>"
```

This comprehensive example targets high-definition content delivery for iOS devices accessing version 2 assets, specified by a path and query parameter, under a particular content network domain, thereby achieving precision through a layered route logic.

Considerations for Employing Advanced Routing Techniques

Employing advanced routing techniques and custom logic necessitates a meticulous approach to avoid misconfigurations, unintended route overlaps, or performance issues:

- **Complexity Management**: Keep routing logic as clear and simple as possible, applying advanced logic only where truly necessary, thus avoiding complications that accompany unwieldy configurations.

- **Performance Optimization**: Choose routing methodologies judiciously to preempt latency, especially where regex or multi-header routes add computational load. Benchmarks and simulations are essential to gauge impact.

- **Security and Compliance**: As with all configurations involving client metadata, maintain vigilance against routing logic that unwittingly exposes services to abuse, ensuring compliance with privacy requirements.

- **Dynamic Adaptation**: Regularly revisit routing setups to accommodate evolving API strategies, business needs, or performance checkpoints, adapting strategies to leverage emerging technologies or user demands.

- **Testing and Validation**: Rigorously test advanced configurations in staging environments, confirming that complex logic routes correctly under varying conditions without introducing regressions or data drift.

By deploying advanced routing configurations within Kong, organizations embody a strategic gateway that harmonizes disparate traffic streams, ensuring consistent and performant service while adapting flexibly to future demands. This ability enables businesses to maximize throughput, optimize resource utilization, and achieve responsive adaptability, flourishing within an ecosystem where API management is pivotal to overarching operational achievements.

4.6   Traffic Splitting and Canary Releases

Traffic splitting and canary releases represent innovative techniques in modern software deployment strategies, primarily aimed at reducing risk and enhancing user experience when introducing new service versions or features. These methodologies allow organizations to incrementally release changes to a small subset of users before doing a full-scale rollout, thereby ensuring reliability, performance, and user satisfaction.

In the context of Kong API Gateway, traffic splitting and canary releases involve the strategic routing and analysis of API traffic to manage and deploy changes effectively. This section explores the mechanics of these approaches, their implementation within Kong, and the underlying benefits they offer to digital service frameworks.

Understanding traffic splitting involves distributing a subset of traffic to different service endpoints or versions concurrently. This dynamic allocation allows organizations to route real customer traffic across multiple versions of a service simultaneously, facilitating comparative performance assessments or feature evaluation.

With Kong, traffic splitting can be implemented to weigh traffic distribution among multiple upstream targets constituting different application versions or service endpoints. This process empowers teams to achieve meaningful insights during different stage evaluations while enabling seamless transitions.

Weighted Traffic Distribution In basic terms, traffic distribution in Kong can be designed using weight allocations across service targets within upstream configurations. Weighted algorithms determine how traffic is distributed among available nodes, influencing how different service instances receive traffic.

```
curl -i -X POST http://localhost:8001/upstreams \
  --data "name=split-traffic-service"

curl -i -X POST http://localhost:8001/upstreams/split-traffic-service/targets \
  --data "target=service-v1.local:80" \
  --data "weight=70"

curl -i -X POST http://localhost:8001/upstreams/split-traffic-service/targets \
  --data "target=service-v2.local:80" \
  --data "weight=30"
```

In this case, traffic directed to split-traffic-service is split such that version 1 (service-v1) receives 70% of the traffic, and version 2 (service-v2) receives 30%. This configuration is instrumental for comparing performance and stability under live conditions.

Implementing canary releases involves launching a new software version to a small subset of users, monitoring behavior, and then making a data-driven decision to continue or rollback based on observable outcomes. This method reduces exposure risk and ensures that new features do not negatively impact the user experience.

Within Kong, canary releases thrive through routing configurations

111

that channel specific user segments to the canary version, differentially observing KPIs (Key Performance Indicators) such as response times, error rates, or engagement metrics.

Targeted Canary Traffic Strategy Targeting specific user segments more precisely maps with feature flagging or strategic header-based routing, enabling precise targeting of the canary cohort.

```
curl -i -X POST http://localhost:8001/routes \
  --data "hosts[]=api.example.com" \
  --data "headers.x-canary-user=beta" \
  --data "service.id=<canary-service-id>"
```

Here, requests containing the header x-canary-user=beta are routed to the canary service, thereby restricting the new deployment exposure to users specially labeled for trials or experimentation.

Phased Rollout Using Request Proxies Kong's capabilities can be extended through custom plugins to further refine traffic segmentation and ensure only desired user interactions benefit from new features without global exposure until validation.

```
curl -i -X POST http://localhost:8001/plugins \
  --data "name=custom-canary-wordpress" \
  --data "service.id=<main-service-id>" \
  --data "enabled=true" \
  --data "config.percentage=10"
```

With a custom plugin proxy, 10% of the traffic intermittently redirected to the canary version empowers the quick detection of anomalies and benchmarking scenarios.

The primary benefits of employing traffic splitting and canary techniques revolve around customer satisfaction, operational continuity, and analytical insights. However, they also present specific challenges requiring careful planning:

Benefits

- **Risk Mitigation:** The minimal exposure of initial deployments reduces potential disruption risk, allowing for an empirical rollout once metrics indicate stability.

- **Incremental Improvements:** Allows for progressive improvement, gathering user feedback and environmental data before firm commitments to broader distribution.

- **User Insights and Engagement:** Direct interaction under new versions reveals improved user experiences and pain points, translating to insightful product refinement.

- **Quick Rollbacks:** Fault detection in early phases permits proactive rollback actions, preventing widespread impact across the user base.

Challenges

- **Complexity in Configuration:** Accurate setup for traffic splitting and canary releases demands detailed configuration of routing rules and segments.

- **Performance Measurement:** Monitoring impact across staggered releases necessitates sound procedures and infrastructure for consistent tracking of usage metrics.

- **Consistency in Data Management:** Synchronizing data states across service versions introduces complications in data processing, storage, and eventual consolidation.

- **Load Variability:** Fluctuating loads may affect service feedback when small sample sizes reflect isolated conditions.

To capitalize on the ability to conduct effective traffic splitting and canary deployments, Kong users should consider adopting strategic best practices:

- **Comprehensive Monitoring:** Implement thorough logging and analytics tools tracking both qualitative and quantitative performance indicators during canary releases.

- **Structured Traffic Incrementalization:** Conduct structured phases for traffic increment, beginning with minute percentages, scaling further with confidence in stable operations.

- **User Segmentation Based Strategy:** Establish user segments based on history, engagement class, or user profile, allowing targeted canary exposure.

- **API Consumer Feedback Loop:** Deploy API consumer feedback mechanisms capturing direct input or automated surveys, enhancing understanding as features are trialed.

- **Documenting the Deployment Pipeline:** Establish and articulate thorough documentation providing end-to-end traffic management policies and configurations for clarity and revisitability.

Implementing these intelligent traffic management solutions requires foresight and deliberate methodologies, yet rewarding organizations with significantly improved service delivery, minimized risk during releases, and heightened user satisfaction. Kong empowers these strategies with the robust configurability of Kong Gateway, enabling a flexible, service-oriented approach to continuous delivery and innovation within modern application landscapes.

Chapter 5

Securing APIs using Kong

This chapter addresses the critical aspect of securing APIs using Kong API Gateway, detailing the various mechanisms available to protect API endpoints. It outlines methods for implementing robust authentication and authorization protocols, including API key management and OAuth 2.0 integration. The chapter also explores techniques for rate limiting, throttling, and encryption to safeguard sensitive data in transit. Additionally, it covers IP whitelisting for access control and strategies for mitigating automated attacks through bot detection. By understanding these security measures, readers can ensure their APIs are effectively protected against unauthorized access and exploitation.

5.1 Authentication and Authorization

Authentication and Authorization are fundamental processes within any architectural framework designed to protect resources from unauthorized access. In the context of an API gateway like Kong, these processes are essential to ensure secure communication between clients and services. Through Kong, various methods can be leveraged to implement authentication and authorization, thus safeguarding APIs against unauthorized usage.

Authentication is the process of validating the identity of a user or a client application. This validation ensures that users are who they say they are, allowing them to prove their identity using various strategies, including API keys, OAuth2.0, JWTs, etc. Authorization, on the other hand, determines whether an authenticated identity has permission to access a resource or perform a specific operation. While authentication is about verifying identity, authorization is about verifying access rights.

Authentication with API Keys:

API keys serve as one of the most straightforward methods for authenticating a client. These keys act as an identifier for the client application to access the API and can be generated and managed through Kong. To implement API key authentication, Kong's key-auth plugin can be used, which checks for valid keys in the incoming requests.

The **key-auth** plugin in Kong requires keys to be passed in the request headers, query string, or request body. Developers can control how keys are accepted and assign them specific expiration periods. Below is a basic example of how you might configure and use API key authentication in Kong.

```
// Enable key-auth plugin for a service
curl -X POST http://localhost:8001/services/{service_id}/plugins \
  --data "name=key-auth" \
  --data "config.key_names=apikey"
```

This command enables the key-auth plugin for a specified service where the client requests must include a key named **apikey**. Once the plugin is enabled, the API consumer must include their key with each request.

```
// Example of a client request with the API key in the header
curl -X GET http://localhost:8000/{api_endpoints} \
  -H 'apikey: YOUR_API_KEY'
```

OAuth 2.0 Integration:

OAuth 2.0 is a more robust and secure framework compared to API keys. It helps to secure APIs by defining a standardized way for users

116

to grant web or mobile applications access to their resources without sharing personal credentials. OAuth 2.0 roles include resource owner, client, resource server, and authorization server. In Kong, the **oauth2** plugin facilitates OAuth 2.0 integration.

OAuth 2.0 processes involve obtaining an access token that a client uses to authenticate and access resources. There are multiple grant types available in the OAuth 2.0 protocol, including Client Credentials, Password, and Authorization Code, each serving different scenarios.

Using Kong's OAuth 2.0 plugin involves a few steps:

- Enable the oauth2 plugin on your service.

- Create an OAuth 2.0 credential for your consumers.

- Manage access tokens with appropriate expiration and scope settings.

For example:

```
// Enable OAuth2 plugin for a service
curl -X POST http://localhost:8001/services/{service_id}/plugins \
  --data "name=oauth2" \
  --data "config.scopes=email,phone,address" \
  --data "config.mandatory_scope=true" \
  --data "config.enable_client_credentials=true"
```

This command sets up the OAuth2 plugin to require specific scopes and allows the client credentials grant type. Following this setup, consumers can be issued OAuth2 credentials:

```
// Create OAuth2 credential for a consumer
curl -X POST http://localhost:8001/consumers/{consumer_id}/oauth2 \
  --data "name=YourApp" \
  --data "client_id=YourClientID" \
  --data "client_secret=YourClientSecret" \
  --data "redirect_uri=http://yourapp.com/callback"
```

In the structured OAuth flow, once the client has obtained the access token, it needs to be included in the Authorization header for subsequent requests:

```
// Client making an authorized request with the access token
curl -X GET http://localhost:8000/{api_endpoints} \
  -H 'Authorization: Bearer ACCESS_TOKEN'
```

117

JSON Web Tokens (JWT):

Another method to authenticate users involves using JSON Web Tokens (JWTs). JWTs are compact, URL-safe mechanisms that encode
claims to be transmitted between two parties, typically a client and
a server. The claims in a JWT are encoded as a JSON object that is
used as the payload of a JSON Web Signature (JWS) structure or as
the plaintext of a JSON Web Encryption (JWE) structure, enabling the
claims to be digitally signed or integrity protected with a Message Authentication Code (MAC) and/or encrypted.

The **jwt** plugin in Kong helps in validating the authenticity of JWTs
passed with incoming requests. This mechanism involves fewer server-
side storage requirements since the token contains all required information.

To configure JWT with Kong, follow these steps:

- Enable the jwt plugin for a service.

- Create JWT credentials for a consumer.

- Make authenticated requests with the JWT.

Example configuration:

```
// Enable JWT plugin for a service
curl -X POST http://localhost:8001/services/{service_id}/plugins \
  --data "name=jwt"
```

Next, JWT credentials can be issued:

```
// Create JWT credential for a consumer
curl -X POST http://localhost:8001/consumers/{consumer_id}/jwt \
  --data "key=Your_Key" \
  --data "algorithm=HS256"
```

Once configured, clients can use a JWT in their requests:

```
// Example of a client request with JWT
curl -X GET http://localhost:8000/{api_endpoints} \
  -H 'Authorization: Bearer YOUR_JWT_TOKEN'
```

Authorization Strategies:

Upon successful authentication, the authorization process decides
which resources and actions the authenticated user should have

118

access to. Kong supports various techniques to enforce authorization, including ACLs (Access Control Lists), RBAC (Role-Based Access Control), and custom lua authorizers.

ACLs: ACLs allow you to define group-based permissions. Users or consumers are added to groups, and resources are tagged with required group memberships. The **acl** plugin in Kong can facilitate this setup.

```
// Enable ACL plugin for a service
curl -X POST http://localhost:8001/services/{service_id}/plugins \
  --data "name=acl" \
  --data "config.whitelist=group1,group2"
```

Consumers are subsequently assigned to groups, which aligns with access scenarios suitable for environments requiring shared or inherited permission structures.

Role-Based Access Control (RBAC): RBAC implementations further refine access based on roles assigned to identities. Kong's RBAC model extends administrator privileges through user-defined roles, which can also be programmatically enforced using Kong Enterprise's advanced feature set. This way, service administrators can narrowly define the operations available to users based on their assigned roles.

These authentication and authorization methods facilitate the creation of a secure, manageable, and scalable API ecosystem. By leveraging Kong's comprehensive set of plugins, developers are empowered to enforce the integrity of their applications while providing reliable and robust solutions for client-server communications.

In practice, choosing the right authentication and authorization strategy will depend on specific business requirements, sensitivity of the data, and client interaction patterns. By integrating multiple complementary layers of security mechanisms, one can significantly enhance API safety and efficiency while providing seamless access control tailored to each use case.

5.2 API Key Management

Effective API key management is a critical aspect of securing access to web services, allowing developers to precisely control client access to

API resources. As a lightweight yet powerful authentication method, API keys provide a straightforward mechanism to identify and authenticate calling programs or users. Kong, as a leading API gateway platform, offers robust API key management capabilities, enabling the creation, distribution, and validation of API keys as part of securing client-server interactions.

API keys are unique tokens assigned to an application or user, and they must be communicated in API requests for authentication. These keys allow developers to monitor and limit the usage of the API, prevent service abuse, and manage consumer access more effectively.

Generating API Keys:

API key generation is the initial step in the API key management process. Kong provides mechanisms to dynamically generate keys for consumers. These keys can be single-use or long-term, depending on the needs of the service and access policy definitions.

Example of generating an API key using Kong:

```
// Create a new consumer
curl -X POST http://localhost:8001/consumers \
  --data "username=new_user"

// Generate an API key for the consumer
curl -X POST http://localhost:8001/consumers/new_user/key-auth \
  --data "key=YOUR_UNIQUE_API_KEY"
```

This sequence of commands first creates a new consumer in Kong and then associates a unique API key with that consumer. Kong will store the key and can validate it during subsequent API requests.

Distributing API Keys:

Upon generation, API keys need to be securely distributed to clients. It is crucial to use secure communication channels, such as HTTPS, to transmit these keys in order to protect them from unauthorized interception. Documentation accompanying the distribution should advise clients on best practices for handling and incorporating these keys into their applications.

For developers, integrating API keys into applications typically involves storing keys within configuration files or environment variables, leveraging secure storage locations to prevent key leakage through source code repositories.

Validating API Keys:

API key validation in Kong is handled using the 'key-auth' plugin, which checks for the presence and correctness of a key before allowing access to an API endpoint. This plugin is activated on a per-service basis and allows for flexible configurations depending on requirements.

Example of enabling the 'key-auth' plugin:

```
// Enable key-auth plugin for a service
curl -X POST http://localhost:8001/services/{service_id}/plugins \
  --data "name=key-auth" \
  --data "config.key_names=api_key"

// Make an authenticated request
curl -X GET http://localhost:8000/{api_endpoints} \
  -H 'api_key: YOUR_API_KEY'
```

Through this configuration, the 'key-auth' plugin checks incoming requests for the 'api_key' parameter in either the header, query string, or request body, ensuring seamless client access verification.

Best Practices for Managing API Keys:

- *Key Rotation:* Regularly rotating API keys can significantly mitigate the risk of unauthorized access due to key leakage or exposure. Automating key rotation using cron jobs or integrated APIs is recommended to periodically update keys without manual intervention.

- *Scope and Quota Restrictions:* Define and enforce scope limitations and usage quotas per API key. This involves restricting what endpoints a key can access and how frequently it can access them. Applying these measures in Kong can be achieved through additional plugins like rate-limiting.

```
// Rate limiting a specific API key
curl -X POST http://localhost:8001/consumers/new_user/plugins \
  --data "name=rate-limiting" \
  --data "config.minute=10"

// Scope limiting using ACL
curl -X POST http://localhost:8001/services/{service_id}/plugins \
  --data "name=acl" \
  --data "config.whitelist=group_name"
```

- *Monitoring and Analytics:* Track key usage through logs and analytic tools to detect patterns indicating potential misuse or abuse. Kong's integration with analytics platforms and logging services aids in providing insights, making it easier to take timely actions in response to anomalies.

- *Design for Robustness:* Avoid hardcoding API keys in source code. Instead, they should be loaded from configuration files or key management systems at runtime. Utilizing environmental variables or secure vaulting tools can provide additional protection against accidental exposure.

- *Educating Consumers:* It's essential to educate API consumers about the importance of maintaining key confidentiality and secure usage practices. This includes avoiding public exposure of keys in URLs, using encrypted transmission, and adhering to minimum privilege principles when granting access via keys.

- *Testing and Staging:* Regular testing of API key validation and management workflows in a staging environment can reveal gaps or inefficiencies in the provisioning or authentication pipeline before deployment into production. This also provides an opportunity to fine-tune monitoring dashboards and response automation for common incident responses.

Advanced Key Management with Kong:

For enterprises looking to extend beyond basic key management, Kong offers advanced features in its Enterprise edition that provide additional layers of security and control.

Kong's Enterprise version includes features like:

- *Consumer Group Management:* Enables complex policy definitions based on consumer groups. Enterprises can define global, per-group, and per-key policies, providing granular control over resource access.

- *Analytics Dashboards:* Enable deep insights into API usage patterns, assisting in informed decision-making regarding API scaling, user engagement, and monetization potential.

- *Integrated Secret Management:* Out-of-the-box integration with secret management solutions ensures that API keys are stored and accessed with rigorous security protocols.

For the evolving landscape of API development, adopting a comprehensive API key management strategy is indispensable. It balances user experience with stringent security requirements, ensuring legitimate access to services while preventing unauthorized interactions.

As teams adopt DevSecOps practices emphasizing security as an integrated part of the development lifecycle, API key management remains a cornerstone in achieving secure, scalable, and resilient service architectures. With Kong, teams can leverage a well-defined set of best practices and plugins to instantiate a robust, user-centric API key management environment.

5.3 OAuth 2.0 Integration

OAuth 2.0 is an open standard for access delegation commonly used as a method for internet users to grant websites or applications limited access to their information without exposing credentials. The primary focus of OAuth 2.0 is to provide a secure and efficient process for authorization and delegation, making it a critical component in API security. Integrating OAuth 2.0 with Kong provides a robust framework for managing access to APIs, enhancing both security and user management capabilities.

The OAuth 2.0 protocol defines four key roles: resource owner, client, resource server, and authorization server. The interactions between these roles are facilitated by access tokens, which act as credentials allowing clients to access specific resources on behalf of the resource owner.

OAuth 2.0 Grant Types:

OAuth 2.0 specifies several grant types to address different authorization scenarios, including:

- **Authorization Code Grant:** Utilized primarily by web applications, it involves the client redirecting the resource owner to the authorization server's authorization endpoint, obtaining an authorization code upon user consent, and then exchanging it for an access token.

- **Implicit Grant:** Typically used by mobile and web applications with OAuth 2.0 implemented on the client-side, offering reduced security since the access token might be exposed in URLs.

- **Resource Owner Password Credentials Grant:** Suitable when the resource owner has a trust relationship with the client, this is often used for first-party apps where the client requests the resource owner's credentials.

- **Client Credentials Grant:** Suitable for server-to-server communication where the client accesses resources in its local scope, typically used for background or automation processes.

Enabling OAuth 2.0 in Kong:

Kong provides a comprehensive oauth2 plugin that facilitates the seamless integration of OAuth 2.0 into the API gateway. To initiate OAuth 2.0 integration with Kong, the following configurations are undertaken:

```
// Enable OAuth2 plugin for a service
curl -X POST http://localhost:8001/services/{service_id}/plugins \
  --data "name=oauth2" \
  --data "config.scopes=read,write,admin" \
  --data "config.mandatory_scope=true" \
  --data "config.enable_client_credentials=true"
```

This command enables the OAuth2 plugin on a specific service. Here, the authorization flows are initiated according to configured scopes. The mandatory_scope ensures that requests must include the scope parameter, while enabling the client credentials grant type which is useful for server-to-server interactions.

Registering OAuth 2.0 Clients:

Once the plugin is activated, clients need to be registered with the necessary OAuth credentials. Kong associates these credentials with existing consumer entries, aligning client authentication with Kong's core user management system.

```
// Register a new OAuth2 application for a consumer
curl -X POST http://localhost:8001/consumers/{consumer_id}/oauth2 \
  --data "name=ExampleApp" \
  --data "client_id=YourClientID" \
  --data "client_secret=YourClientSecret" \
  --data "redirect_uri=http://example.com/callback"
```

The client_id and client_secret are crucial for the client's identification and authorization workflow, while the redirect_uri specifies the callback endpoint post-authorization.

Handling Authorization Flows:

OAuth 2.0 flows involve multiple steps and redirections, necessitating clear understanding and accurate implementation to avoid security pitfalls. The most commonly used flow, the Authorization Code Grant, functions as follows:

- **Client Redirects User:** The client redirects the resource owner to the authorization server to gain authorization.

- **User Consents:** After successfully authenticating, the user consents to the permissions requested by the client.

- **Authorization Code Issuance:** Upon consent, the authorization server redirects the user back to the client with an authorization code.

  Example request for authorization:

  ```
  // Redirect user to authorization URL
  GET /authorize?response_type=code&client_id=YourClientID&redirect_uri=
      http://example.com/callback&scope=read%20write
  ```

- **Authorization Code Exchange:** The client exchanges the authorization code for an access token.

  ```
  // Exchange authorization code for access token
  curl -X POST http://localhost:8000/{token_endpoint} \
    -d 'grant_type=authorization_code' \
    -d 'client_id=YourClientID' \
    -d 'client_secret=YourClientSecret' \
    -d 'redirect_uri=http://example.com/callback' \
    -d 'code=AUTHORIZATION_CODE'
  ```

- **Access Token Utilization:** The client uses the obtained access token to access protected resources.

  ```
  // Access protected resource with access token
  curl -X GET http://localhost:8000/{api_endpoints} \
    -H 'Authorization: Bearer ACCESS_TOKEN'
  ```

Advanced OAuth 2.0 Features:

Kong's integration with OAuth 2.0 introduces several advanced capabilities designed to enhance security and token management:

- **Refresh Tokens:** These allow clients to obtain a new access token without user intervention. Tokens can be extended or renewed seamlessly, improving user experience and minimizing disruptions.

```
// Refresh access token
curl -X POST http://localhost:8000/{token_endpoint} \
  -d 'grant_type=refresh_token' \
  -d 'client_id=YourClientID' \
  -d 'client_secret=YourClientSecret' \
  -d 'refresh_token=REFRESH_TOKEN'
```

- **Token Revocation:** Allowing resource owners or administrators to revoke tokens that are compromised or no longer needed, effectively terminating active sessions.

- **Scope Management:** Centralized policies that govern API access granularity through scoping, ensuring clients only access the data required for their use case.

- **Dynamic Client Registration:** Facilitating seamless client onboarding by allowing clients to register dynamically rather than through manual configuration.

Best Practices for OAuth 2.0 Security:

Securing the OAuth 2.0 flows and protecting tokens involves adherence to security best practices:

- **SSL/TLS Enforcement:** Always use SSL/TLS to protect data integrity and confidentiality during API interactions, preventing man-in-the-middle attacks.

- **Token Lifetime Management:** Short-lived access tokens reduce the impact of compromised tokens. Implement token expiration policies and leverage refresh tokens appropriately.

- **Rotate Tokens Regularly:** Employ token rotation strategies to invalidate tokens periodically and update authentication protocols, minimizing misuse risks.

126

- **Validate Scopes:** Ensure that scopes are properly defined and validate that clients' requests abide by these restrictions.

- **Mitigate Phishing:** Implement strong user verification mechanisms at the authorization server to reduce the chances of phishing attacks.

OAuth 2.0 provides a high level of security when implemented properly. The Kong API Gateway enhances these capabilities with its advanced plugin system, enabling detailed and accurate access token management. When executed correctly, OAuth 2.0 integration using Kong ensures a secure, flexible, and scalable platform for managing user access across various applications and services. Through diligent application of OAuth 2.0, developers can maintain high security standards while delivering seamless user experiences.

5.4 Rate Limiting and Throttling

Rate limiting and throttling are essential traffic management practices implemented in an API gateway such as Kong to control the number of requests a client can make to an API within a given period. These techniques are vital for safeguarding APIs against abuse, ensuring fair usage, optimizing performance, and maintaining the availability of backend services. By regulating the traffic flow, rate limiting and throttling prevent the potential overloading of resources.

Rate Limiting Concepts:

Rate limiting controls the frequency of requests, measured in requests per second, minute, hour, or day, that an API client can make. When the limit is exceeded, the server can reject further requests and may return an HTTP status code such as 429 (Too Many Requests). Clients are advised to adhere to the defined limits, often specified in API documentation, to prevent disruptions in service.

Rate limiting addresses several key concerns:

- **Preventing Abuse:** By setting thresholds on the number of permissible requests, rate limiting deters potential abuse by preventing excessive calls from singular clients.

- **Ensuring Fair Usage:** This process ensures equitable distribution of resources among multiple consumers, safeguarding service integrity.

- **Service Protection:** Rate limiting acts as a shield against poor API implementations or malicious traffic patterns that could inadvertently impact backend processing capabilities.

Implementing Rate Limiting in Kong:

Kong facilitates rate limiting through the 'rate-limiting' plugin. This plugin offers multiple configurations to control traffic based on various parameters, such as the number of requests per consumer, service, or route.

Configuring Rate Limiting on a Service:

Below is an example of enabling the 'rate-limiting' plugin on a specific service with a defined request cap:

```
// Enable rate-limiting plugin on a service
curl -X POST http://localhost:8001/services/{service_id}/plugins \
  --data "name=rate-limiting" \
  --data "config.minute=10" // Limit to 10 requests per minute
```

In this configuration, the 'rate-limiting' plugin enforces a limit of 10 requests per minute for the specified service. The plugin counts requests based on consumer data, such as API keys, and imposes restrictions upon reaching the defined threshold.

Global vs. Consumer-Specific Limits:

Kong's rate limiting can be applied globally or tailored to individual consumers:

- **Global Rate Limiting:** This applies limits uniformly across all clients, ensuring that no single consumer compromises service availability for others.

```
// Global rate limit across a service
curl -X POST http://localhost:8001/plugins \
  --data "name=rate-limiting" \
  --data "config.minute=1000" // Allow 1000 requests total per minute
```

- **Consumer-Specific Rate Limiting:** This design allows different limits for specific consumers based on their usage agreements or SLA.

```
// Rate limit for a specific consumer
curl -X POST http://localhost:8001/consumers/{consumer_id}/plugins \
  --data "name=rate-limiting" \
  --data "config.hour=200" // Allow 200 requests per hour for the consumer
```

Throttling Mechanisms:

Throttling complements rate limiting by staggering request execution over time, rather than blocking or rejecting excess requests. This practice helps maintain smooth service operation, prioritizing essential tasks while delaying non-urgent queries. Throttling is especially useful for:

- **Traffic Spikes:** In situations where traffic peaks occur naturally or inadvertently, throttling adjusts the request handling pace to align with backend or processing capacity.

- **Resource Protection:** By spreading out demand, throttling reduces pressure on shared or finite resources.

- **Improving Resilience:** It enhances the system's ability to remain responsive under load by preventing bottlenecks in processing operations.

Implementing Throttling in Kong:

Kong doesn't have a dedicated throttling plugin, but the rate limiting capabilities inherently function as a throttling mechanism by evenly spacing requests over given time intervals. For instances requiring advanced throttling controls, custom logic may be implemented using Lua scripting within Kong to manage deferred execution needs.

Advanced Rate Limiting Strategies:

- **Burst Rate Allowance:** Permitting occasional bursts of request traffic while maintaining average limits permits flexibility without compromising core resource limitations.

- **Sliding Window Algorithm:** Employing sliding windows, often seen in token bucket and leaky bucket models, enables more dynamic and precise rate calculations by measuring the window continuously rather than in fixed intervals.

- **Variable Rate Limits:** These can adjust dynamically based on time of day, system load, profile of the consumer, geographic origin, or other contextual parameters.

- **Rate Limit Headers:**   Letting clients know about limit status through headers like X-RateLimit-Limit, X-RateLimit-Remaining, and Retry-After provides transparent feedback on their request capacity. These are typically enforced within service logic or plugins managing responses.

Best Practices for Rate Limiting and Throttling:

- **Monitor and Adjust:** Continuous monitoring allows the tuning of thresholds based on historical and real-time data.

- **Align with Business Goals:**   Determine rate limits and throttling rules aligned with API business goals to accommodate bursts during promotional events, peak times, or unexpected usage growth.

- **Educate API Consumers:** Transparent communication of rate limits and expected behaviors helps consumers integrate APIs more effectively without frustrating over-limit scenarios.

- **Use Caching Wisely:** Implement caching strategies to reduce the load on APIs, which complements rate limiting while aiding performance optimization.

- **Consider Backoff Strategies:** Instruct clients to implement exponential backoff strategies, especially on 429 HTTP responses, to gracefully handle retries.

- **Leverage Analytics:** Utilize logging tools and analytics plugins to glean insights from usage patterns, spikes, and regular behaviors for informed configuration adjustments.

The harmonious application of rate limiting and throttling strategies helps ensure that APIs remain stable, reliable, and perform optimally even under diverse and challenging circumstances. When integrated into API management protocols using Kong, these techniques empower developers to maintain control over resource allocations, protect backend services, and enrich the end-user experience through seamless service delivery.

5.5 Securing Data with SSL/TLS

The fundamental aim of securing data in transit is to ensure that sensitive information remains confidential, intact, and authentic between communicating parties. Transport Layer Security (TLS), and its predecessor Secure Sockets Layer (SSL), provide the cryptographic backbone required to secure communications over networks. When integrated with Kong, SSL/TLS facilitates encrypted channels between clients and API services, guaranteeing that transmitted data remains protected from interception and tampering.

Understanding SSL/TLS:

TLS is a cryptographic protocol designed to provide secure communication over a computer network. It is the successor of SSL and offers enhanced security features. The development from SSL to TLS attempted to address known vulnerabilities and improve upon the handshake protocol and cipher functionalities, thus yielding a more robust security framework.

TLS ensures data privacy and integrity through:

- **Encryption:** All communication contents are encrypted, prohibiting eavesdroppers from gaining unauthorized insight into the data being exchanged. Modern TLS relies on advanced symmetric cryptographic techniques offering a high level of security with minimal performance overhead.

- **Integrity:** Ensures message integrity using cryptographic hash functions, detecting any data alterations in transit.

- **Authentication:** Servers and optionally clients are authenticated through digital certificates to establish trust. Certificates are verified by a Certificate Authority (CA), fortifying against man-in-the-middle attacks.

Configuring SSL/TLS in Kong:

To employ SSL/TLS with Kong, users configure a secure listener on the API gateway. This process involves setting up digital certificates and keys that define the security parameters for the communication sessions.

- **Generating a Self-Signed Certificate:**

  For development or testing purposes, generating a self-signed certificate provides an easy way to enable SSL. Example of generating a certificate and key using openssl:

  ```
  // Generate a self-signed SSL certificate
  openssl req -x509 -newkey rsa:2048 -keyout kong-selfsigned.key -out kong-
      selfsigned.crt -days 365 -nodes -subj "/CN=localhost"
  ```

  This command creates a certificate for localhost valid for one year. While suitable for testing, self-signed certificates should not be used in production environments due to lack of trust by clients.

- **Installing an SSL/TLS Certificate in Kong:**

  Once you possess the certificates, Kong can be configured with a new SSL listener to accept secure HTTP (HTTPS) requests.

  ```
  // Configuring SSL certificates in Kong
  curl -i -X POST http://localhost:8001/certificates \
    --data "cert=@/path_to/kong-selfsigned.crt" \
    --data "key=@/path_to/kong-selfsigned.key"

  // Set up a service to use HTTPS
  curl -X PATCH http://localhost:8001/services/{service_id} \
    --data "protocol=https" --data "host=your-domain.com"
  ```

Purchasing and Managing Trusted Certificates:

For production environments, using certificates signed by a trusted Certificate Authority (CA) is imperative. Trusted CA-signed certificates are recognized by most clients (web browsers, API clients), eliminating common security alerts and establishing legitimate trust mechanisms.

- **Certificate Types:**

  - **Domain Validated (DV):** Basic validation confirming domain ownership only.

  - **Organization Validated (OV):** Includes organization authentication, providing enhanced credibility over DV.

  - **Extended Validation (EV):** In-depth scrutiny of the organization, resulting in prominent browser trust indicators.

  Selecting the appropriate certificate type correlates with security needs, brand trust, and the level of assurance desired.

TLS Configurations and Best Practices:

While Kong's default TLS configuration provides robust security, additional configurations can align with specific security requirements or organizational policies.

- **Cipher Suite Selection:** Define strong cipher suites for encryption. Disable outdated protocols and algorithms that present known vulnerabilities, such as SSLv3 and weak ciphers like Triple-DES.

- **Forward Secrecy:** Implement cipher suites that provide forward secrecy, ensuring session keys are not compromised even if a long-term key is breached.

- **Strict Transport Security (HSTS):** Enforce HSTS policy by setting HTTP headers indicating that browsers can only communicate using secure connections. This practice reduces the risk of protocol downgrade attacks.

```
// Enable HSTS for all responses in Kong (via plugin)
curl -X POST http://localhost:8001/plugins \
  --data "name=hsts" \
  --data "config.max_age=63072000"
```

- **OCSP Stapling:** Optimize certificate verification performance by enabling OCSP (Online Certificate Status Protocol) stapling, which reduces latency by delivering certificate status information directly in the TLS handshake.

- **Regular Key Rotation:** Regularly renew and update TLS certificates and keys to maintain current security standards and respond to potential compromises.

Testing SSL/TLS Implementations:

Continuous testing of your SSL/TLS configuration using tools like SSL Labs' SSL Test ensures that your setup retains strong security characteristics and aligns with best practices.

- A test should assess:
    - Protocol support and algorithm strength.
    - Cipher suite preferences and fallbacks.
    - Implementation of forward secrecy.
    - Cross-referencing against hardening guidelines and testing tools' configurations.

```
// Example OpenSSL command to validate server SSL setup
openssl s_client -connect your-domain.com:https -servername your-domain.com
```

TLS for API Security: Focus Areas:

- **API Communications:** All API interactions should leverage TLS for confidentiality and integrity, shielding sensitive data from transit interception.

- **Mutual TLS (mTLS):** Particularly valuable in highly secure environments, mTLS requires both client and server authentication, providing enhanced trust verification.

- **Certificate Lifecycle Management:** Automate certificate issuance, renewal, and invalidation to streamline operational workflows and minimize human error potential.

SSL/TLS form the backbone of secure communications over the internet. Successfully integrating these protocols with Kong not only protects API traffic from interception and tampering but also elevates user trust and compliance with regulatory standards. In a landscape increasingly aware of privacy and security, adhering to SSL/TLS best practices through Kong provides both security assurance and stability for robust API deployments.

5.6   IP Restrictions and Whitelisting

IP Restrictions and Whitelisting are crucial mechanisms for enhancing the security posture of APIs within an enterprise environment. Employing these techniques allows API providers to control and filter incoming traffic based on IP addresses, thus mitigating unauthorized access and reducing the attack surface.

Understanding IP Restrictions:

IP restrictions limit access to API resources by allowing or denying requests based on the client's IP address. These controls can prevent unauthorized devices from connecting to critical endpoints and help safeguard sensitive information. By analyzing client IP addresses, API gateways like Kong can make informed decisions about which requests to serve and which to block.

Types of IP Address Filtering:

- **Blacklist Approach:** This method blocks specific IP addresses that are known to be malicious or undesired. However, blacklists require continuous updates as new malicious IPs emerge, and there's a risk of blocking legitimate traffic.

- **Whitelist Approach (Preferred):** A whitelist explicitly designates approved IP addresses that can access the API, effectively denying all other traffic. Whitelisting is inherently more secure than blacklisting since, by default, it blocks any non-whitelisted IPs.

- **IP Ranges and CIDR Blocks:** Instead of individual IPs, providers often specify entire ranges or CIDR (Classless Inter-Domain Routing) blocks to manage expected traffic patterns efficiently.

Implementing IP Whitelisting in Kong:

Kong offers an 'ip-restriction' plugin for exacting control over which IPs can access your services. It supports both blacklisting and whitelisting strategies, giving administrators flexibility based on their unique requirements.

```
// Enable IP Restriction Plugin on a service
curl -X POST http://localhost:8001/services/{service_id}/plugins \
  --data "name=ip-restriction" \
  --data "config.whitelist=203.0.113.0/24,198.51.100.24"
```

The 'whitelist' configuration parameter takes a comma-separated list of IP addresses or CIDR blocks, permitting access only to these specified networks.

Configuring IP Blacklisting:

In cases where a blacklist is preferable or serves as an augmentation to existing security strategies:

```
// Enable and configure IP blacklist
curl -X POST http://localhost:8001/services/{service_id}/plugins \
  --data "name=ip-restriction" \
  --data "config.blacklist=192.0.2.0/24,198.51.100.23"
```

Requests from the specified IPs and CIDR networks are automatically rejected by Kong.

Dynamic IP Management:

Networks may change, or you may need to adjust access based on evolving security needs. Therefore, the ability to update IP restrictions dynamically is vital. Kong allows administrators to add or remove IPs from blacklists or whitelists using scriptable endpoints or APIs, ensuring rapid adjustment to threat intelligence developments without requiring services to restart.

```
// Updating an existing whitelist
curl -X PATCH http://localhost:8001/plugins/{plugin_id} \
  --data "config.whitelist=203.0.113.0/24,203.0.113.10"
```

Considerations for Efficient IP Management:

- **Regular Audits and Updates:** Frequent audits of whitelists and blacklists align access controls with the latest security policies and operational changes, preventing unauthorized access and enhancing responsiveness to new threats.

- **Monitoring and Logging:** Implement comprehensive monitoring and logging for all access attempts. Analyzing logs helps to detect anomalies, refine IP policies, and understand geographic access distributions, yielding insights into normal and abnormal traffic flows.

- **Geolocation Control:** Integrating geolocation filtering complements IP-based strategies. By considering IP origin country or region, further refined policies can be developed to align access with geographical business objectives.

- **Rate Limiting Synergies:** Combine IP restrictions with rate limiting mechanisms for an additional layer of security. Detect particular IPs attempting rate limit exploits, and dynamically adjust list entries to temporarily block those infringing entities.

- **Utilizing Cloud-Based Intelligence:** Leverage threat intelligence feeds from cloud services providing real-time data on compromised IPs. Integration with Kong enables automatic updates of IP restrictions according to global threat trends.

Challenges with IP Restrictions:

While effective in many cases, IP restriction and whitelisting approaches have inherent limitations:

- **Dynamic IP Address Allocation:** In modern networking environments, IPs are not static. Technologies such as DHCP, NAT, and the growing use of IPv6 can obscure actual origin IPs, complicating efforts to maintain accurate lists.

- **Corporate Proxy Gateways:** Traffic sources routed through proxies or corporate gateways may obscure end-user IPs, leading to potential false positives and access challenges.

- **VPN Services:** Widespread use of VPNs can mask true IP origins, complicating whitelist management. Enhanced policies or additional user authentication methods may be required to thoroughly verify client identity beyond IP checks.

Best Practices for Securing APIs using IP Filtering:

- **Layered Security Approach:** IP restrictions should not be the singular method of access control. Combine with authentication mechanisms, such as OAuth2.0 or JWT, to provide comprehensive security coverage.

- **Documentation and Change Control:** Maintain comprehensive documentation on current IP policies and procedural guidelines for adjustments. Controlled change and adherence to established maintenance practices will minimize disruptions.

- **Testing and Validation:** Regularly test IP-based controls to ensure they function as anticipated under various network conditions and configurations.

Conclusion:

IP restrictions and whitelisting provide an effective method of controlling access to API endpoints, directly filtering traffic based on defined parameters. When used alongside other security controls, they add a valuable layer of defense, protecting services, preserving data integrity, and ensuring services are accessed as intended. By harnessing the capabilities within Kong, organizations can efficiently implement these strategies to enhance their API security framework with both precision and agility.

5.7 Bot Detection and Prevention

In the digital landscape, bots—a term referring to software applications that automatically perform tasks over the internet—can present significant security challenges. While some bots serve useful purposes, such as search engine indexing, others are malicious and can lead to data breaches, service disruptions, and fraudulent activities. Therefore, effectively detecting and preventing malicious bot activity is an integral component of API security and management.

Understanding Bot Threats:

Bots can engage in various activities that undermine the integrity and performance of web services:

- **Credential Stuffing:** Bots attempt to gain unauthorized access by systematically trying stolen username/password pairs.

- **Denial-of-Service (DoS) Attacks:** Bots generate high volumes of traffic, aiming to overwhelm systems and render services unavailable to legitimate users.

- **Data Scraping and Stealing:** Bots extract confidential data and intellectual property, which can lead to financial losses and competitive disadvantages.

- **Inventory Hoarding and Skewing:** Bots can automatically purchase or hold products in e-commerce, distorting inventory and affecting genuine transactions.

- **Comment and Review Spam:** Automated content generated by bots can degrade the user experience and dilute authentic user interactions.

Bot Detection Techniques:

- **Traffic Analysis:** One of the primary detection mechanisms is analyzing traffic patterns relative to established baselines. Unusual spikes or behaviors may indicate bot activity.

- **Behavioral Analysis:** Bots often behave predictably and differ from genuine user interactions. Machine learning models can be trained to identify such patterns through request analysis, click behavior, and session engagement.

- **User-Agent Analysis:** Malicious bots frequently expose telltale identifiers with non-standard User-Agent headers or attempt to mask as common browsers; deviations from expected patterns can signify unwanted activity.

- **IP Reputation:** Cross-referencing request origins with IP reputation databases enables identification of known malicious hosts.

- **Challenge-Response Tests (e.g., CAPTCHAs):** These tests can effectively discern humans from bots by demanding activity beyond a bot's capabilities, like image recognition tasks.

Bot Prevention Strategies:

Kong's plugin architecture provides a flexible platform for implementing bot detection and prevention strategies.

Below is an array of strategies to mitigate bot threats:

- **Rate Limiting and Throttling:** Deploy strict rate limits to reduce the possibility of automated requests swamping servers. Aggressively rate-limiting responses can deter unwanted bots.

```
// Enable rate limiting to control request volume
curl -X POST http://localhost:8001/services/{service_id}/plugins \
  --data "name=rate-limiting" \
  --data "config.minute=60" // Limit 60 requests per minute
```

- **IP Blacklisting:** Leverage an IP restriction strategy to block known bot-originating addresses, dynamically managing these lists based on traffic analysis and intelligence feeds.

```
// Blacklist known bot IP addresses
curl -X POST http://localhost:8001/services/{service_id}/plugins \
  --data "name=ip-restriction" \
  --data "config.blacklist=192.0.2.0/24"
```

- **User-Agent Filtering:** Identify and either block or scrutinize requests exhibiting suspicious or non-standard User-Agent strings associated with bots.

- **Behavioral Analysis and Machine Learning:** Integrate anomaly detection systems capable of recognizing automated patterns not typical of legitimate user behavior. This involves real-time analysis of session lengths, request intervals, and input patterns.

- **Access Tokens and API Keys:** Protect endpoints behind keys and tokens, ensuring that only authenticated clients with valid credentials can access services. Each request may be assessed for legitimacy based on token status and origin.

```
// Use access tokens for additional security
curl -X POST http://localhost:8001/services/{service_id}/plugins \
  --data "name=jwt"
```

- **CAPTCHAs and Computational Puzzles:** Use CAPTCHAs, particularly for endpoints prone to abuse (e.g., login, signup, or query-heavy requests), to differentiate legitimate users from bots.

Implementing Bot Detection in Kong:

Kong's versatility allows for custom middleware or third-party integrations beyond its core plugins to address diverse security needs involving bots. Using Lua scripting or external monitoring systems, APIs can employ advanced detection algorithms that adapt to evolving bot tactics.

Here is a Kong Lua script snippet to log and identify potentially risky requests:

```
local function is_suspicious_ip(ip)
  -- Dummy function for illustration purposes that checks IP reputation
  local suspicious_ip_addresses = {
    ["198.51.100.23"] = true,
    ["203.0.113.45"] = true
  }
  return suspicious_ip_addresses[ip]
end

-- Check incoming requests
local req_ip = ngx.var.remote_addr
if is_suspicious_ip(req_ip) then
  ngx.log(ngx.ERR, "Suspicious IP detected: "..req_ip)
  return ngx.exit(ngx.HTTP_FORBIDDEN)
end
```

Challenges with Bot Management:

Although sophisticated approaches exist to detect and mitigate bots, certain challenges persist:

- **Adaptive Bot Technologies:** Advanced bots leverage AI and machine learning to mimic human behavior effectively, demanding equally advanced detection paradigms.

- **False Positives/Negatives:** Errors in bot detection may inadvertently block legitimate users (false positives) or allow malicious bots (false negatives). Calibrating systems for precision requires nuanced tuning.

- **Legitimate Automated Use Cases:** Implementing too stringent measures might disrupt or degrade service for intentional and valuable automated integrations, like business analytics tools.

Best Practices for Bot Management:

- **Regular Updates and Intelligence Integration:** Use threat intelligence sources to keep abreast of emerging bot patterns and suspicious IP addresses.

- **Comprehensive Monitoring and Alerts:** Establish real-time monitoring to identify anomalies quickly, backed by alert systems that notify administrators of potential bot traffic.

- **User Education and Awareness:** Inform users about account safety and encourage security measures like strong passwords and two-factor authentication, reducing bot-facilitated compromises.

- **Iterative Testing and Adaptation:** Continuously evaluate bot detection systems to understand newly adapted behaviors. Regular testing optimizes systems against novel attack vectors.

Conclusion:

Bot detection and prevention are pivotal for maintaining API integrity, performance, and user trust. By leveraging Kong's extensible platform, organizations can deploy a multitude of defensive strategies, from simple rate limiting to sophisticated machine learning techniques, effectively curbing malicious bot activities. As threats evolve, a proactive and flexible approach to bot management ensures that APIs remain resilient amidst a dynamic threat environment.

Chapter 6

Plugins and Customization in Kong

This chapter provides an in-depth examination of the plugins system within Kong API Gateway and the extensive customization opportunities it offers. It discusses the configuration and use of built-in plugins to enhance functionality and address specific API management needs. The chapter further guides readers through the process of creating custom plugins, detailing the development stages and best practices for integration. Additionally, it explores how plugins are executed during request and response lifecycles, allowing for tailored workflows and increased control over API operations. By mastering these aspects, users can effectively extend Kong's capabilities to suit unique business requirements.

6.1 Understanding Kong Plugins

Kong, a powerful and flexible API gateway, enables developers to extend its core functionalities through the use of plugins. These plugins serve as modular components that can be integrated to customize the behavior and extend the capabilities of the Kong API gateway. This section delves into the fundamental concept of Kong plugins, defining their roles, capabilities, and advantages, alongside practical examples that illustrate their usage within an application.

Kong plugins are defined by Lua code and operate within the Kong process, providing a seamless method of intercepting request and response flows. They can perform actions such as authentication, logging, traffic control, transformation, and analytics integration. These capabilities are crucial in adapting the behavior of the gateway to fit specific business requirements and improving the overall management of APIs.

Kong plugins can be enabled globally for all services or selectively applied to specific services, routes, or consumers. This flexibility allows for precise control over the behavior of each API endpoint, ensuring that only the necessary plugins are active for a given context. At their core, Kong plugins enrich the Kong ecosystem by introducing new capabilities without the need for a complete overhaul of existing infrastructure.

To better understand how Kong plugins function, consider a scenario where an API requires multiple layers of security with detailed logging. Two plugins are enabled: one for authentication and another for logging. Upon receiving a request, the authentication plugin verifies the client's identity. If the request passes authentication, it proceeds to the logging plugin, which records details of the transaction before the request is finally routed to its intended service.

```
{
    "name": "my-service",
    "url": "http://my-api.service",
    "routes": [
        {
            "name": "my-route",
            "methods": ["GET", "POST"],
            "paths": ["/api/v1"],
            "strip_path": true,
            "plugins": [
                {
                    "name": "key-auth",
                    "config": {
                        "key_names": ["apikey"],
                        "key_in_body": false,
                        "run_on_preflight": true
                    }
                },
```

```
{
    "name": "file-log",
    "config": {
        "path": "/var/log/my-api-log.log",
        "reopen": true
    }
}
        ]
    }
]
}
```

In the provided example, the service "my-service" is configured with two plugins at the route "/api/v1". The "key-auth" plugin imposes an authentication requirement using a user-specified API key, and the "file-log" plugin logs request details into a specified file. The configuration includes tailored settings, such as re-opening the log file after each log operation. This facilitates real-time logging without necessitating service restarts.

Kong plugins are executed at various stages of the request and response lifecycle. The key execution phases include:

- **Access Phase:** This phase handles incoming requests. Plugins such as authentication and IP restriction operate here to validate and potentially modify requests before they are forwarded to the upstream service.

- **Response Phase:** Post-upstream service response, this phase allows plugins to modify or process the response before it is sent back to the client. Transformation plugins may be active in this phase to alter the response payload.

- **Log Phase:** Finalizing the interaction, this phase enables logging plugins to register information about the request-response cycle. Plugins such as statsd and file-log typically execute here.

- **Rewrite Phase:** Here, directives can change request properties before they advance to other processing phases.

Each of these phases corresponds to specific plugin handlers within the Lua plugin code, allowing developers to precisely control how and when their plugins interact with traffic.

145

Creating a simple custom plugin involves developing a Lua module structured to fit within Kong's plugin architecture. To illustrate a basic Kong plugin, consider this simplified Lua script that acts as a rudimentary request transformer.

```
local BasePlugin = require "kong.plugins.base_plugin"

local CustomPlugin = BasePlugin:extend()

function CustomPlugin:new()
  CustomPlugin.super.new(self, "custom-plugin")
end

function CustomPlugin:access(conf)
  CustomPlugin.super.access(self)

  -- Example: Add a custom header to the request
  ngx.req.set_header("X-Custom-Header", "Processed by CustomPlugin")
end

return CustomPlugin
```

This plugin intercepts requests during the access phase, adding a custom header "X-Custom-Header". To enable this plugin, it must be correctly set up in the Kong plugin registry and configured within Kong's key-value store, which requires updating the database schema accordingly.

Plugins extend beyond mere request and response modifications. They can provide intricate observability into traffic patterns by integrating with third-party analytics solutions. Integrating such capabilities requires a clear understanding of required data and configured plugin parameters, which often involves sending metrics to an external analytics platform through the "log" phase plugins.

Kong provides several official plugins, supplying common, well-tested functionalities out of the box. Examples include rate-limiting, enabling fair usage policies by restricting the number of permitted requests per consumer over a defined time interval, or the basic-auth plugin, implementing simple username and password authentication.

To illustrate practical usage, consider using the rate-limiting plugin. First, it's necessary to configure it through the Admin API, defining a rate limit based on consumer identifiers, IP addresses, or service-specific rules. Below is an example of how to enable and configure the rate-limiting plugin via curl commands on a hypothetical service.

```
curl -i -X POST http://localhost:8001/services/my-service/plugins \
    --data "name=rate-limiting" \
    --data "config.second=5" \
    --data "config.hour=1000" \
    --data "config.policy=local"
```

This command configures the rate-limiting plugin, allowing up to 5 requests per second and 1000 requests per hour for the "my-service" service. The local policy ensures rate-limiting operates only through the local Kong node, without relying on any external datastore.

Beyond pre-existing plugins, developers often find it imperative to craft custom solutions to address specialized requirements. The bespoke development of plugins permits the lodging of intricate business logic right at the gateway level, offering transformative potential to manage API traffic more effectively.

Developing custom plugins involves setting up a development environment, typically including LuaRocks for dependency management, and the Kong development framework to facilitate testing. Testing custom plugins demands a clear understanding of unit, integration, and performance testing to ensure their robustness in the face of production-grade traffic.

The flexibility introduced by Kong plugins necessitates a solid grasp of the data flow and API lifecycle within Kong, as the interactions between different plugins and their configurations can complexly intertwine. Managing these interactions precisely can significantly enhance or detract from the overall performance and reliability of the API gateway.

Therefore, an understanding of the Kong plugin ecosystem not only empowers the configuration and customization of critical gateway functionalities but also capacitates the innovation required to tailor a highly responsive API management strategy. Mastery of plugin development and deployment redefines the operational possibilities, enabling seamless adaptability to the evolving technological landscape.

147

6.2 Managing Built-in Plugins

Kong's array of built-in plugins provides a comprehensive toolkit for implementing a range of functionalities that enhance API management, security, and analytics. These plugins are crafted to address common use cases, offering pre-validated solutions that mitigate the need for custom plugin development when generic functionality suffices. Effective management of these built-in plugins is crucial for leveraging their full potential to meet specific organizational needs, ensuring security, performance, and compliance.

The management of built-in plugins in Kong involves several key activities: enabling, configuring, updating, and monitoring plugins. Each activity must be performed with a keen understanding of the plugin's purpose, capabilities, and limitations to optimize API gateway operations.

Built-in plugins are available on both the global and granular levels, allowing users flexibility in their application and scope of influence. They can be applied globally across all services and routes, or targeted specifically at certain services, routes, or consumers. This hierarchical application means that plugins can be finely tuned to the specific requirements of each API endpoint.

Enabling and configuring a built-in plugin in Kong generally starts with the Admin API, an essential component of Kong that provides HTTP endpoints for managing services, routes, consumers, and plugins. Using RESTful practices, the Admin API enables users to define how and where plugins are applied, as illustrated in the following example with the CORS (Cross-Origin Resource Sharing) plugin:

```
curl -i -X POST http://localhost:8001/services/my-service/plugins \
    --data "name=cors" \
    --data "config.origins=http://example.com" \
    --data "config.methods=GET,POST" \
    --data "config.headers=X-Custom-Header" \
    --data "config.exposed_headers=X-Exposed-Header"
```

This command enables the CORS plugin on "my-service", configured to allow requests from "http://example.com" and to expose the custom header "X-Exposed-Header". The CORS plugin configuration is concise yet demonstrates essential aspects such as specifying allowed origins, HTTP methods, and headers, empowering developers to secure cross-origin requests.

For effective deployment, configuration details of plugins must match the operational needs closely. Incorrect configurations can lead to unintended access or denial, reduction in performance, or incomplete data analytics. Built-in plugins serve functions such as:

- **Security:** Plugins like basic-auth, key-auth, and OAuth2 provide various methods of authentication and authorization, while plugins like IP restriction ensure only approved network addresses access the service.

- **Traffic Control:** Rate-limiting and response-rate-limiting plugins help manage the request flow, preventing abuse and ensuring fair use.

- **Transformation:** Transformation plugins, including request-transformer and response-transformer, allow modification in request and response headers and bodies to meet specific API requirements.

- **Logging and Analytics:** These plugins, such as syslog, file-log, or statsd, are crucial for monitoring and understanding traffic patterns and system performance.

Given this broad applicability, it is useful to examine in detail some common scenarios where built-in plugins provide optimal solutions in API management. Consider, for example, securing an API using the basic-auth plugin to mandate that clients authenticate using a username and password:

```
curl -i -X POST http://localhost:8001/services/my-private-service/plugins \
    --data "name=basic-auth" \
    --data "config.hide_credentials=true"
```

By enabling the basic-auth plugin, as demonstrated, a service "my-private-service" requires client requests to be authenticated with basic authentication credentials. The configuration hides credentials from proxy logs to enhance security by preventing the unintentional logging of sensitive information. Following this, credentials must be added using consumers and their respective endpoints within the Admin API.

149

Understanding the interplay between different plugins is essential for effective management, as the order of execution and presence of multiple plugins can significantly affect the system's behavior. For example, using both rate-limiting and IP restriction requires understanding of how requests might be throttled or denied based on their source IP and the set limits.

When managing plugins, consider the deployment spectrum, from development to production environments. The chosen strategy for enabling and configuring plugins should include environment-specific details and adhere to an automated continuous integration and deployment pipeline, ensuring consistency and reducing human error. Here is an example using Terraform to manage Kong configurations declaratively:

```
resource "kong_plugin" "rate_limit_my_service" {
  name = "rate-limiting"
  service_id = kong_service.my_service.id

  config_json = jsonencode({
    second = 10
    hour = 1000
    policy = "cluster"
  })
}
```

Terraform files can be version controlled, providing a robust framework for managing infrastructure as code, including Kong API Gateway plugins. This approach supports consistency across multiple environments and facilitates audits and disaster recovery processes.

In addition to management through APIs and infrastructure-as-code tools, monitoring and analyzing plugin performance and effectiveness are also crucial tasks. Tools such as Grafana, Prometheus, and various logging solutions can be integrated with Kong to provide rich, real-time analysis of traffic, plugin performance, and gateway health.

Monitoring involves setting up dashboards and alerts that track metrics outputted by plugins, such as request traffic, latency, error rates, and authentication successes or failures. For plugins like statsd or prometheus, ensure the necessary metric collectors and recorders are configured to capture plugin-generated data.

Finally, as requirements evolve, regular reviews of existing plugin configurations are necessary to adjust parameters to meet new needs or remove no longer relevant plugins. Updates and configuration changes must be rigorously tested in a staging environment before production rollout to ensure plugin behavior aligns with expectations.

Through diligent management of built-in plugins, organizations benefit from a holistic suite of capabilities necessary for maintaining API performance and security in dynamic environments. The highly flexible nature of Kong's built-in plugin system, when properly leveraged, enables seamless scaling and adaptation to emerging trends and business challenges in API management.

6.3 Creating Custom Plugins

Creating custom plugins in Kong allows developers to extend the functionality of the API gateway beyond the capabilities offered by built-in plugins. These plugins become necessary when specific business logic or functionality is required that cannot be satisfied by the existing set of plugins. The process involves a series of steps including design, coding, testing, and deploying, each of which is crucial to building a robust and functional plugin.

Developing a custom plugin requires a thorough understanding of Kong's plugin architecture, which is built around the Lua programming language and nginx's event-driven model. Custom plugins operate through finely defined execution phases, such as 'rewrite', 'access', 'header_filter', 'body_filter', and 'log' that hook into various points of the request/response lifecycle.

- **Designing a Custom Plugin**

    Before developing a custom plugin, a comprehensive design phase should determine its functional requirements and outline how it will interact within Kong. Key considerations include determining what the plugin needs to accomplish, which lifecycle phases it must interact with, and how it will handle configuration.

    For instance, consider a scenario where a plugin is needed to append a unique transaction identifier to each request and log this identifier along with other request details. This plugin might need to interact with the access phase to modify the request headers and the log phase to record the detailed request log.

- **Setting Up the Development Environment**

A conducive development environment is essential for efficient custom plugin development. The environment typically includes:

- **Lua:** Kong plugins are written in Lua, thus a Lua interpreter and package manager such as LuaRocks are necessary.
- **Docker:** For creating a controllable environment, Docker can run a local instance of Kong, allowing testing of plugins without affecting the production setup.
- **Kong Development Framework (Kong PDK):** Provides interfaces and functions that facilitate interaction with Kong's core.

Here's a basic setup using LuaRocks and Docker:

```
# Install LuaRocks and dependencies
sudo apt-get install luarocks

# Install Kong-specific libraries
luarocks install kong
```

- **Coding the Plugin**

Coding involves implementing the business logic in Lua. A custom plugin usually extends the base plugin class and implements necessary lifecycle phase handlers. Below is a basic example of a custom plugin that modifies request headers and logs requests:

```
-- Import the base plugin class
local BasePlugin = require "kong.plugins.base_plugin"

-- Create a new custom plugin class extending the base class
local TxnIDPlugin = BasePlugin:extend()

-- Constructor
function TxnIDPlugin:new()
  TxnIDPlugin.super.new(self, "txn-id-plugin")
end

-- Access phase: Modify request headers
```

```
function TxnIDPlugin:access(conf)
  TxnIDPlugin.super.access(self)
  -- Generate and set a unique transaction ID
  local txn_id = "TXN-" .. tostring(math.random(100000, 999999))
  ngx.req.set_header("X-Txn-Id", txn_id)
end

-- Log phase: log transaction details
function TxnIDPlugin:log(conf)
  TxnIDPlugin.super.log(self)
  ngx.log(ngx.INFO, "Request processed with Transaction ID: ", ngx.req.
    get_headers()["X-Txn-Id"])
end

return TxnIDPlugin
```

This plugin attaches a 'Transaction ID' to requests and logs it, demonstrating basic plugin handling for access and log phases.

- **Packaging the Plugin**

Once developed, the plugin must be packaged for deployment. Packaging involves making sure the plugin files are located in the proper directory structure expected by Kong. Plugins can be organized as Lua modules and placed in a directory where Kong expects custom code, such as '/usr/local/share/lua/5.1/kong/plugins/'.

Create the following directory structure:

```
/usr/local/share/lua/5.1/kong/plugins/txn-id-plugin/
    handler.lua
    schema.lua
```

The 'schema.lua' file defines the plugin configuration schema, against which plugin configurations are validated.

- **Testing the Plugin**

Testing is critical to ensure the plugin behaves as expected. This involves unit testing individual components and integration testing within the Kong environment. Unit tests may employ Lua-specific testing frameworks, while integration tests require deploying the plugin in a controlled Kong instance.

Run an automated test suite using Busted or other frameworks to ensure code reliability:

153

```
busted spec/
```

- **Deploying the Plugin**

Deploying the plugin involves integrating it into a running Kong instance. The deployment process should follow best practices like using staging environments, automated testing pipelines, and gradual rollout strategies.

Sample deployment steps:

1. **Copy the plugin files to the Kong setup:**

```
cp -r /local/path/txn-id-plugin /usr/local/share/lua/5.1/kong/
    plugins/
```

2. **Modify the 'kong.conf' file to include the plugin:**

```
custom_plugins = txn-id-plugin
```

3. **Restart Kong to enable the new plugin:**

```
kong restart
```

4. **Enable the plugin via the Admin API:**

```
curl -i -X POST http://localhost:8001/services/my-service/plugins
    \
    --data "name=txn-id-plugin"
```

- **Best Practices for Custom Plugin Development**

  - **Thorough Documentation:** Document plugin functionality and configuration parameters to facilitate maintenance and handover.

  - **Interactive Configuration:** If a plugin requires configuration, ensure it includes a schema to validate inputs, thereby reducing misconfiguration risk.

  - **Efficiency Considerations:** Minimize processing overhead to maintain Kong's high-throughput model. Efficiently handle requests without blocking or unnecessary computation.

154

  – **Security:** Implement secure coding principles to safeguard
    against injection attacks and sensitive data exposure.

  – **Compliance with Kong PDK:** Adhere to the public Kong
    Developer Kit API to ensure compatibility with Kong's core
    updates and improvements.

Through careful design, development, testing, and deployment, custom plugins can significantly extend Kong's capabilities. They provide developers with the flexibility to inject bespoke logic into the request/response processing lifecycle, enabling powerful, tailored API management solutions. By capitalizing on this power and flexibility, organizations can transform the Kong API gateway to meet unique, evolving technical demands and business objectives effectively.

6.4 Plugin Execution Phases

The lifecycle of a request through the Kong API Gateway is intricately structured through several execution phases, during which plugins can interact with incoming requests and outgoing responses. Understanding these phases is fundamental for both using existing plugins effectively and developing custom plugins that leverage the full capability of the Kong platform.

Kong's plugin execution model is tightly integrated with the nginx event-driven architecture, where each phase presents an opportunity to execute specific logic pertinent to that stage of the request-response cycle. This capability allows developers to apply transformations, enforce policies, log data, and more, as suited to the organizational requirements or application logic.

  • **Overview of Execution Phases:**

The primary phases within the Kong plugin lifecycle are as follows:

  • **Rewrite Phase:** Initial processing of requests, allowing
    changes to URL components and request headers.

155

- **Access Phase:** Authentication, authorization, and input validation checks are implemented here.

- **Header Filter Phase:** Modifications can be made to the headers right before forwarding the response to clients.

- **Body Filter Phase:** Enables transformation or inspection of the response body.

- **Log Phase:** Final phase, where logging or analytics data is collected and sent to external systems.

Each phase serves a distinct purpose aligned with the request's journey through the gateway, allowing for granular control over handling actions and optimizations.

- **Detailed Examination of Each Phase:**

Rewrite Phase:

In the Rewrite Phase, the request URL, headers, and other properties can be dynamically altered before proxying it to the upstream service. This phase is ideal for plugins that require conditionally adjusting routing or injecting metadata into requests.

Example Rewrite Phase Plugin Handler:

```
function CustomPlugin:rewrite(conf)
  CustomPlugin.super.rewrite(self)
  -- Redirect requests to a maintenance page
  ngx.req.set_uri("/maintenance.html")
end
```

In this example, every request is redirected to a maintenance webpage, demonstrating rewrite capabilities for routing traffic conditionally.

Access Phase:

This is arguably the most critical phase, responsible for safeguarding services through authentication, rate-limiting, or endpoint access control. It's during the Access Phase that plugins enforce policies based on request metadata, user credentials, or other parameters.

Implementation in the Access Phase typically involves interacting with request headers and consumer credentials. Below is an example where an Access Phase plugin verifies API key validity:

```
function APIKeyAuthPlugin:access(conf)
  APIKeyAuthPlugin.super.access(self)

  -- Extract API Key from request header
  local api_key = ngx.req.get_headers()["api-key"]

  if not api_key or api_key ~= "valid-api-key" then
    return kong.response.exit(403, "Forbidden, invalid API Key")
  end
end
```

In the code above, an API key is extracted from the request header and validated, demonstrating authentication enforcement within the Access Phase.

Header Filter Phase:

In the Header Filter Phase, plugins can modify response headers just before they are sent to the client. This is ideal for plugins needing to append security headers, modify cache control directives, or enable cross-origin resource sharing.

An example of a Header Filter Phase handler adding a custom security header is shown below:

```
function SecurityHeadersPlugin:header_filter(conf)
  SecurityHeadersPlugin.super.header_filter(self)

  ngx.header["Content-Security-Policy"] = "default-src 'self'"
end
```

This example demonstrates setting a Content Security Policy header, which helps protect clients against various types of attacks, like XSS.

Body Filter Phase:

Plugins that perform content transformation or logging sensitive data often use this phase to inspect and potentially alter the response body, typically for data masking, compression, or generating analysis metrics.

Example Body Filter Plugin Handler:

```
function ResponseTransformerPlugin:body_filter(conf)
  ResponseTransformerPlugin.super.body_filter(self)

  local chunk, eof = ngx.arg[1], ngx.arg[2]

  local modified_chunk = string.gsub(chunk, "sensitive", "****")
  ngx.arg[1] = modified_chunk
```

```
end
```

The example above shows a plugin that replaces instances of the word "sensitive" with asterisks in the response body as it streams back to the client.

Log Phase:

Once the request/response cycle completes, the Log Phase handles after-effects logging and communication with monitoring systems. Plugins collect metrics, structure enriched logs, or push analytics information to an external system for real-time observability.

Example Log Phase Plugin Handler:

```
function MonitoringPlugin:log(conf)
  MonitoringPlugin.super.log(self)

  local message = string.format("Request from %s took %d ms", ngx.var.remote_addr,
      (ngx.now() - ngx.req.start_time()) * 1000)
  -- Send log to an external system
  ngx.log(ngx.INFO, message)
end
```

As demonstrated, this plugin logs request execution time and the client's IP address, intended for performance monitoring or auditing.

- **Considerations for Plugin Development Across Phases:**

While each phase allows rich plugin interactions, developers must consider some vital factors during development:

- **Execution Order:** Ordering can be crucial where multiple plugins handle the same phase. Defining execution precedence prevents conflicts, especially within the Access and Log Phases.

- **Resource Constraints:** Plugins must be efficient to avoid impacting gateway performance. Operational logic that might introduce latency should be profiled and optimized.

- **State Management:** Use appropriate caching for repeated data lookups or processing to reduce duplicative processing load, especially during the Access Phase.

158

- **Asynchronous Operations:** Consider calling asynchronous functions when interacting with external resources or processing-intensive tasks, preventing blocking.

- **Importance of Testing in Lifecycle Phases:**

Each plugin phase should be thoroughly verified through unit, integration, and stress tests to validate its anticipated behavior and ensure compatibility with the gateway's other aspects. Focus on edge cases and failure modes specific to each phase, particularly testing under production-like loads.

For instance, testing a plugin intended for the Header Filter Phase should validate that headers are set correctly under typical and stress-tests scenarios. Likewise, plugins operating during the Access Phase should be subjected to security testing, ensuring authentication, rate limiting, and access controls behave correctly.

- **Conclusion:**

The Kong plugin execution model provides a varied assortment of hooks that developers can leverage to implement dynamic, bespoke behavior in their API management workflows. These phases ensure that custom and built-in plugins can operate efficiently across multiple layers of the request and response lifecycle, allowing for high levels of customization and operational effectiveness. Through astute application of these phases, businesses can attain precise control and optimize interactions at the API Gateway, producing highly tailored and responsive service orchestration.

6.5 Configuring Plugins for Routes and Services

In Kong, the ability to configure plugins for specific routes and services provides targeted control and customization over how requests are processed and managed. This level of granularity enables developers to apply plugins with precision, ensuring that the appropriate logic and transformations are applied only to the desired endpoints. Understanding how to configure plugins at the route and service levels is fundamental to optimizing API management and enhancing performance, security, and functionality.

Kong Configuration Model Overview

Kong's configuration model is hierarchical, with entities like services, routes, consumers, and plugins being the primary building blocks. A service represents an API backend. Routes define how requests are mapped to these services based on criteria such as hosts, paths, and HTTP methods. Plugins, in turn, are attached to either services or routes, where they can tailor the request processing according to predefined logic.

A single plugin might be configured for a:

- **Service:** Affecting all requests routed to a particular upstream service.

- **Route:** Applying only to requests that match the specific route criteria.

- **Globally:** Affecting all traffic handled by a Kong instance, unless overridden.

Configuring Plugins for Services

Configuring plugins at the service level applies their functionality to every request processed by that service. Use this approach when the plugin logic should be consistent across all paths and endpoints of a backend service. Consider configuring security-focused plugins like authentication or authorization plugins at the service level to ensure uniform security policies.

Suppose a service requires a default set of security headers for all its routes for security compliance:

```
curl -i -X POST http://localhost:8001/services/my-service/plugins \
    --data "name=response-transformer" \
    --data "config.add.headers=X-Security-Policy:Secure"
```

This command uses the response-transformer plugin to add default security headers to responses from the my-service. It ensures consistent security implementations across all its endpoints.

Configuring Plugins for Routes

Route-level plugin configurations allow for fine-grained control, enabling developers to apply distinct logic to different parts of an API. This is beneficial when different endpoints require specific treatments, such as varied authentication methods across routes or one-off transformations.

For example, suppose there are different authentication requirements between a public and a private API route; they can be handled distinctly:

```
curl -i -X POST http://localhost:8001/routes/my-private-route/plugins \
  --data "name=basic-auth"
```

And for a public-facing route, maybe a custom header manipulation might be applied:

```
curl -i -X POST http://localhost:8001/routes/my-public-route/plugins \
  --data "name=request-transformer" \
  --data "config.add.headers=X-Public-Access:Granted"
```

Plugin Configuration Properties

When configuring plugins, multiple properties and parameters dictate their behavior. These configurations typically include functionality-specific settings, scope, and reliability factors, tailored according to the plugin's role.

For example, when configuring an authentication plugin:

- service_id or route_id: Defines the scope where the plugin operates.

- enabled: Boolean value determining if the plugin is active.

- config parameters: Plugin-specific options like secret keys, validating IPs, or rate threshold.

Coding a detailed JWT plugin setup at a service level can look as follows:

```
curl -i -X POST http://localhost:8001/services/my-service/plugins \
  --data "name=jwt" \
```

161

```
--data "config.run_on_preflight=true" \
--data "config.claims_to_verify=exp"
```

This setup ensures the JWT claims' validity for every request routed through my-service. It leverages claims verification options, such as checking for token expiration (exp).

Hierarchical Plugin Configuration

In Kong, hierarchical configurations imply that plugins applied globally will affect all requests handled by Kong unless explicitly overridden at the service or route level. This forms a cascade of configurations where the most specific plugins take precedence.

Suppose a rate-limiting plugin is set globally to manage traffic, but my-service requires a dedicated limit due to different operational requirements:

```
# Apply a global rate-limiting for all services
curl -i -X POST http://localhost:8001/plugins \
    --data "name=rate-limiting" \
    --data "config.second=100"

# Override with a distinct rate-limiting for a specific service
curl -i -X POST http://localhost:8001/services/my-service/plugins \
    --data "name=rate-limiting" \
    --data "config.second=200"
```

Here, requests processed by my-service will adhere to its specific rate limit of 200 requests per second, overriding the global configuration that imposes a stricter 100 requests per second.

Advanced Conditional Logic

In more complex scenarios, conditional logic can be employed by combining multiple plugins to achieve advanced configurations. Consider a logging configuration where both request headers and certain payloads must be logged based on request criteria:

- Request path filtering to log requests to the /admin path.

- Conditional request payload inspection for specific sensitive attributes.

Set up a combination using more than one plugin:

162

```
# Log requests only at /admin route
curl -i -X POST http://localhost:8001/routes/admin-route/plugins \
   --data "name=file-log" \
   --data "config.path=/var/log/admin-log.log"

# Additionally, use a transformer to mask sensitive payloads conditionally
curl -i -X POST http://localhost:8001/routes/admin-route/plugins \
   --data "name=request-transformer" \
   --data "config.replace.json.root.data.ssn=****"
```

This example shows how combining /admin specific logging and request transformation plugins achieves both comprehensive logging and sensitive data protection.

Orchestrating Multiple Plugins

For comprehensive management, orchestrating multiple plugins across routes and services should follow a considered strategy:

- **Ensure Plugins Are Complimentary:** Plugins should not conflict but instead complement each other's functionality.

- **Enforce Security and Compliance at Strategic Points:** Apply security fleet-wide but reserve specific transformations or specialized logging at individual services/routes.

- **Test Coverage of All Combinations:** Simulate real-world traffic conditions in testing stages to validate plugin interactions under load.

- **Version Control Configurations:** Integrate with CI/CD pipelines to ensure plug-in configurations follow software development best practices, supporting rollback and environment-specific adjustments as needed.

Monitoring and Optimizing

The efficacy of plugin configurations can only be guaranteed through active monitoring and periodic reviews. By employing logging and analytics plugins or integrating external monitoring systems like Prometheus or Grafana, detailed insights into plugin performance and gateway traffic patterns can be obtained.

Criteria for optimization based on monitoring data are:

- **Adjust Plugin Configurations According to Usage Patterns:** Scale up traffic limits or refine transformation rules as inferred from analytics.

- **Audit Plugin Effectiveness Regularly:** Determine if plugins achieve expected outcomes; e.g., validate access policies, evaluate logged data for completeness.

- **Refine Routing and Service Structures:** Reorganize services/routes to better fit usage, ensuring plugin application remains effective.

By employing meticulous configurations, frequent auditing, and proactive monitoring, plugins can be effectively managed, ensuring they maximize their intended benefits with minimized operational overhead, adapting rapidly to changing needs and technical landscapes.

6.6   Plugin Development Best Practices

Developing plugins for the Kong API Gateway is a powerful way to extend its capabilities and customize the handling of requests and responses. However, the flexibility that custom plugin development offers also demands a sound strategy and adherence to best practices to ensure reliability, maintainability, and performance. This section outlines a comprehensive set of best practices for the development of high-quality Kong plugins.

Understanding the Kong Architecture

An essential preliminary step in developing effective plugins is a thorough understanding of the Kong architecture and its underlying technologies, such as NGINX and LuaJIT. Developers must be familiar with the Kong Plugin Development Kit (PDK), which provides essential interfaces and utilities for plugin development.

The PDK abstracts complexities, offering functions for handling HTTP requests, logging, data transformations, and more. A deep dive into the PDK documentation is indispensable, as it ensures using supported and efficient API calls within the plugin codebase.

Code Organization and Structure

Following a clear structure and organization for plugin code assists maintainability and scalability. A typical Kong plugin comprises the following essential components:

- **Handler Module:** Implements the core plugin logic and phases of execution.

- **Schema Module:** Defines configurable parameters and constraints the plugin supports.

- **Tests:** A suite of unit and integration tests validating functionality.

A structured plugin directory might look something like:

```
/my-kong-plugin/
    handler.lua
    schema.lua
    spec/
        handler_spec.lua
        schema_spec.lua
        ...
```

Efficient Code Practices

Efficiency in execution is paramount given Kong's role as a central component of the API architecture. Some aspects of efficient code include:

- **Minimize Blocking Operations:** Avoid blocking I/O operations, favor asynchronous counterparts using Kong's async libraries or expose minimal synchronous operations.

  ```
  local ngx = require "ngx"
  -- Instead of blocking call
  local response = some_blocking_function()

  -- Use asynchronous handler
  ```

165

```
ngx.timer.at(0, function()
  some_async_function(callback)
end)
```

- **Optimize Data Access and Manipulation:** Utilize caching
  mechanisms for data fetched repeatedly and judiciously restruc-
  ture loops to avoid redundant work.

```
local cache = {}
function fetch_user_data(user_id)
  if cache[user_id] then return cache[user_id] end
  local data = fetch_from_db(user_id) -- Hypothetical, replace accordingly
  cache[user_id] = data
  return data
end
```

- **Memory Management:** Lua's garbage collector is efficient,
  but consciously managing memory can prevent performance bottlenecks, especially with large payloads.

Comprehensive Testing

Robust testing is non-negotiable for plugin development:

- **Unit Tests:** Focus on individual functionalities, ensuring behaviors align with expected outcomes even in edge scenarios.

- **Integration Tests:** Include Kong's entire lifecycle, validating
  the plugin interacts correctly with the gateway and other plugins.

- **Load Tests:** Simulate high traffic conditions to profile performance, verifying the plugin maintains efficacy at scale.

Employ tools like Busted for Lua testing to automate and simplify the
testing framework. An example setup might use logical assertions and
condition checks:

```
describe("Example Plugin", function()
  it("adds a header", function()
    local plugin = require "kong.plugins.example_plugin.handler"
    assert.is.truthy(plugin:access{})
  end)
end)
```

166

Secure Coding Practices

Security is critical since plugins often handle sensitive data or influence control flows:

- **Data Validation and Sanitization:** Validate all inputs to avoid injection vulnerabilities or malformed data that could break logic.

- **Least Privilege Principle:** Reduce access to external resources or Kong internals, restricting use only where necessary.

- **Sensitive Data Handling:** Securely manage and rarely persist sensitive data. Always opt for in-transit encryption where applicable.

```
local validation = require "kong.tools.validation"
local input_data = get_sensitive_input()
assert(validation.is_non_empty(input_data), "Invalid input, should be non-empty")
```

Configuration and Flexibility

Configuration schemas empower Kong users to customize plugins according to their needs. Define clear, well-documented configurations with sensible defaults:

- **Schema Module:** Use it to declare all accepted plugin parameters, constraints, and validation logic.

- **Environment Agnostic:** Plugin behavior shouldn't rely on a fixed environment; environment variables and configurations offer flexibility.

```
local typedefs = require "kong.db.schema.typedefs"
return {
  name = "example-plugin",
  fields = {
    { config = {
        type = "record",
        fields = {
```

167

```
        { flag = { type = "boolean", required = true, default = false }},
        { rate = { type = "number", required = true, gt = 0 }}
    }
}}
}
```

Logging and Monitoring

Transparent operation is achieved via informed logging and proactive monitoring:

- **Granular Debugging Logs:** These logs can be toggled on for troubleshooting and should be kept concise. Use different log levels where appropriate: trace for fine details, debug for general development, and error for fault logging.

- **Integrate with Monitoring Tools:** Expose relevant metrics that align with business metrics using tools like Prometheus or StatsD, providing actionable insights into plugin operations.

Documentation and Maintenance

Comprehensive documentation ensures plugin longevity and facilitates handover between development teams:

- **Usage Instructions:** Capture deployment steps, runtime configurations, and FAQs to guide users in leveraging the plugin effectively.

- **Internal Documentation:** Maintain inline comments explaining logic flows, edge cases handled, and reasons for particular design decisions.

- **Version Control and Semantic Versioning:** Keep track of changes through a version control system like Git, and adopt semantic versioning to communicate plugin updates easily.

Engage with the Kong Community

Benefit from wider learning and insights by engaging with the Kong community. This involves participation in forums, contributing to open-source plugins, and sharing insights that might advance community knowledge. Collective learning from community contributions often helps avoid common pitfalls and gathers innovative ideas, richly influencing future development.

Through assiduous adherence to these best practices, plugin development for Kong can yield robust, scalable, and effective solutions that greatly enhance the native capabilities of the API Gateway. This structured approach ensures not only the initial success of plugin deployments but their continued relevance and resilience in an evolving technological landscape.

6.7   Troubleshooting Plugin Issues

Troubleshooting plugin issues in the Kong API Gateway is essential for maintaining operational efficacy and ensuring that the configured logic runs seamlessly. When a plugin, whether built-in or custom-developed, does not perform as expected, identifying and resolving the problem quickly is crucial to minimize disruption and maintain service reliability. This section provides an in-depth exploration of systematic approaches and tools for diagnosing and fixing plugin-related issues.

Initial Diagnosis and Problem Identification

The first step in troubleshooting is to isolate the problem. This involves identifying symptoms, such as unusual behavior of APIs, unexpected outputs, errors in processing, or abnormal response times. The key to efficient troubleshooting is systematic consideration of possible causes, ranging from misconfigurations, code issues, to performance bottlenecks, and logical errors.

- **Understanding Symptoms**: Start by defining the observed issues clearly. For example, is the plugin crashing, causing in-

169

creased latency, or blocking traffic unexpectedly?

- **Check Kong Logs**: Kong provides extensive logging capabilities. Examine the error logs (typically located at '/usr/local/kong/logs/error.log') for any messages related to your plugin.

```
tail -f /usr/local/kong/logs/error.log | grep "plugin-name"
```

Logs often contain stack traces or error numbers that can hint at misconfigurations or runtime errors in the plugin code.

Configuration Review and Verification

Common sources of plugin issues include errors in configuration and environment setup. Reviewing these configurations for typos, missing fields, or incorrect values is an initial low-friction step:

- **Verify Plugin-Specific Parameters**: Check if requisite configurations like authentication tokens, rates, or target URLs are defined and correctly formatted.

- **Service and Route Mapping**: Ensure that plugins are correctly mapped to the intended services or routes, avoiding global misconfiguration that might affect performance adversely.

```
curl -i -X GET http://localhost:8001/routes/{route_id}/plugins
```

This command retrieves all plugins associated with a specific route, allowing a verification of whether the expected plugins are active and correctly configured.

Code Analysis and Debugging

For custom plugins, delve into the plugin's source code. Common pitfalls include logic errors, incorrect API usage, or Lua-specific issues such as nil references or syntax errors.

- **Lua Debugging**: Use Lua unit testing tools like Busted to detect unexpected behaviors, incorporating assertions that validate function output and logic paths.

```
describe("Functionality Test", function()
  it("should return true", function()
    assert.True(your_plugin_function("input"), "Expected true but got false
        ")
  end)
end)
```

- **Use ngx and PDK Functions**: Ensure correct application of ngx API and Kong PDK methods, respecting calling conventions and expected usages. Review the Kong PDK documentation for correct method usage.

Performance and Load Considerations

Should plugins introduce noticeable performance reductions, investigate via load testing and performance profiling methodologies:

- **Load Testing Tools**: Use tools like Apache JMeter or k6 to simulate traffic and observe impact across plugin phases. Monitor latency, throughput, and error rates attributable to plugin processing.

```
jmeter -n -t test_plan.jmx -l test_results.jtl
```

- **Optimize for Efficiency**: Identify bottlenecks within the plugin logic. Consider caching repeated data lookups, avoiding unnecessary computations, and employing asynchronous processing models where latency may significantly affect performance.

Systematic Approach to Plugin Dependencies and Conflicts

Plugins can occasionally conflict with others, leading to unexpected behaviors:

171

- **Dependency Management**: Double-check LuaRocks dependencies for custom plugins. Ensure correct versions and compatibility matrix, resolving any LuaRocks dependency issues.

- **Order of Operations**: Confirm that plugins execute in an intended order. If order affects the output, adjust priorities in configurations to reflect desired control flow.

Validate using:

```
curl -i -X GET http://localhost:8001/plugins
```

Advanced Monitoring and Observability

If initial diagnostics do not reveal clear outcomes, deeper observability tools can assist:

- **Kong Dashboard**: Utilize dashboards that integrate with Kong, giving visualizations of request flows, plugin activations, and traffic indices.

- **External Monitoring Solutions**: Prometheus and OpenTracing can be integrated to provide in-depth analysis with granular metrics, following request paths through plugins, collecting duration, hit rates, or failure frequencies.

Continuous Improvement through Feedback Loop

Troubleshooting not only resolves current issues but contributes to improving future development processes:

- **Document All Findings**: Maintain runtime logs, error fixes, and changes in configurations within a knowledge base for reference on similar future cases.

- **Iterative Improvements**: Based on learnings, refine development processes, including enhanced validation, more comprehensive testing, and systematic reviews, incorporating automation where possible.

- **Feedback to Developers**: Channel information from support teams and system users back into development pipelines, guiding future architectural decisions or plugins' updates/enhancements.

Conclusion and Steps Forward

By following a structured approach to troubleshooting, organizations significantly improve their ability to resolve plugin issues proactively, minimizing downtime and maintaining resilience in API gateway operations. Emphasizing an observational strategy enriched by automated tools and community-best practices establishes a proactive troubleshooting model, enabling strong, sustained API Gateway integrity. This fosters broader insights across development and operational landscapes, yielding not only immediate resolutions but adaptive strategies for future endeavors.

Chapter 7

Load Balancing and Scaling with Kong

This chapter focuses on the essential aspects of load balancing and scaling within Kong API Gateway, crucial for ensuring efficient traffic distribution and high availability of services. It covers the setup and configuration of load balancers, delves into various strategies for managing upstreams, and discusses the implementation of health checks and failover mechanisms. Additionally, the chapter examines the use of DNS-based load balancing to enhance distribution across nodes and illustrates techniques for auto-scaling Kong clusters to meet dynamic demand. Through understanding these practices, users can optimize their API infrastructure for performance and reliability.

7.1 Concepts of Load Balancing in Kong

In distributed systems architecture, load balancing is an integral component that ensures the equitable distribution of incoming network traffic across multiple servers or server clusters. This section elucidates the fundamental principles of load balancing,

175

particularly focusing on its application within the Kong API Gateway, a high-performance, open-source API gateway and microservices management layer. By understanding how Kong facilitates load balancing, developers can effectively manage network traffic, optimize resource usage, and enhance overall system resilience.

Load balancing in Kong is primarily focused on managing upstream services. An upstream in Kong represents a target service group that receives client requests. The gateway dynamically distributes these requests among available upstream nodes based on predefined load balancing algorithms, ensuring optimal service delivery.

- *Core Load Balancing Algorithms in Kong*

Kong natively supports several load balancing algorithms, each tailored to suit specific application requirements and traffic patterns. Understanding these algorithms is critical for configuring an efficient load balancing strategy.

- *Round Robin:* This method distributes requests sequentially across all available targets. It's an equitable approach when all targets have equivalent processing capacity. Despite its simplicity, round-robin may not cater effectively to scenarios with targets of varying capacities. The inherent assumption of homogeneity among servers can lead to suboptimal resource utilization if not appropriately matched with the target configuration.

- *Least Connections:* Requests are directed to the target with the fewest active connections. This algorithm excels in environments where persistent connections prevail, such as when long-lived connections consume resources differently across servers. By ensuring that no single node is overwhelmed while others remain underutilized, the least connections method actively contributes to a balanced workload distribution.

- *IP Hash:* In this technique, requests are allocated based on the hash of the client's IP address. This ensures that a particular client always interacts with the same upstream target, thereby maintaining session persistence. IP hashing is advantageous in scenarios necessitating consistent session data across requests,

176

thus negating the need for additional state-sharing mechanisms among servers.

```
{
    "name": "upstream-name",
    "targets": [
        {"target": "192.168.1.11:80", "weight": 10},
        {"target": "192.168.1.12:80", "weight": 10}
    ],
    "algorithm": "round-robin"
}
```

The configuration of each algorithm requires meticulous calibration regarding the target parameters. For instance, targets may be assigned weights to influence selection probability under particular algorithms, such as weighted round robin or weighted least connections. An understanding of these intricacies facilitates creating a tailored load balancing configuration that aligns strategically with application needs.

- *Dynamic Scaling and Load Balancing*

Kong incorporates mechanisms for dynamic scaling, providing resilience against fluctuating load conditions. Targets can be added or removed dynamically without significant impact on service continuity. This elasticity ensures that the upstream service topology remains responsive to real-time demands.

```
curl -i -X POST http://localhost:8001/upstreams/upstream-name/targets \
--data "target=192.168.1.13:80" \
--data "weight=10"
```

Integrating such dynamic capabilities with automated monitoring scripts or scaling policies enables a self-regulating system capable of automatically adjusting in response to volumetric changes. Moreover, by leveraging Kong's Health Checking APIs, upstream targets are automatically marked as healthy or unhealthy, determining their eligibility to receive traffic. This ensures robust failover capabilities, a subject explored further in the subsequent sections.

- *Session Persistence in Load Balancing*

Ensuring session persistence or sticky sessions can be crucial under certain application contexts such as online shopping carts or similar application states. Kong allows session persistence mainly via IP Hashing as elaborated earlier, where the client's IP address plays a critical role in determining the request path. This persistence can often be complemented with cookie-based strategies implemented at the application level to enhance state management.

Kong's architecture is inherently extensible, allowing developers to integrate custom logic through the use of plugins. As such, implementing sophisticated load balancing strategies that go beyond what Kong natively provides becomes feasible by employing custom plugins. Such plugins can perform additional inspection on requests, allowing a more granular routing logic as required by complex enterprise workloads.

```
{
    "name": "upstream-name",
    "targets": [
        {"target": "192.168.1.11:80", "weight": 5},
        {"target": "192.168.1.12:80", "weight": 5}
    ],
    "algorithm": "ip-hash"
}
```

The strategic utilization of plugins can influence how Kong handles requests, altering the native load balancing characteristics to accommodate almost any desired operational requirement.

- *Integrating Load Balancer Metrics*

Successful load balancing requires comprehensive monitoring. Kong provides extensive metrics that developers can exploit to gauge the performance of their load balancing strategy. By collecting data on request latencies, throughput, and error rates, insightful analysis can be performed to optimize load distribution policies further.

```
Kong Metrics:
---------------
Total Requests per Target
Successful Response Ratio
Request Latency Distribution
Error Rate per Upstream
```

These metrics, accessible via Kong's Admin API and potentially visualized using external systems like Prometheus or Grafana, equip system administrators with actionable insights on upstream performance and load balancer efficiency. Systematic observation of these metrics enables tuning load balancing policies to eliminate bottlenecks and align with evolving performance goals.

7.2 Setting Up Load Balancers

Setting up load balancers in Kong is a multifaceted process that involves configuring various components to ensure effective traffic management across distributed architectures. This section delves into the intricate details of configuring load balancers within Kong, highlighting strategic approaches and step-by-step instructions that facilitate a robust implementation.

To commence, it's essential to understand the role of load balancers in managing traffic and maintaining high availability. In Kong, a load balancer is essentially an orchestrator that routes incoming requests to multiple upstream nodes based on predefined criteria. Setting up load balancers involves defining services, creating upstreams, and configuring targets.

- A service in the context of Kong refers to any upstream API or microservice that processes client requests. To set up a service in Kong, it's paramount to define its attributes accurately, such as the protocol, host, port, and path. This definition ensures that Kong understands how to route requests appropriately.

```
{
    "name": "example-service",
    "url": "http://example.com"
}
```

The basic configuration above specifies an HTTP service hosted at example.com. Kong leverages this information to construct upstream requests, translating incoming client requests into actionable service calls. It's imperative to ensure that this configuration aligns with the actual service endpoints to prevent routing errors.

- Once services are defined, the next step involves creating upstreams. An upstream in Kong is a logical abstraction representing a cluster of targets, typically application servers, grouped to

179

manage load balanced traffic. Within an upstream, Kong distributes client requests based on the associated load balancing algorithm.

```
{
    "name": "example-upstream"
}
```

```
curl -i -X POST http://localhost:8001/upstreams/example-upstream/targets \
--data "target=192.168.1.10:80" \
--data "weight=10"
```

```
curl -i -X POST http://localhost:8001/upstreams/example-upstream/targets \
--data "target=192.168.1.11:80" \
--data "weight=10"
```

The example above demonstrates setting up an upstream named example-upstream with two targets. Each target, such as 192.168.1.10:80, can have a weight assigned to indicate its relative capacity or preference in receiving traffic. By manipulating these weights, operators can fine-tune how requests are balanced across available targets. The capability to dynamically add or remove targets affords the system the flexibility to adapt to traffic changes without incurring downtime.

- Selecting the appropriate load balancing strategy is crucial. Different algorithms may be optimal based on the specific traffic patterns and service characteristics. As discussed in the previous section, strategies such as round-robin, least connections, and IP hash each offer distinct advantages and operational considerations.

Utilizing heuristics and metrics helps determine which strategy best suits the given service conditions. For example, if a service experiences highly variable connection loads, a least connections algorithm might be preferable. Conversely, if the services predominantly require session affinity, an IP hash-based strategy would ensure consistent routing for repeated client interactions.

- The configuration of routes is integral to linking defined services with consumer requests. Routes determine how incoming requests should map onto service endpoints. Various attributes

180

such as paths, hosts, methods, or headers can conditionally trigger the invocation of specific services.

```
{
    "service": {
        "id": "example-service-id"
    },
    "hosts": ["example.org"],
    "paths": ["/v1/path"],
    "methods": ["GET", "POST"]
}
```

This example depicts a route configuration targeting requests to example.org, matching the specified path and HTTP methods. The association between routes and services is pivotal in achieving a granular level of traffic management, ensuring that requests are directed to the appropriate business logic executed via the invited upstreams.

Properly defining routes ensures precise control over how API calls traverse through Kong, essentially serving as the switchboard for request flow. Given the criticality, configurations are typically validated and tested to mitigate routing discrepancies.

- To maintain high availability and optimal performance, Kong can perform health checks on upstream targets. These checks ascertain the operational status of the targets and dynamically adjust routing policies to exclude unhealthy nodes from the pool of eligible targets. By precluding defective targets, the system averts potential disruptions.

```
{
    "active": {
        "http_path": "/status",
        "healthy": {
            "interval": 5,
            "successes": 2
        },
        "unhealthy": {
            "interval": 5,
            "http_failures": 3
        }
    },
    "passive": {
        "healthy": {
            "successes": 2
        },
        "unhealthy": {
```

```
        "http_failures": 3
      }
    }
}
```

Active checks actively probe targets via specified endpoints (/status in this case), determining health based on successes or failures over time. Meanwhile, passive checks react to anomalies encountered during normal traffic flow, marking targets based on response quality. Configuring both types strengthens resilience by ensuring continuous traffic flow despite individual target failures.

- The ability to assign weights to targets introduces additional control over traffic distribution. By setting distinct weights, different targets can adopt varying proportions of the total request load corresponding to their respective processing capabilities or intended balance.

```
{
    "target": "192.168.1.12:80",
    "weight": 15
}
```

Higher weights increase the likelihood a target is selected for provisioning incoming requests relative to its peers. By carefully structuring these weights, operators can optimize available resources, ensuring neither overutilization nor underutilization persists across nodes, contributing to more stable operation during unpredictable traffic scenarios.

- Kong's extensible plugin architecture empowers developers to implement custom logic, which can complement or override the default load balancing mechanics. This ecosystem supports a wide range of additional functionalities, such as rate limiting or bespoke routing logic to address domain-specific requirements that conventional load balancing strategies cannot adequately accomplish.

Kong's comprehensive suite of functionalities, when combined with its flexible configuration capabilities, affords system architects unparalleled control in setting up and managing load balancers, facilitating the construction of reliable and scalable network infrastructures. Through thoughtful consideration and informed implementation of these capabilities, Kong equips organizations to adeptly handle complex operational demands.

7.3   Health Checks and Failover

In maintaining high availability and performance for distributed systems, health checks and failover mechanisms are essential components that allow the detection and management of unhealthy service nodes. Within the Kong API Gateway, implementing these features ensures that client requests are continuously routed to only those upstream targets that are operationally fit, thereby minimizing service disruption and enhancing user experience.

The importance of health checks and failovers cannot be overstated. They provide a system of checks and balances that enables dynamic response to evolving system conditions, mitigating downtime, and preserving data integrity. This section explores the intricacies of configuring and optimizing health checks and failover strategies in Kong.

Understanding Active Health Checks

Active health checks involve proactive monitoring wherein Kong independently checks the health status of upstream targets at regular intervals. By using a defined endpoint, such as /health or /status, the system sends periodic requests to each target to determine their operational status.

```
{
    "active": {
        "type": "http",
        "http_path": "/health",
        "healthy": {
            "interval": 10,
            "successes": 3
        },
        "unhealthy": {
            "interval": 5,
            "http_failures": 2
        }
    }
}
```

In this configuration, the system checks the /health endpoint on each target every 10 seconds. A target is marked as healthy after 3 consecutive successful responses. Conversely, it is marked as unhealthy after 2 consecutive failures within a 5-second interval.

Such frequent probing ensures that unhealthy targets are quickly detected and removed from the active pool, while recovering targets can be reintegrated expediently once their operational state stabilizes. The detail and frequency of such checks should be carefully configured to balance system sensitivity against performance overhead.

Implementing Passive Health Checks

Passive health checks complement active checks by responding to failure patterns observed during regular traffic flow. They are particularly useful for capturing transient or momentary issues that may not be detected during periodic active probes.

```
{
    "passive": {
        "healthy": {
            "successes": 5,
            "tcp_failures": 0,
            "timeouts": 0,
            "http_statuses": [200, 201]
        },
        "unhealthy": {
            "http_failures": 4,
            "tcp_failures": 1,
            "timeouts": 2,
            "http_statuses": [429, 500, 503]
        }
    }
}
```

This example demonstrates a passive health check configuration. A target rebounds to a healthy state after 5 consecutive successful requests with specific HTTP status codes, such as 200 (OK) or 201 (Created). Conversely, a target is labeled as unhealthy upon 4 HTTP failures, a single TCP failure, or 2 timeouts, indicating significant connectivity or server-side issues.

By utilizing passive checks, Kong accounts for real-world request handling issues that proliferate through normal operations, thereby aiding in cautiously adjusting target status based on empirical evidence.

Integrating Health Checks with Failover Strategies

184

The successful implementation of health checks directly influences the efficacy of failover mechanisms in Kong. Failover is the process by which requests are automatically rerouted to alternative nodes upon detection of target failure. Effective failover strategies minimize client impact during disruptions, maintaining seamless request servicing.

Implementing failover entails configuring the load balancer to quickly switch over to healthy targets in the event of identified failures:

```
{
    "name": "example-upstream",
    "algorithm": "least-connections",
    "healthchecks": {
        "active": {
            "type": "http",
            "http_path": "/health",
            "healthy": {
                "interval": 10,
                "successes": 3
            },
            "unhealthy": {
                "interval": 5,
                "http_failures": 2
            }
        }
    }
}
```

The above configuration combines health checks with a load balancing algorithm, specifically least connections, to promptly exclude or reinclude targets based on their health status. The least connections strategy is beneficial in this context as it diminishes the load on currently stressed nodes, diverting traffic to those with greater processing headroom.

Monitoring and Alerting

For health checks and failover strategies to be genuinely effective, there must be robust monitoring and alerting systems in place. Information from health checks should be logged and analyzed to detect trends or recurring patterns. Various metrics such as the frequency of server failures, average response times, and success/failure ratios are key indicators of upstream health.

Kong's integration with observability tools such as Prometheus and Grafana offers visualization of these metrics, transforming raw data into actionable insights:

```
Kong Health Check Metrics:
----------------------------
Upstream Targets Monitor
Request Latency
HTTP Failures Count
TCP Failures Count
Timeout Events
```

Through comprehensive monitoring, potential infrastructure bottle-necks or failure modes can be identified and addressed preemptively, allowing system administrators to enforce continuous improvement over deployed failover measures.

Enhancing Resilience with Traffic Control Plugins

Beyond intrinsic health checks and failover configurations, plugins within the Kong ecosystem further enhance high availability setups. For instance, plugins such as traffic throttling, circuit breaking, and request retries provide additional layers of fault tolerance:

- *Traffic Throttling*: Guards against overwhelming upstream targets by capping the volume of traffic directed towards them during periods of congestion.

- *Circuit Breaking*: Automatically detects failure surges, temporarily halts traffic to the affected targets, and resumes once stability is restored.

- *Request Retries*: Implements retry logic, automatically reissuing requests after transient failures to ensure successful delivery wherever feasible.

Utilizing these plugins allows Kong to absorb and adapt to failure instigators effortlessly, diverting workload away from problematic nodes while ensuring an unbroken request flow.

Strategic Considerations and Best Practices

Implementing health check and failover strategies within Kong requires strategic deliberations to achieve operational excellence. Key considerations and best practices include:

1. **Determining Appropriate Check Frequencies:** Strike a balance to minimize latency while avoiding undue load caused by excessive health check requests.

186

2. **Defining Clear Thresholds:** Set precise success and failure counts for each target type, aligning them closely with known operational baselines.

3. **Matching Checks with System Capabilities:** Integrate contextually appropriate monitoring and observability tools to detect performance anomalies in real-time.

4. **Planning Redundancy and Load Spreading:** Deploy multiple, geographically distributed upstream clusters to mitigate failures and maintain connectivity regardless of location-specific issues.

The deployment of a resilient health check and failover framework within Kong ensures the continuity of enterprise-grade service delivery, notwithstanding the challenges posed by routine fluctuations or unanticipated disruptions in network service conditions.

7.4 DNS-Based Load Balancing

DNS-based load balancing is a pivotal technique in managing traffic across distributed systems, especially in the context of large-scale deployments leveraging the Kong API Gateway. This approach utilizes the Domain Name System (DNS) to distribute client requests efficiently by associating multiple IP addresses with a single domain name. As such, it serves as a fundamental mechanism for enhancing system scalability and redundancy.

This section delves into the operational principles of DNS-based load balancing, how it is implemented within Kong, and the considerations for effectively leveraging it to maximize availability and performance.

- **Principles of DNS-Based Load Balancing**

At its essence, DNS-based load balancing operates by returning a set of IP addresses for a given domain name query. When a client requests access to a service via its domain name, the responding DNS server provides multiple A (IPv4) or AAAA (IPv6) records, each pointing to an operational instance of the service. The client or intermediate resolver then selects one of these addresses, distributing the load organically across nodes.

The inherent simplicity of this scheme provides a stateless yet effective method for spreading requests:

- **Statistical Distribution**: DNS responses vary each time, achieving a statistical spreading of requests over the set of available service nodes.

- **Geo-Location Awareness**: Proximity-based DNS resolutions can reduce latency by directing clients to geographically nearer instances.

- **Redundancy**: Multiple IP assignments offer fault tolerance; should a node fail, alternate addresses remain reachable.

In Kong, DNS load balancing is particularly advantageous as it inherently supports the dynamic scaling of services, allowing organizations to elastically add or remove nodes without necessitating complex reconfiguration.

- **Enhancing Kong with DNS Load Balancing**

Kong natively supports DNS-based load balancing, facilitating transparent integration with its upstream mechanisms. This capability ensures smooth interaction with service backends, leveraging DNS to translate service names into routable addresses that Kong can use to distribute requests.

```
{
    "name": "example-upstream",
    "targets": [
        {"target": "backend.example.com", "weight": 10},
        {"target": "backup.example.com", "weight": 5}
    ],
    "algorithm": "round-robin"
}
```

In this configuration, upstream targets are specified using DNS hostnames (e.g., backend.example.com), with each hostname potentially resolving to multiple IP addresses. Kong handles these target definitions in conjunction with load balancing algorithms like round-robin to evenly spread requests among the resolved addresses.

Such flexibility extends usability by decoupling upstream configurations from fixed IP assignments. This decoupling is critical in cloud and microservices environments where service endpoints are subject to frequent changes.

- **Leveraging TTL Values for Dynamic Resolutions**

The role of Time To Live (TTL) values in DNS responses is crucial. TTL dictates how long a DNS resolver caches a given entry before re-querying the authoritative servers. In the context of load balancing, shorter TTLs encourage frequent updates, allowing clients to adapt rapidly to changes in the set of available service nodes:

- **Stale Cache Prevention**: By employing short TTL values, stale entries are minimized, and DNS A/AAAA records are refreshed more frequently, ensuring the client list of potential endpoints is current.

- **Responsive Load Adjustments**: With real-time updates to DNS records, systems can respond to changes, such as scaling operations or node failures, more dynamically.

While beneficial, short TTLs can also induce higher query traffic to DNS servers, posing a trade-off between freshness of data and system load. Optimizing TTL requires a strategic analysis of the expected churn rate and network conditions.

- **Challenges and Mitigation Strategies**

DNS-based load balancing, while powerful, must navigate certain limitations and operational challenges:

- **DNS Caching Behavior**: Client or intermediate DNS resolver caching can lead to uneven load distributions, particularly if certain IP addresses remain cached disproportionately longer than others.

- **Failure Detection**: DNS itself lacks inherent health checks for endpoint availability. Without additional mechanisms, clients may be directed towards non-functional nodes, necessitating supplementary health monitoring and failover strategies.

- **Propagation Delays**: DNS record updates can take time to propagate depending on TTL configurations across the DNS hierarchy, potentially delaying failure response times.

To alleviate these challenges, ensure comprehensive DNS health checking and leverage hybrid models that incorporate both DNS and application-layer load balancing methods. Techniques such as DNSSEC can authenticate DNS responses for improved trustworthiness.

- **Using Service Discovery for Enhanced DNS Integration**

For Kong to maximize DNS-based strategies, especially in microservices environments, service discovery systems can be leveraged to dynamically register and deregister service endpoints. Tools such as Consul or etcd provide automated service registration, enabling platforms to adaptively align DNS records with actual service states:

- **Automated Health Checks**: Continuously validate service health and update DNS records accordingly to reflect operational realities.

- **Eureka Integration**: Incorporate DNS-based load balancing with solutions like Netflix Eureka, which streamlines service instance management and lightens DNS procedural loads on Kong.

This service-centric approach complements Kong's architecture by ensuring that DNS responses reflect current system states, facilitating efficient request routing without manual intervention.

- **Advanced Use Cases and Best Practices**

Understanding when and how to utilize DNS-based load balancing in Kong involves strategic considerations:

190

- **Adapting to Cloud Environments**: Integrate with multi-region and cloud-native settings where IP address fluidity is prevalent. By decentralizing endpoint management, DNS not only addresses load balancing but also mitigates latency through geo-aware resolutions.

- **Combining with Application Layer Balancing**: Deploy application-layer enhancements atop DNS foundations, allowing for sophisticated resource allocations or session affinity considerations beyond DNS's capability.

- **Resilience Through Redundancy**: Structure resilient DNS architectures by deploying redundant nameservers, guaranteeing DNS availability and mitigating the impact of DNS failures themselves.

- **Testing and Simulation**: Conduct load testing and failure simulations to evaluate DNS performance characteristics, focusing on edge cases such as misconfigurations, bursty load patterns, and TTL-induced delays.

Through strategic configuration and optimization, DNS-based load balancing can act as a cornerstone of effective traffic management in Kong, weaving together the threads of scalability, reliability, and efficiency into a cohesive fabric suitable for modern distributed applications. This agility is crucial as systems evolve to meet the demands of increasingly dynamic operational environments, underscoring the pivotal role of DNS solutions in contemporary networking paradigms.

7.5 Auto-scaling Kong Clusters

Auto-scaling is an essential capability for managing the dynamic nature of workloads in cloud environments. Within the context of Kong API Gateway, auto-scaling facilitates the seamless adaptation of computing resources in response to varying traffic demands. Through the automation of scaling processes, organizations can maintain service performance while optimizing resource utilization and cost efficiency.

This section elucidates the principles and implementation of auto-scaling Kong clusters, exploring key strategies, practical considerations, and integrating automation into a continuous deployment pipeline for adaptive infrastructure management.

Core principles of auto-scaling include:

- **Elasticity**: The ability to scale compute resources up or down automatically in response to demand fluctuations, ensuring ideal performance levels.

- **Efficiency**: Optimal resource usage, reducing costs associated with over-provisioning while preventing performance degradation during peak loads.

- **Resiliency**: Maintaining redundancy and availability across nodes to handle node failures transparently.

Auto-scaling Strategies

Several strategies may be employed when configuring auto-scaling within Kong:

- **Reactive Scaling**: Involves scaling actions driven by observable metrics such as CPU utilization, memory usage, or request latencies. This relies on monitoring current loads and triggering scaling events when metrics surpass thresholds.

- **Predictive Scaling**: Incorporates machine learning algorithms to forecast demand based on historical data, allowing preemptive scaling ahead of anticipated spikes.

- **Scheduled Scaling**: Implements fixed scaling based on known activity patterns, such as increasing capacity during business hours and reducing during off-hours.

Deciding on an appropriate strategy often involves evaluating system requirements, traffic patterns, and operational objectives to tailor the scaling solution efficiently.

Implementing Auto-scaling with Cloud Providers

Most cloud platforms, such as AWS, Google Cloud Platform, and Microsoft Azure, provide native services to manage auto-scaling efficiently. These services can be configured to handle scaling for Kubernetes-based deployments, where Kong typically operates:

For example, AWS's Elastic Kubernetes Service (EKS) combined with its Auto-Scaling Groups enables dynamic resource management:

```
{
    "AutoScalingGroupName": "Kong-ASG",
    "LaunchConfigurationName": "KongLaunchConfig",
    "MinSize": 2,
    "MaxSize": 10,
    "DesiredCapacity": 4,
    "AvailabilityZones": ["us-west-2a", "us-west-2b"],
    "HealthCheckGracePeriod": 300,
    "Targets": [
        {
            "MetricName": "CPUUtilization",
            "Statistic": "Average",
            "ComparisonOperator": "GreaterThanThreshold",
            "Threshold": 70.0,
            "Period": 60,
            "EvaluationPeriods": 2,
            "ScalingAdjustment": 1
        }
    ]
}
```

This configuration specifies an auto-scaling group with a minimum of 2 nodes and a maximum of 10. Based on CPU utilization exceeding 70% over two consecutive evaluations, a scaling event increases the node count.

Integrating Kubernetes Horizontal Auto-scaling

In Kubernetes, Horizontal Pod Autoscaler (HPA) provides native support for managing pods based on observed metrics, automatically adjusting the number of replicas deployed within Kubernetes clusters. For an API gateway like Kong, this assists in balancing load against the system's internal components:

```
apiVersion: autoscaling/v2beta2
kind: HorizontalPodAutoscaler
metadata:
  name: kong-hpa
spec:
  scaleTargetRef:
    apiVersion: apps/v1
    kind: Deployment
    name: kong-deployment
```

```
minReplicas: 2
maxReplicas: 10
metrics:
- type: Resource
  resource:
    name: cpu
    target:
      type: Utilization
      averageUtilization: 75
```

In this setup, HPA applies to a Kong deployment, ensuring that at least 2 pods are always running, while allowing up to 10 if average CPU utilization surpasses 75%.

Monitoring and Alerting for Auto-scaling

Active monitoring is vital to an effective auto-scaling architecture. By equipping scaling setups with robust monitoring and alerting systems, potential scaling inefficiencies or failures can be readily identified:

- **Prometheus and Grafana**: Provide a framework to monitor operational metrics and visualize trend data. This historical insight aids in detecting anomalies or justifying adjustments in scale policies.

  ```
  Prometheus Metric Examples:
  ----------------------------
  Kong Request Rate
  Kong Latency Percentiles
  CPU and Memory Utilization
  Pod and Node Availability
  ```

- **Alertmanager**: Part of the Prometheus ecosystem, it automates notifications when metrics indicate potential scale issues, prompting investigation or intervention.

Incorporating Canary Deployments and Rollback Strategies

When scaling in tandem with continuous integration and deployment pipelines, adopting sophisticated deployment strategies enhances scalability outcomes:

- **Canary Deployments**: Incrementally introduce changes to a subset of users or nodes, validating updates under scaled operations without impacting the entire environment.

194

- **Automated Rollbacks**: Enhance resiliency through rapid roll-back procedures in the event incorrect scaling causes disruption.

These strategies contribute to overall system stability by measured roll-out of changes alongside adaptive scaling.

Cost Considerations and Optimization

While auto-scaling offers dynamic responsiveness, it introduces new cost vectors that must be managed to ensure budgetary alignment:

- **Resource Allocation Redundancy**: Avoid over-allocating resources by periodically assessing usage patterns and refining threshold values to better match actual demand.

- **Spot and Preemptible Instances**: Utilize cheaper instance options where feasible, especially in non-critical services, to reduce operational expenditure.

Effective auto-scaling achieves cost-efficient scaling, maintaining a delicate balance between resource availability and fiscal responsibility.

Best Practices for Auto-scaling Kong Clusters

- **Thorough Testing**: Simulate scaling scenarios to assess resilience and evaluate system performance under anticipated loads.

- **Adaptive Policies**: Deploy policies that can dynamically adjust thresholds and limits based on environmental feedback.

- **Comprehensive Documentation**: Maintain detailed records of scaling configurations and changes to inform ongoing refinement processes.

- **Cross-regional Considerations**: Enhance geographic distribution to ensure disaster recovery readiness and minimize the impact of regional failures.

Implementing auto-scaling within Kong clusters is crucial for creating responsive, perpetually optimized systems capable of thriving under variable load conditions. By leveraging modern cloud-native technologies and integrating advanced monitoring tools, scaling becomes not just a matter of necessity but a core operational competency, propelling efficient service delivery across a landscape of constant change.

7.6   Optimizing Performance

In the modern landscape of digital services, optimizing performance is critical to maintaining seamless user experiences and meeting operational goals. For API gateways like Kong, which sit as intermediaries between clients and microservices, performance tuning is essential to ensure efficiency, reliability, and scalability. This section explores a comprehensive strategy for optimizing performance within Kong deployments, encompassing various layers from configuration, resource tuning, to leveraging advanced features.

- **Understanding Performance Factors**

Several factors influence the overall performance of Kong within an infrastructure:

- Network Latency: The time required to send requests to and receive responses from upstream services can impact perceived performance.

- Resource Utilization: CPU, memory, and network bandwidth usage of Kong instances must be monitored to prevent bottlenecks.

- Plugin Overhead: Plugins provide advanced functionalities but can introduce processing overhead if not properly configured.

- Load Balancing: Efficient distribution of requests across upstreams is crucial for minimizing load imbalance and contention.

A successful optimization strategy combines addressing each factor by tuning configurations and observing system behavior under load.

- **Tuning Kong Configuration Settings**

Optimization begins with configuring Kong itself. Certain parameters within Kong's configuration can be tuned based on specific workloads and environmental characteristics:

```
{
  "worker_processes": 4,
  "worker_connections": 1024,
  "client_max_body_size": "10m",
  "upstream_keepalive": 60
}
```

- Worker Processes: Configuring the number of worker processes affects concurrency. Adjusting this value based on CPU cores can enhance throughput, especially in high-load scenarios where demand for concurrent request handling escalates.

- Worker Connections: Defines the maximum number of simultaneous connections per worker. This effectively dictates how well Kong handles large numbers of requests, making it pivotal in high-traffic environments.

- Client Max Body Size: Setting this parameter appropriately ensures responses can accommodate maximum expected payload sizes without rejection.

- Upstream Keepalive: Enabling keepalives preserves persistent connections to upstreams, reducing handshake times for repeated requests and boosting efficiency.

- **Strategic Plugin Management**

Kong's powerful plugin architecture offers flexible request processing capabilities, but these plugins must be managed judiciously:

- Selective Activation: Use only necessary plugins to minimize processing overhead. Each active plugin examines incoming requests, adding latency.

- Prioritization: Assign execution order to plugins based on importance and computational demand. Critical path plugins like authentication should precede others to expedite request completion.

- Custom Plugins: Develop bespoke plugins where needed, optimizing internal logic for performance-critical paths.

Plugins should be reviewed periodically to ensure they deliver value against the incurred processing cost.

- **Leveraging Caching Mechanisms**

Caching is pivotal in minimizing response times and reducing load on backend services:

- Proxy Caching: Employ caching strategies to store and serve frequently requested resources, thereby reducing the number of requests reaching upstream services.

Kong can be configured with caching plugins that support varying cache strategies:

```
{
  "name": "api-cache",
  "config": {
    "cache_ttl": 300,
    "strategy": "disk"
  }
}
```

- Cache TTL (Time to Live): Properly configuring TTL values balances freshness against the overhead of fetching new content.

- Cache Invalidation: Monitor and purge cache entries that may become stale due to updates or deletions in source data.

- **Monitoring and Observability**

Optimizing performance is an iterative process driven by monitoring and analytics:

- Analytics Tools: Utilize tools like Prometheus and Grafana to obtain a comprehensive view of key metrics concerning Kong's performance.

- Focus Metrics: Prioritize metrics such as response time distributions, request rates, error rates, and resource utilization when assessing performance:

```
Prometheus Metrics Collection:
-------------------------------
Kong Latency Statistics
Kong Throughput Over Time
Kong Memory and CPU Usage
Upstream Availability
```

- Alerting Systems: Deploy alerting mechanisms via tools such as Alertmanager to promptly act on threshold breaches or anomalous conditions.

Effective observability permits timely interventions to rectify suboptimal performance by ascertaining root causes of issues.

- **Load Balancer Optimization**

Load balancers impact how Kong distributes incoming requests among backend services. Fine-tuning these mechanisms helps streamline performance:

- Algorithm Selection: Adopting suitable load balancing algorithms, such as least connections or consistent hash, aligns with application demands and minimizes resource contention.

- Session Stickiness: While typically discouraged for stateless application design, session stickiness might alleviate performance issues for state-dependent architectures by ensuring continuity.

Intelligent balance of trailer headers and weight allocations also assist in achieving fair resource distribution.

- **Infrastructure and Resource Scaling**

Beyond optimizing configurations, scaling infrastructure proportionate to demand ensures consistent performance:

- Auto-scaling: Configure auto-scaling for Kong nodes based on set performance metrics. This includes both horizontal scaling (adding more instances) and vertical scaling (increasing resources per instance).

```
{
  "scaling_metric": "load",
  "thresholds": {
    "max_cpu_usage": 80,
    "max_latency": 200
  },
  "scale_up_factor": 2,
  "scale_down_factor": 1
}
```

- Resource Management: Provision adequate network, storage, and compute capacities aligned to operational needs to maintain peak performance.

Flexibility through cloud hosting solutions allows rapid adaptation under scaling protocols.

- **Strategies for Content Distribution Networks (CDNs)**

Content Delivery Networks (CDNs) are instrumental in distributing content closer to clients, markedly reducing latency and load:

- CDNs Usage: Direct static and cacheable content through CDNs, relieving proxies from extraneous bandwidth consumption.

- Dynamic Content Combinations: Explore methodical CDNs applications over dynamic APIs, reducing server footprint through intelligent caching practices.

CDNs deployment reshapes geographical distribution impact, ensuring routing efficiency and user experience parity.

- **Best Practices for Performance Optimization**

- Review and Iterate: Regularly revisit configuration and plugins, adapting according to insights from monitoring data and evolving traffic patterns.

- Controlled Experiments: Conduct experiments such as canary deployments to test configuration hypotheses, assess their impact before widespread adoption.

- Cross-Functional Collaboration: Involve teams beyond developers, including network administrators and operations staff, to align on infrastructure strategies and share a performance-oriented culture.

- Holistic Optimization: Extend efforts beyond Kong, assessing database schemas, networking policies, and application logic as part of an inclusive optimization endeavor.

By systematically applying these strategies, optimizing performance within Kong becomes a dynamic, evidence-led process that underpins reliable and efficient service provision. It facilitates the fulfillment of operational objectives while ensuring that end-users receive consistent, superior experiences as they engage with APIs mediated by Kong.

7.7 Handling Traffic Spikes

In the digital age, where user engagement levels can vary unpredictably, it is crucial for API gateways like Kong to handle sudden traffic spikes effectively. Traffic spikes occur due to a variety of reasons, including marketing campaigns, seasonal peaks, unexpected user behavior, or viral success. This variability necessitates a well-architected system capable of scaling promptly and maintaining service reliability.

This section examines strategies and techniques for handling traffic spikes in Kong environments, focusing on architectural adjustments, technical configurations, real-time monitoring, and the implementation of effective mitigation tactics.

Architectural Scalability

The foundation of handling traffic spikes lies in a scalable architecture that can elastically adjust to increased load:

- **Microservices Architecture**: Adopting a microservices architecture inherently supports scaling by distributing individual ser-

vice components independently. Kong, deployed as the API gateway, should ideally sit at the interface of well-constructed microservices with clear interaction patterns, facilitating isolated
scaling based on individual service demand.

- **Cloud-Native Deployments**: Leveraging cloud infrastructures provides flexibility with built-in services to automate
  scaling operations through managed clusters or container
  orchestration platforms like Kubernetes, which supports
  Horizontal Pod Autoscaling:

```
apiVersion: autoscaling/v2beta2
kind: HorizontalPodAutoscaler
metadata:
  name: kong-hpa-spike
spec:
  scaleTargetRef:
    apiVersion: apps/v1
    kind: Deployment
    name: kong-deployment
  minReplicas: 2
  maxReplicas: 12
  metrics:
  - type: Resource
    resource:
      name: cpu
      target:
        type: Utilization
        averageUtilization: 70
```

The HPA ensures that additional replicas are deployed when CPU utilization exceeds 70%, allowing the system to manage load spikes without manual intervention.

Real-Time Monitoring and Load Predictions

Proactive monitoring forms the backbone of detecting and reacting to
traffic spikes:

- **Comprehensive Monitoring**: Implement comprehensive
  monitoring with tools like Prometheus and Grafana, enabling
  visualization of critical metrics like request rates, latency
  distributions, and resource utilization:

```
Essential Metrics to Monitor:
--------------------------------
Real-time Request Throughput
```

Latency Percentile (95th/99th)
Error Rate Tracking
Scalable Resource Usage Index

- **Anomaly Detection**: Use machine learning models for traffic prediction, allowing recognition of patterns that precede spikes, which can trigger preparatory measures before spikes escalate.

- **Automated Alerts**: Establish alerts to inform operational teams of emerging spikes based on threshold violations, enabling immediate attention and action.

Rate Limiting and Throttling

Rate limiting is a tactical tool used to manage client requests during peak times, protecting the core services from overload:

- **Rate Limiting Plugin**: Configure the Kong Rate Limiting plugin to enforce per-second, per-minute, or per-hour limits on traffic to avoid resource saturation:

```
{
  "name": "rate-limiting",
  "config": {
    "second": 100,
    "minute": 2000,
    "policy": "local"
  }
}
```

This configuration restricts requests to 100 per second, safeguarding resources, while accommodating a limited increase in traffic.

- **Planned Throttling**: Gracefully throttle incoming requests, providing informative error responses, encouraging retries instead of abrupt denials.

Implementing Caching and Content Delivery

Caching mechanisms reduce the load on backends by serving repeat requests more efficiently:

- **HTTP Caching**: Deploy caching strategies using plugins compatible with Kong to speed response times and reduce processing overhead. Establishing strategic cache invalidation policies preserves data relevance without overloading traffic conduits.

- **CDN Integration**: Direct static assets and cacheable content through Content Delivery Networks (CDNs), redistributing load away from the main stack, especially useful when spikes owe to geographic concentration.

Graceful Degradation

Ensuring that a system degrades gracefully under stress is crucial to maintaining user experience even when full service levels cannot be sustained:

- **Load Shedding**: Implement techniques to prioritize critical traffic paths or degrade non-essential features, ensuring that primary functionalities remain responsive.

- **Feature Toggling**: Temporarily disable features contributing to excessive load until traffic stabilizes, reducing resource pressure without channeling away all interactions.

Response Queueing and Prioritization

Establishing queuing mechanisms allows the system to manage traffic influx effectively, ordering processing based on priority:

- **Work Queues**: Integrate message queues for processing-intensive tasks, allowing non-urgent requests to queue and deplete load gradually.

- **Priority Channels**: Implement differentiated service levels, directing priority traffic over dedicated channels ensuring quality-consistent delivery, especially in premium service offerings.

Testing and Simulation

Conducting stress testing and scenario simulations prepares systems for handling real-world scenarios:

- **Load Testing**: Use tools like Apache JMeter or Locust to simulate high traffic levels, testing configurations under controlled stressors, evaluating the system's capacity to throttle, shed loads, or scale.

- **Chaos Engineering**: Engage in controlled fault conditions to explore robustness, discovering system limits and refining strategies based on findings.

Strategic Considerations

Strategic measures bolster system capability to absorb and diffuse traffic spikes:

- **Geo-distributed Deployments**: Deploy instances in multiple regions to diffuse concentrated spikes and bolster redundancy.

- **Preemptive Scalability Clustering**: Pre-provision resources when traffic prediction foresees incoming spikes, maintaining global pressure balance.

Best Practices for Managing Traffic Spikes

- **Holistic Approach**: Consider entire system architecture, anticipating specific entry points where spikes are likely and planning responses proteanly.

- **Documentation and Communication**: Maintain detailed records of strategies and infrastructure changes, ensuring dissemination across teams for cohesive impact mitigation.

- **Cross-Functionality for Resilience**: Aggregate knowledge from diverse teams including developers, operations, and network engineers shaping robust, adaptable load strategies.

- **Iterative Optimization**: Monitor, learn from past traffic spikes, and regularly iterate on mitigation and enhancement techniques based on evolving usage patterns.

Effectively preparing Kong instances to handle traffic spikes through robust techniques provides a safeguard against performance degradation, ensuring continuity and reliable service in dynamic conditions.

By integrating a balanced blend of swift adaptation, strategic foresight, and predictive insights, architecture remains resiliently prepared to manage sudden demand bursts, affording optimal service even amidst the bustling digital tides.

Chapter 8

Monitoring and Logging in Kong

This chapter examines the frameworks and tools for effective monitoring and logging in Kong API Gateway, essential for maintaining optimal performance and security. It describes how to configure logging and integrate Kong with external logging tools for enhanced data analysis. The chapter also explores setting up monitoring solutions using metrics to provide real-time insights into API usage. Guidelines on configuring alerting and notifications enable proactive management of potential issues. By leveraging these practices, administrators can ensure comprehensive oversight of their API operations, allowing for informed decision-making and timely troubleshooting.

8.1 Importance of Monitoring and Logging

Monitoring and logging are foundational components in managing and maintaining the health, performance, and security of APIs, particularly in an environment like Kong API Gateway where robust handling of API traffic is essential. These two practices provide API administrators with the ability to observe the ongoing status of their systems, identify and diagnose issues proactively, and make informed decisions based on real-time and historical data analysis.

Effective monitoring involves tracking and analyzing the metrics that represent the behavior and state of the applications. This includes data such as request rates, error rates, latency, and server health statuses. Logging, on the other hand, captures detailed records of various events that occur, providing a chronological trail that can be instrumental for troubleshooting and auditing purposes.

In a large-scale deployment such as Kong, which serves as an intermediary layer between clients and services, the importance of monitoring and logging cannot be overstated. Logging ensures that every request, response, and error is recorded, allowing developers to pinpoint issues accurately and swiftly. Monitoring provides a macro-level view over time, highlighting trends and patterns that might otherwise go unnoticed.

The logging mechanisms within Kong are typically designed to capture essential data points, such as request paths, response times, status codes, and headers. Here's an example of a typical log entry for a request handled by Kong, formatted for clarity:

```
{
  "request": {
    "method": "GET",
    "url": "http://example.com/api/resource",
    "headers": {
      "Host": "example.com",
      "User-Agent": "PostmanRuntime/7.26.5"
    }
  },
  "response": {
    "status": 200,
    "headers": {
      "Content-Type": "application/json"
    }
  },
  "latency": 53,
  "timestamp": "2023-10-25T12:30:45Z"
}
```

This log entry not only provides insight into the request and response but also the latency, allowing for performance tuning and optimization efforts.

Real-time monitoring in Kong can be achieved through metrics such as latency, request counts, throughput, and error percentages. A common toolset for such purposes includes Prometheus for data collection and Grafana for visualization. These tools allow the setup of dashboards that reflect the current state of the API Gateway at a glance.

Establishing a monitoring system typically involves the following steps: metrics definition, data collection, data storage, and alert configuration. Each plays a crucial role in ensuring that the system remains responsive and reliable. The configuration in a typical Prometheus setting might include:

```
[monitor-prometheus]
enabled = true
metrics = ["kong_latency", "kong_requests", "kong_errors"]
```

Analysis of the logged data and metrics can be enhanced by integrating Kong with advanced analytics tools like the ELK stack (Elasticsearch, Logstash, and Kibana) or Splunk, which offer advanced searching and visualization capabilities. This integration not only improves the ease of managing and visualizing data but also helps in identifying API usage patterns, potential security breaches, and operational anomalies.

In the context of security, monitoring and logging offer invaluable insights into potential security threats. Logging every access attempt and monitoring for unusual patterns help detect anomalies such as repeated unauthorized attempts or abnormally high traffic volumes that may signal distributed denial-of-service (DDoS) attacks.

Consider the scenario where API consumption patterns must be understood. By analyzing the logs, it is possible to ascertain which APIs are most frequently accessed, at what times, and by which users. This insight can guide capacity planning and highlight opportunities for API feature enhancements. A sample analytics query that could be used in Kibana might look like:

```
GET /_search
{
  "query": {
    "range": {
      "timestamp": {
        "gte": "now-1d/d",
        "lte": "now/d"
      }
```

209

```
    }
  },
  "aggs": {
    "top_apis": {
      "terms": {
        "field": "request.url",
        "size": 10
      }
    }
  }
}
```

This query retrieves the top 10 most frequently accessed API endpoints over the last day, allowing administrators to conduct further analysis on traffic patterns.

From a compliance perspective, logging provides an audit trail for ensuring regulatory adherence. Regulatory standards such as GDPR, HIPAA, and PCI DSS often mandate meticulous logging practices as a part of their compliance requirements. This requirement underscores the necessity for a logging solution within Kong that can maintain comprehensive, immutable logs, while also ensuring data protection and privacy.

Moreover, troubleshooting and diagnostics are made more efficient with detailed logs and thorough monitoring processes. Logs help trace the sequence of events leading to an issue, enabling rapid identification and resolution, significantly mitigating downtime and performance degradation. Monitoring tools can provide alerts in real-time, allowing for immediate corrective actions.

The effectiveness of monitoring and logging in a Kong environment hinges on their configuration and the tools employed to analyze and visualize the collected data. For instance, configuring proper log levels—such as INFO, DEBUG, WARN, or ERROR—ensures that logs remain useful and manageable without being overwhelming.

A critical aspect of setting up logging is considering the volume and retention policy of log data. High-traffic apps might generate significant amounts of data, which can be expensive to store and analyze. It is, therefore, crucial to establish clear policies and utilize cloud-based log management solutions that can scale with the needs of your deployment.

Finally, it is imperative for API administrators to regularly review both logs and monitoring dashboards to ensure they accurately reflect the current API traffic and operational state. Proactive regular audits and updates to these systems will accommodate changes in the architecture or user behavior, maintaining operational efficiency and security.

By leveraging a structured, comprehensive approach to monitoring and logging, API administrators working with Kong can achieve operational excellence through improved visibility, enhanced security, and optimized performance of their API ecosystems. This holistic understanding empowers informed decision-making and ensures that issues are addressed before they escalate into critical failures.

8.2 Configuring Logging in Kong

Configuring logging in Kong is a critical task that ensures comprehensive visibility into each transaction processed by the API Gateway. Logging provides the detailed information necessary for monitoring applications, diagnosing issues, complying with regulations, and performing detailed data analysis. This section delves deeply into the procedures and considerations for setting up efficient logging in Kong, covering log formats, configuration settings, target endpoints, and best practices.

Kong provides various plugins for logging, enabling flexibility and extensibility to meet diverse needs. Commonly used logging plugins include HTTP Log, File Log, Syslog, TCP Log, UDP Log, and Loggly, among others. The choice of logging plugin should be dictated by scalability needs, performance requirements, and existing infrastructure architecture.

To begin configuring logging in Kong, one must first select the proper plugins based on the target systems desired for log storage. For instance, if consolidated logs are needed in an HTTP endpoint, the HTTP Log plugin is appropriate. Basic configuration for the HTTP Log plugin involves specifying the endpoint and methods for authentication, if required.

Here is an example of configuring the HTTP Log plugin using the declarative configuration in Kong:

```
plugins:
- name: http-log
  config:
    http_endpoint: http://logs.example.com/collect
    method: "POST"
    timeout: 1000
    keepalive: 60000
```

In this configuration, the http_endpoint parameter specifies where logs will be sent. Adjusting timeout and keepalive is critical for controlling how Kong manages connections to the log server, balancing between resource consumption and logging efficiency.

Another option is the File Log plugin, which writes logs to a file on the server. This is useful for local audit trails but may require more setup for external log aggregation:

```
plugins:
- name: file-log
  config:
    path: /var/log/kong/kong.log
```

The path specifies the file location where logs are written. Ensure that the Kong user has the necessary file permissions to write logs and that there is sufficient disk space to accommodate the expected log volume.

Syslog is also a versatile option available with Kong, especially useful in environments where logging needs to be centralized across distributed systems. Example configuration of the Syslog plugin is as follows:

```
plugins:
- name: syslog
  config:
    host: 127.0.0.1
    port: 514
    facility: kern
    severity: info
```

The parameters such as host, port, and facility determine where and how the logs are forwarded. Ensure that the syslog daemon is properly configured to accept the incoming log data.

A significant aspect of managing logs in Kong is handling log formats. Kong typically uses structured logging, often in JSON or Logfmt formats, to facilitate easy parsing and analysis by log management systems. Here is a JSON formatted log entry example:

```
{
```

```
"service": "example_service",
"consumer": "user_123",
"method": "POST",
"uri": "/api/v1/resource",
"status": 200,
"response_size": 512,
"request_time": 0.35
}
```

Such structured logs simplify integration with log analysis and processing tools like ELK Stack or Splunk, which automatically recognize and process JSON objects.

When configuring logging, it is paramount to balance between detail and volume—capturing excessive detail may lead to overwhelming data sizes, slowing down the analysis, and increasing storage costs. It is recommended to begin by logging critical events and gradually extending the detail level as needed.

The efficiency of logged data management can be further optimized by partitioning logs based on tags, such as services or routes. This structured logging approach allows for filtering and querying log data with precision. For instance, annotating logs by route might allow a query like:

```
GET /logs/_search
{
  "query": {
    "term": {
      "route.id": "example_route_id"
    }
  }
}
```

This Elasticsearch query demonstrates retrieving logs specifically for a given route, reducing noise and focusing analysis.

When it comes to managing the effect of logging on performance, it's critical to offload logs to dedicated systems outside of the main application path. Utilizing asynchronous logging approaches helps avoid slowing down request processing. This consideration is crucial in high-throughput environments where logging overhead could impact application responsiveness.

Kong provides rate-limiting on logs, allowing administrators to define thresholds that prevent excessive log generation from overwhelming the system. For instance:

```
plugins:
- name: rate-limiting
  service: example_service
  config:
    second: 5
    minute: 100
    policy: local
```

This configuration ensures that the log generation rate does not exceed defined limits, safeguarding system resources.

Kong's integration capabilities allow for seamless connections with cloud-based log management solutions such as Amazon CloudWatch, Azure Monitor, or Google Cloud Logging. These integrations provide scalable storage and powerful querying capabilities, often bundled with alerting systems.

Security of logs is another critical area. Ensure that logs do not inadvertently contain sensitive user information, such as passwords or personal data, to comply with privacy laws and regulations. Properly configure log redaction and masking when necessary.

In sum, configuring logging in Kong requires careful consideration of plugin selection, format specifications, infrastructure integration, and compliance with security and performance standards. Each choice, from structured data formats to the specifics of log destinations, plays a role in ensuring the effectiveness of the logging strategy for a Kong deployment. By systematically analyzing logging needs and infrastructure capabilities, Kong administrators can design a logging architecture that supports robust observability and operational intelligence without sacrificing performance or security.

8.3 Integrating with Logging Tools

Integrating Kong's logging capabilities with external logging tools enhances data analysis, visualization, and retention. These integrations are essential for extracting actionable insights from logs, streamlining monitoring operations, optimizing system performance, and maintaining compliance with organizational or regulatory standards. An array of robust logging tools, such as the ELK Stack (Elasticsearch, Logstash,

Kibana), Splunk, or cloud-based solutions like Amazon CloudWatch, Azure Monitor, and Google Cloud Logging, offer advanced functionalities that, when combined with Kong's data, allow for a deeper understanding of an API's operations.

The first step in this integration process involves selecting a logging tool that aligns with your organization's technical environment and analytical needs. Consider factors such as scalability, ease of integration, costs, and the depth of analytical features. For many organizations, the ELK Stack presents a compelling option due to its open-source nature and extensive customization capabilities. It encompasses Elasticsearch for data indexing and search, Logstash for data processing and transformation, and Kibana for visualization and exploration.

To integrate Kong logs with the ELK stack, begin by configuring the appropriate Kong logging plugin such as the Syslog, HTTP Log, or File Log to export logs in a format compatible with Logstash, the data processing layer. A sample configuration using the HTTP Log plugin might look like:

```
plugins:
- name: http-log
  config:
    http_endpoint: http://logstash.example.com:5044
    method: "POST"
    timeout: 1000
    keepalive: 60000
```

In this example, logs are sent from Kong to a Logstash instance using a specified 'http_endpoint'. Logstash then processes these logs, potentially applying filters, enrichment, or transformations, and forwards them to Elasticsearch where they are indexed.

Logstash configuration represents the core of ELK's flexibility, allowing you to parse and process Kong logs according to your specific requirements. Below is a sample configuration snippet for a Logstash pipeline that receives Kong logs:

```
input {
    http {
        port => 5044
    }
}

filter {
    json {
        source => "message"
```

```
    }
    date {
        match => ["timestamp", "ISO8601"]
    }
    mutate {
        remove_field => ["headers"]
    }
}

output {
    elasticsearch {
        hosts => ["http://elasticsearch:9200"]
        index => "kong-logs-%{+YYYY.MM.dd}"
    }
}
```

This configuration accepts HTTP input on port 5044, parses log messages as JSON, reinterprets timestamps to a standardized format, and indexes the output into Elasticsearch under a time-based index pattern, ensuring efficient storage and query performance.

Once logs are stored in Elasticsearch, Kibana serves as the interface for visualization and analysis. It allows for the creation of custom dashboards and panels that offer real-time insights into API usage, latency, error rates, traffic patterns, and more. The integration is seamless once the Elasticsearch indices are correctly configured and logs are consistently indexed. An example use case would be setting up a dashboard to monitor request counts by API endpoint:

- Define an index pattern in Kibana corresponding to the time-based indexing logic used in Logstash.

- Use the 'Visualize' functionality in Kibana to create a new visualization, selecting 'bar chart.'

- Set the X-axis to be the API endpoint field, and Y-axis to show count of requests.

Splunk offers another popular solution for log integration with advanced search, filtering, and analytical capabilities. The integration with Splunk can be achieved using Splunk's HTTP Event Collector (HEC) which facilitates streaming of logs directly from Kong. Here's an example Kong configuration for integrating with Splunk:

```
plugins:
- name: http-log
```

216

```
config:
  http_endpoint: http://splunk.example.com:8088/services/collector/event
  method: "POST"
  timeout: 1000
  keepalive: 60000
  headers:
    Authorization: Splunk <HEC_TOKEN>
```

In this instance, logs are sent to Splunk's HEC endpoint using a secure token ('<HEC_TOKEN>'), authenticating and logging events without disruptive configuration changes or potential security lapses.

Cloud-based logging services like Amazon CloudWatch, Azure Monitor, and Google Cloud Logging offer integrated solutions tailored to their environments. These platforms offer seamless log collection, long-term storage, integrative dashboards, alerting capabilities, and query interfaces. Utilizing these services involves configuring appropriate endpoints or agents to forward logs from Kong, often relying on Kong's HTTP Log or TCP Log plugins. Here is a sample configuration for sending to CloudWatch using AWS Lambda to streamline the log delivery process:

```
plugins:
- name: http-log
  config:
    http_endpoint: https://<API_GATEWAY_ID>.execute-api.<region>.amazonaws.
        com/PROD/log
    method: "POST"
    timeout: 1000
    keepalive: 60000
    headers:
      Authorization: AWS4-HMAC-SHA256 <Signature>
```

Ensure the Lambda function is properly set up to receive logs, process them, and then forward these logs to CloudWatch Logs by configuring the execution role with the requisite permissions.

Once integrated with any external logging tool, careful consideration should be given to privacy, retention policies, data security, and permissible levels of access among users and systems. Ensuring compliance with standards like GDPR or HIPAA often necessitates employing encryption in transit, anonymization, or obfuscation strategies to protect sensitive user data.

Furthermore, as the volume and complexity of generated log data grow, the importance of automating processes within the log analysis workflow increases. Leveraging alerting capabilities of the logging solution ensures that system administrators are notified of significant events or anomalies in real time. For instance, configuring alerts in Amazon CloudWatch might involve setting threshold criteria on API request error rates, generating notifications through AWS SNS when exceeded.

Incorporating machine learning models into the log analysis pipeline can also provide proactive insights into potential issues through anomaly detection or predictive trend analysis. Several logging solutions either natively include or integrate with machine learning frameworks, extending operational intelligence gathered from Kong's rich logging data.

By establishing a robust log integration strategy with these tools, organizations significantly improve operational visibility and responsiveness to API-related events, transforming raw data into a powerful asset for system performance optimization and strategic decision-making. The harmonization of Kong's logging output with robust logging infrastructure fosters an environment conducive to investigative analysis, continuous improvement, and compliance enforcement, empowering teams to extend their operational capabilities with confidence.

8.4   Metrics and Monitoring Solutions

Metrics and monitoring solutions in the context of the Kong API Gateway constitute a fundamental aspect of operations management, providing the ability to observe, measure, and improve the performance and reliability of API services. This section explores the core principles of metrics-based monitoring, the specific metrics pertinent to a Kong deployment, and how tools like Prometheus, Grafana, and others can be leveraged to effectively visualize and respond to these metrics.

The concept of monitoring revolves around the continuous assessment of a system through the collection and evaluation of metrics. Metrics, in essence, are quantifiable measures that reflect the performance and health of a system. In Kong, these metrics facilitate an in-depth understanding of various aspects of API traffic such as request counts, latencies, error rates, throughput, and server health.

To initiate monitoring in Kong, one must first identify the critical metrics that need to be tracked. In a typical API environment, essential metrics may include:

- Total Requests: Counts of all requests received by the system.

- Successful Responses: Counts of successful request responses (HTTP status codes 2xx).

- Client Error Responses: Alerts regarding client-side issues (HTTP status codes 4xx).

- Server Error Responses: Notifications of server-side errors (HTTP status codes 5xx).

- Request Latency: Time taken to fulfill requests.

- Request Rates: Analysis of the number of requests over a time interval.

- Active Connections: Number of active connections to upstream services.

- Data Volumes: Measurement of ingested and emitted data quantities.

The process of gathering and visualizing these metrics can be effectively handled by monitoring solutions like Prometheus, which is a powerful, open-source system for service monitoring and time series databases. Prometheus collects metrics from monitored targets at specified intervals, evaluates rule expressions, displays the results, and triggers notifications if certain conditions arise.

In deploying Prometheus with Kong, the first step involves setting up the Prometheus plugin. This allows Kong to expose its metrics in a format that Prometheus understands. An example of configuring the Kong Prometheus plugin might look like the following:

```
plugins:
- name: prometheus
```

This configuration activates Prometheus monitoring, exposing a '/metrics' endpoint on Kong from which Prometheus can scrape data. It is crucial to appropriately configure Prometheus scraping settings, defining the target endpoints and scrape intervals. A basic Prometheus configuration file might appear as follows:

```
scrape_configs:
 - job_name: 'kong'
   scrape_interval: 15s
   static_configs:
     - targets: ['localhost:8001']
```

This setup directs Prometheus to scrape metrics from Kong every 15 seconds. The choice of scrape intervals should reflect the desired granularity and timeliness of data collection balanced against resource consumption.

Once data is collected by Prometheus, visualization tools like Grafana can be layered on to create insightful dashboards that present metrics in an easily digestible format. Grafana's flexibility allows users to create tailored visual representations such as bar charts, line graphs, heat maps, and singlestat panels.

To integrate Grafana with Prometheus, configure Grafana to connect to the Prometheus instance as a data source. This process usually involves specifying the Prometheus server URL within Grafana's data source configuration interface. After establishing the connection, users can leverage predefined dashboards templates such as the Kong API Gateway dashboard available from Grafana's community, or build custom dashboards suited to specific monitoring requirements.

Building an effective monitoring dashboard in Grafana involves selecting relevant queries that yield meaningful insights. A typical Grafana panel configuration might query Prometheus with:

```
rate(kong_http_requests_total[5m])
```

This PromQL expression calculates the rate of HTTP requests within a five-minute window, providing an indication of request velocity changes over time. By harnessing Grafana's alerting capabilities, thresholds can be set up to react to certain metric conditions, ensuring proactive responses to anomalies. For instance, if average request latency exceeds a predefined level, automated alerts via email, Slack, or PagerDuty can be dispatched.

In addition to Prometheus and Grafana, Kong can be integrated with other monitoring ecosystems provided by cloud service providers. Amazon CloudWatch, Azure Monitor, and Google Cloud Operations are some leading solutions, offering extensive APIs for integrating and extending monitoring capabilities with external environments. Their seamless integration allows for scalable monitoring, leveraging native cloud resources and advanced analytical tools.

Many of these platforms offer pre-built integration features with third-party platforms for expanded analytical processing of collected data. Consider Amazon CloudWatch offering AWS Lambda functions for more complex metric transformations, or Azure Monitor providing Azure Logic Apps for advanced workflows and alerts.

As part of a comprehensive monitoring strategy, organizations should consider implementing custom metrics. These metrics prove invaluable in cases where predefined metrics do not adequately reflect specific business logic or operational performance aspects. Custom metrics can be instrumented through various methods such as Kong Lua plugins, introducing additional complexity but providing tailored insights.

Monitoring should not be static, and rather evolve with the system developments and business needs. Ensuring optimal configuration involves regular reviews and updates to the monitored metrics, thresholds, and visualization tools. It is vital to continue reassessing which metrics truly contribute to understanding API health and performance to avoid neglecting KPIs or over-inflating data relevance.

Security remains a pivotal focus within metrics monitoring, especially regarding access controls and data handling, ensuring sensitive information remains secure. Establish permissions within monitoring tools to restrict access to sensitive data and always employ encryption on metrics data transmitted across networks.

A well-executed metrics and monitoring setup bolstered by Kong serves as the backbone of operational intelligence, enabling timely, informed decisions that improve system resilience and performance. By seamlessly integrating Kong with these sophisticated monitoring solutions, infrastructure teams are empowered to not only maintain but enhance their API operations with dexterity and precision. This proactive approach ensures that businesses can deliver reliable and consistent services to end-users, embodying the primary organizational objective of operational excellence.

8.5   Alerting and Notifications

Alerting and notifications are key components of a comprehensive monitoring strategy, enabling organizations to respond swiftly to issues by automatically informing relevant stakeholders about system anomalies. Within the context of Kong API Gateway management, integrating alerting and notification mechanisms ensures that administrators are immediately aware of performance degradations, security incidents, or any deviation from expected operational behaviors. This section delves into the design, implementation, and management of effective alerting systems, highlighting best practices and solutions available for Kong deployments.

Effective alerting starts with a clear understanding of what constitutes a significant event or threshold that warrants an alert. These events can range from API response time exceeding a certain threshold, error rates surpassing defined limits, unauthorized access attempts, or abnormal traffic patterns indicating potential DDoS attacks. Identifying these conditions involves establishing baseline metrics and employing statistical detection techniques to articulate alerts precisely.

A typical alerting workflow involves several steps: defining alert rules, configuring actions upon trigger events, determining notification channels, and managing alert lifecycle. This workflow is often complemented by alert aggregation and suppression mechanisms to prevent alert fatigue or noise.

Prometheus, coupled with Alertmanager, provides a robust framework for creating alert rules and managing alert flow. Alerting rules in Prometheus are configured using the Prometheus query language (PromQL), which allows for programmatically defining conditions under which alerts should be fired.

An example alert rule in Prometheus might be:

```
groups:
- name: kong_alerts
  rules:
  - alert: HighErrorRate
    expr: rate(kong_http_status{status=~"5.."}[5m]) > 0.05
```

```
for: 5m
labels:
  severity: critical
annotations:
  summary: "High error rate detected"
  description: "The error rate has been over 5% for the last 5 minutes."
```

This rule triggers an alert named 'HighErrorRate' when the proportion of 5xx responses exceeds 5% over a five-minute window, categorizing the alert with a severity level of 'critical'. Using annotations, additional context can be provided, assisting in understanding the alert's nature and scope.

Once alerts are defined in Prometheus, Alertmanager assumes responsibility for handling alert notifications. Alertmanager can route alerts to various destinations based on predefined configurations, avoiding redundant notifications and providing group-based notifications for related alerts. Integrations include email, SMS, Slack, OpsGenie, Pager-Duty, Webhooks, and more, with configuration settings allowing for conditional routing based on alert labels.

A sample Alertmanager configuration might look like this:

```
route:
  group_by: ['alertname']
  group_wait: 30s
  group_interval: 5m
  repeat_interval: 1h
  receiver: 'team-slack'

receivers:
- name: 'team-slack'
  slack_configs:
  - send_resolved: true
    channel: '#alerts'
    api_url: 'https://hooks.slack.com/services/T000/B000/XYZ'
```

In this configuration, alerts are grouped by 'alertname' and sent to a Slack channel. The 'group_wait', 'group_interval', and 'repeat_interval' settings control the timing of alert aggregation and repeated notifications. Routes and receivers can be further refined and extended to accommodate organizational structures and roles.

Beyond baseline alerting, advanced alerting strategies incorporate predictive alerting and anomaly detection, where machine learning and statistical techniques predict future anomalies based on historical data trends. These alerts typically offer more proactive notifications, allowing organizations to resolve issues before they impact system availability.

Real-time notifications are paramount during incidents, yet not all alert conditions necessitate immediate action. To mitigate alert fatigue, integrating severity levels and escalation policies within alert configuration is crucial. Severity levels should define the urgency of an alert, and escalation policies dictate next steps if an alert is unresolved within a specified duration.

Moreover, integrations with IT Service Management (ITSM) systems provide mechanisms to ensure alerts create actionable items within ticketing services like Jira, ServiceNow, or Trello, facilitating streamlined incident management. Automation capabilities within these platforms can further reduce manual interventions, enabling quicker response times.

Dashboards in Grafana or other visualization tools not only display metric data but also visualize alert status. With Grafana, for example, panels can be configured to change appearance based on alert states, providing visual cues that enhance situational awareness.

Setting up alerts within Grafana depends on its integration with the data source. Grafana supports querying Prometheus, Elasticsearch, InfluxDB, and other sources directly for triggering alerts. Alerts in Grafana can be created by selecting specific queries within panels and defining thresholds that, when surpassed, trigger the alert notification.

Example Grafana alert definition might include:

```
Alert: HighLatency
  Condition: avg() of query(A, 5m, now) > 0.3
  Evaluated every: 1m
  Actions: Notify Slack
```

This alert checks if the average latency exceeds 300ms over a five-minute interval, evaluating every minute. Actions define the communication channels to escalate alerts automatically.

Security considerations are fundamental throughout the alerting and notifications configuration, ensuring system integrity and data privacy. Limiting access to alert configurations and applying encryption where applicable across notification channels protect against unauthorized tampering and information breaches.

Additionally, cultural aspects should be factored into alert design. Clear communication about alert severity and prioritization helps align operational expectations and promotes best practices among teams. Training and continuous education about alert management should be integrated into organizational onboarding and professional development programs.

Documentation and post-incident reviews further supplement the alerting process, offering insights into alert efficacy and opportunities for refinement, such as reducing false positives or improving response strategies. Regular audits of the alerting system confirm that all alerts are relevant, actionable, and appropriately directed.

Through thoughtful integration and management of alerting and notification strategies within Kong's ecosystem, operators establish trust that the system is continuously monitored and safeguarded against disruptions. Intelligent alerting not only informs stakeholders of potential issues but enables proactive system administration, fortifying system resilience and availability.

8.6 Analyzing API Traffic Patterns

Analyzing API traffic patterns is a critical practice for optimizing performance, enhancing security, and understanding user behavior within a Kong API Gateway environment. By meticulously examining how, when, and by whom APIs are accessed, organizations can uncover valuable insights that drive strategic decision-making and operational efficiency. This section delves into the methodologies, tools, and practices involved in comprehensively analyzing API traffic patterns, providing a detailed exploration of techniques and technologies that facilitate an in-depth understanding of API interactions.

API traffic analysis begins with the systematic collection of data concerning API usage. Essential data points include request frequencies, geographic locations, user agents, response statuses, and response times. These data facilitate the identification of trends and anomalies in API consumption, informing capacity planning, security measures, and user experience enhancements.

Kong, equipped with robust logging mechanisms, captures log data that can be leveraged for traffic analysis. Log entries typically contain metadata about the request and response cycles. Here's a succinct example of a log structure used for traffic analysis:

```
{
  "client_ip": "192.168.0.1",
  "timestamp": "2023-10-28T14:25:03Z",
  "http_method": "GET",
  "request_uri": "/api/resource",
  "response_status": 200,
  "response_time": 0.204,
  "consumer": "user_a",
  "region": "us-west-1"
}
```

This log encapsulates critical information such as client IPs, timestamps, HTTP methods, and geographic regions, which are pivotal for dissecting API traffic patterns.

Visualizing this data is crucial for interpreting traffic patterns. Tools like ELK Stack and Grafana come in handy, offering an amalgamation of powerful visualization capabilities and real-time analytics. Consider a scenario where Elasticsearch indexes Kong logs. Kibana, as part of the ELK Stack, allows creating visualizations based on time-series data, such as request trends across different endpoints.

Creating a Kibana dashboard that visualizes traffic pattern data could involve:

- **Index Pattern Creation**: Define an index pattern within Kibana that recognizes time-stamped data, aiding in time-based queries and visualizations.

- **Visualization**: Utilize Kibana's 'Visualize' feature to plot request volumes over time with line graphs, decipher geographical distributions using region maps, or identify anomalies with machine learning-enhanced anomaly detectors.

- **Dashboard Composition**: Assemble a comprehensive dashboard displaying multiple visualizations, providing an overarching view of traffic patterns and enabling drill-down analysis for more granular insights.

For example, using Kibana, an administrator might configure a bar chart visualization tracking request counts by endpoint:

```
GET /_search
{
  "aggs": {
    "requests_per_endpoint": {
      "terms": {
        "field": "request_uri.keyword",
        "size": 5
      }
    }
  }
}
```

This query aggregates the top five most requested API endpoints, revealing usage spikes or declines that suggest shifts in user engagement or potentially guide use-case prioritization for development.

Aside from ELK Stack, Prometheus in conjunction with Grafana offers a robust platform for collecting metrics, enabling the monitoring of real-time data and performance trends. While Prometheus excels in handling numerical data, it can be configured to reflect metrics such as request rates, response latencies, and error percentages—integral for evaluating API performance.

A typical setup in Grafana might showcase these metrics through a traffic dashboard, employing panels with queries that encapsulate:

```
rate(api_requests_total[5m])
```

This query calculates the rate of requests over a five-minute interval, an invaluable metric for identifying usage peaks and troughs in API calls. An added dimension can involve breaking down these metrics by route or service, offering insights into specific areas of the API that require scaling or optimization.

Furthermore, machine learning models can be incorporated to enrich traffic analysis by forecasting traffic demands or detecting subtle pattern shifts. Tools such as AWS's machine learning services can analyze data patterns and predict future shifts in API consumption, bolstering preparedness for capacity adjustments and ensuring SLA compliance.

Security is an ever-present concern in API management, and traffic analysis serves as a bulwark against myriad threats. By monitoring traffic patterns, administrators can promptly identify abnormal behavior indicative of threats, such as DDoS attacks or credential-stuffing attempts, and implement mitigation strategies. In practice:

- **Anomaly Detection**: Establish baselines for normal traffic patterns and deploy machine learning algorithms to monitor deviations, triggering alerts when anomalies exceed predefined thresholds.

- **Rate Limiting**: Configure automated actions to limit request rates once unusual patterns are detected, enforcing IP throttling or implementing CAPTCHA challenges to disrupt potential attacks.

- **Access Trends**: Audit logs for repeated failed authentication attempts or excessive access from unusual IP ranges, coupling with automated threat intelligence tools that block malicious actors.

Effective traffic pattern analysis extends beyond security and performance, offering deeper insights into user behavior. By segmenting logs by attributes such as geography or user agent strings, businesses gain a nuanced understanding of audience segments and preferences, guiding marketing strategies or user experience enhancements.

This comprehensive approach mandates incorporating feedback mechanisms whereby user experience improvements derived from traffic data analyses are methodically tested and validated through additional traffic monitoring. Continuous evaluation of these feedback loops enriches API services, aligning with evolving user expectations and technological advances.

Analyzing API traffic patterns through a layered approach that integrates data collection, visualization, security, and user insights comprehensively strengthens API management. With Kong's inherent capabilities and the adoption of external tools, an informed strategy is derived, characterized by constant vigilance and adaptive optimization. This robust analysis forms the backbone for maintaining scalable, secure, and user-centric API ecosystems that confidently support organizational goals.

8.7   Troubleshooting and Diagnostics

Troubleshooting and diagnostics are integral to maintaining the reliability and performance of the Kong API Gateway. As a central point for API traffic management, Kong must operate smoothly; disruptions can significantly affect service availability and user satisfaction. This section explores the methodologies, tools, and strategies essential for effective troubleshooting and diagnostics in Kong environments, offering detailed guidance on identifying, analyzing, and resolving issues.

Effective troubleshooting is a systematic process involving multiple steps: identifying symptoms, defining potential causes, isolating issues, testing hypotheses, implementing solutions, and finally documenting the findings for future reference. This iterative cycle helps ensure minimal disruption and builds knowledge for faster resolutions in subsequent incidents.

Identification of symptoms is the first step in the diagnostic process. Monitoring systems configured for Kong, such as Prometheus with Grafana dashboards and alerts, are often the initial indicator of potential issues. Alerts might be based on deviations from normal traffic patterns, elevated error rates, or increased latencies. Log data collected through Kong's extensive logging capabilities further aid in correlating metrics with specific incidents.

For instance, a consistent increase in request latency triggers an alert. Analyzing log entries at the onset of increased latency might reveal patterns such as specific routes affected or the nature of requests causing the delay. A typical log analysis process using Elasticsearch could employ queries that filter logs by response time:

```
GET /kong-logs/_search
{
  "query": {
    "range": {
      "response_time": {
        "gte": 1.0
      }
    }
  }
}
```

This query identifies API calls that have response times greater than one second, which can be instrumental in pinpointing problematic areas.

Once symptoms are identified, defining potential causes follows. This involves a deep dive into system configurations, observing environmental changes, and reviewing recent deployments or configuration changes. Other common potential causes might include increased load beyond capacity, bottlenecks in backend systems, or misconfigurations within Kong or the network.

Isolation of the issue involves narrowing down the potential causes. Consider a scenario where elevated error rates may suggest backend unavailability or misconfigured routing. Employing Kong's detailed logging facilities, administrators can confirm backend health using direct pings or curl commands to isolate connectivity issues. For instance:

```
curl -I http://backend-service-domain/resource
```

The response received from this command affirms or dismisses backend unavailability. If the backend is responsive, attention shifts to routing configurations, verifying upstream targets and health checks instituted in Kong.

Kong's powerful debugging tools, including HTTP status checks and customizable plugins, can reveal much about its operational state. Using Kong's Admin API, it's possible to inspect configured services, routes, and plugins to ensure intended configurations. For example, retrieving all services configured in Kong can be executed via:

```
curl -s http://localhost:8001/services | jq .
```

This command yields a comprehensive list of services and their attributes, facilitating the identification of discrepancies in service configurations.

Testing hypotheses often involves applying configuration changes in a controlled manner to gauge effects. This might be updating load balancing strategies, altering timeout values, or recalibrating health check settings in Kong. Kong supports dynamic reconfiguration with minimal impact, allowing testing to occur in real-time:

```
curl -X PATCH http://localhost:8001/services/service-name \
--data "connect_timeout=6000"
```

By adjusting timeouts, the interaction between Kong and upstream services can be optimized, potentially resolving latency issues.

Implementing solutions necessitates a collaborative approach, involving insights from developers, operations, and network teams. This might involve deploying updated configurations, scaling infrastructure components, or executing custom plugin logic tailored to circumvent identified bottlenecks.

Documenting the entire troubleshooting process is crucial for institutional knowledge building, arming teams with refined practices for future scenarios. This documentation should capture the symptoms, diagnostic steps, resolutions, and any lasting changes affecting system operation. It supports training efforts, aligns stakeholder understanding, and ensures continuity of quality responses irrespective of personnel changes.

Advanced diagnostics might integrate machine learning models which predict failures or automate anomaly detection. These models analyze historical data to discern patterns preceding failures and propose proactive interventions. Leveraging AI augments human expertise, enabling preemptive maintenance actions that bolster system uptime.

Security remains an overarching concern, ensuring that diagnostics and troubleshooting do not inadvertently expose sensitive data or weaken defense mechanisms. Ensure that access to diagnostic tools and logs is restricted to authorized personnel only, employing encryption and secure communication protocols at all times.

Capacity planning and incident simulation form part of proactive diagnostics. By simulating potential failure events or surges, Kong administrators gain insights into system weaknesses or capacity thresholds, informing bolstered designs or preemptive scaling actions. Automated scaling policies in cloud environments further enhance system resilience to fluctuating loads.

In sum, effective troubleshooting and diagnostics in Kong not only resolve immediate issues but contribute to strategic growth in system reliability and organizational knowledge. By systematically assessing, testing, and refining procedures, Kong administrators ensure API services remain robust, responsive, and secure even as demands evolve and technical landscapes shift. This strategic focus on diagnostics and troubleshooting empowers teams to sustain the integrity and availability of services, fostering trust and satisfaction among users and stakeholders alike.

231

Chapter 9

Advanced Kong Features and Use Cases

This chapter delves into advanced features of Kong API Gateway, showcasing its versatility and adaptability in diverse use cases. It highlights Kong Enterprise capabilities, such as enhanced security and API governance, and explores management strategies for API versioning. The chapter also examines Kong's role as a service mesh for microservices. Advanced topics include rate limiting techniques, handling modern protocols like GraphQL and gRPC, and leveraging real-time analytics for improved decision-making. By analyzing real-world case studies, readers will gain insight into implementing best practices and innovative solutions using Kong's advanced functionalities.

9.1   Kong Enterprise Features

Kong Enterprise extends the functionality of the open-source Kong Gateway with a suite of enhanced features designed for enterprise needs. These features contribute to heightened security, advanced administration, scalability, and robust performance monitoring. This section explores these capabilities in detail, offering insights into how Kong Enterprise augments API management and microservices architecture.

One of the standout features of Kong Enterprise is its advanced security capabilities. With APIs becoming critical components in digital infrastructures, securing them against unauthorized access and breaches is paramount. Kong Enterprise offers several layers of security through key authentication mechanisms, OAuth2.0 integration, and HMAC authentication. This multilayered approach ensures that APIs remain robust against a multitude of potential threats.

Kong Enterprise's implementation of OAuth2.0 is particularly noteworthy. OAuth2.0 serves as an authorization framework enabling third-party applications to access user data without exposing passwords. In the context of Kong, integrating OAuth2.0 authentication is streamlined, allowing for secure API access control. The following configuration script illustrates OAuth2.0 integration within Kong Enterprise:

```
{
  "name": "oauth2",
  "config": {
    "provision_key": "abcd1234",
    "scopes": ["email", "phone"],
    "mandatory_scope": true,
    "auth_header_name": "authorization"
  }
}
```

In the above configuration, we define scopes that limit the data applications can access, enhancing privacy and reducing risks associated with data leakage. The mandatory scope requirement ensures that all authorizations are explicitly scoped.

Kong Enterprise also employs HMAC authentication, leveraging hash-based message authentication codes to verify entities making requests to an API. This method strengthens message integrity by confirming that the message has not been altered during transmission. The following sample code demonstrates configuring HMAC authentication:

```
{
  "name": "hmac-auth",
  "config": {
    "clock_skew": 300,
    "enforce_headers": ["date", "x-consumer-id"],
```

```
    "replay_protection": true
  }
}
```

The configuration highlights the use of enforced headers and replay protection, both crucial in securing communications against man-in-the-middle attacks and replay attacks, thereby enhancing the overall security posture of the API.

Another substantial feature of Kong Enterprise is its advanced API management capabilities, including dynamic load balancing, multi-datacenter redundancy, and canary releases. These features deliver high availability, flexible traffic routing, and sophisticated deployment strategies for API-centric infrastructures.

Dynamic load balancing in Kong Enterprise is achieved through integration with service discovery tools. By monitoring available instances, Kong can smartly distribute incoming requests, optimizing resource utilization and minimizing latency. An example of a service discovery integration script is outlined as follows:

```
{
  "name": "service",
  "labels": {
    "version": "v1"
  },
  "discovery": {
    "provider": "consul",
    "service": "my-api"
  }
}
```

Here, the integration with Consul, a popular service discovery tool, allows Kong to recognize new service instances automatically and route traffic accordingly, ensuring minimal downtime and uninterrupted service.

Multi-datacenter redundancy is facilitated by Kong's ability to replicate data across geographic locations. This redundancy not only enhances reliability but also improves performance by serving requests from the nearest data center. The use of consistent hashing in Kong's implementation ensures that client requests are efficiently distributed across multiple datacenters.

Canary releases are a deployment strategy enabled by Kong Enterprise, allowing a subset of users to experience new API features before a full rollout. This approach helps identify potential issues in the new release without impacting the entire user base, contributing to more stable and reliable deployments.

Moreover, Kong Enterprise supports comprehensive analytics and monitoring capabilities. Real-time analytics aids organizations in understanding how APIs are consumed, discovering usage patterns, and identifying potential bottlenecks. Metrics such as request counts, response times, and error rates are visualized to inform decision-making and capacity planning.

The administrative interface of Kong Enterprise, Kong Manager, provides a powerful GUI for overseeing API entities and configurations. Administrators can effortlessly monitor system health, configure plugins, and setup workflows. Coupled with Kong's robust logging mechanisms, administrators can maintain compliance with audit requirements while performing operational troubleshooting.

Kong Enterprise's alerting and monitoring capabilities are further bolstered through its integration with prominent monitoring platforms such as Prometheus and Grafana. For example, by leveraging Prometheus Exporter, metrics can be effortlessly scraped and visualized through Grafana dashboards, providing holistic visibility over API performance.

Logging plays a critical role in maintaining operational excellence. Kong Enterprise supports extensive logging configurations, capturing a wide range of data elements such that request and response cycles can be thoroughly analyzed. The logs generated can be seamlessly forwarded to aggregation and visualization tools like Elasticsearch, Logstash, and Kibana (ELK Stack) for enhanced traceability.

In addition to security and administration features, Kong Enterprise offers functionalities optimized for large-scale business needs, such as role-based access control (RBAC) and a developer portal. RBAC provides granular permission control over API access, ensuring that only authorized personnel manage critical API functions. This feature is vital in environments that mandate strict compliance adherence and data privacy measures.

The developer portal of Kong Enterprise provides an intuitive platform for developers to access API documentation, manage their API keys, and collaborate on API usage. By supporting the creation of custom documentation and interactive testing, Kong simplifies the integration process and enhances developer productivity.

Finally, Kong Enterprise's plugin architecture supports a wide array of built-in and custom plugins, providing flexibility in addressing specific business needs. Custom plugins can be developed in Lua or other supported languages, allowing organizations to extend functionality and integrate specialized logic into their API ecosystem.

To illustrate, consider a scenario where a custom plugin is required to execute a specific transformation on request headers. The Lua script below demonstrates a simplistic implementation that modifies the incoming request headers:

```lua
local BasePlugin = require "kong.plugins.base_plugin"
local HeaderModifier = BasePlugin:extend()

function HeaderModifier:access(conf)
  HeaderModifier.super.access(self)
  ngx.req.set_header("custom-header", "value")
end

return HeaderModifier
```

This Lua script extends the base plugin class and modifies the 'custom-header' field for every incoming request. Such flexibility empowers organizations to tailor Kong Enterprise functionality across diverse use cases.

Kong Enterprise's comprehensive feature set—spanning security, performance, analytics, and robust administration—presents a compelling solution for enterprises looking to enhance their API management strategies. With its scalability, extensive plugin support, and integration capabilities, Kong Enterprise remains a pivotal tool for managing complex microservices environments effectively.

9.2   API Versioning and Gateway Management

API versioning is an essential practice in maintaining the stability and evolution of APIs as they undergo incremental or significant changes over time. With the global proliferation of APIs facilitating diverse app functionalities, controlled versioning ensures backward compatibility, maintaining consumer trust and seamless service continuation. In this section, we delve into the strategies of API versioning in conjunction with gateway management using Kong, a versatile API management platform.

API versioning involves creating new and distinctive interfaces or endpoints to evolve functionalities while preserving existing ones. Essentially, versioning acts as a contract, allowing APIs to transition without disrupting consumers. Effective versioning strategies include URL path versioning, query parameter versioning, content negotiation, and header-based versioning. Selecting the appropriate strategy often relies on the specific context of the API and organizational requirements.

One prevalent technique is URL path versioning, where the version identifier is embedded in the URL path. This method is remarkably intuitive, providing clear separation between different API versions. An example URL might resemble 'https://api.example.com/v1/resource'. Integrating URL path versioning into Kong involves creating multiple routes, each corresponding to a different API version. Consider the following example:

```
{
  "name": "my-api-v1",
  "protocols": ["http", "https"],
  "paths": ["/v1"],
  "service": {
    "id": "service-id-v1"
  }
}
{
  "name": "my-api-v2",
  "protocols": ["http", "https"],
  "paths": ["/v2"],
  "service": {
    "id": "service-id-v2"
  }
}
```

Here, separate services for versions 'v1' and 'v2' are defined, allowing requests to be routed appropriately based on the version specified in the URL.

Another common approach is query parameter versioning, where the version is defined as a query parameter, such as '?version=1'. This technique is less intrusive to the URL structure but must be clearly documented for API consumers. Proper validation should be implemented to ensure requests without valid version parameters are gracefully handled.

Content negotiation, another viable method, involves using the 'Accept' HTTP header for version determination. This approach allows clients to specify desired response formats alongside the version, albeit requiring explicit application in headers. For instance, using 'Accept: application/vnd.myapi.v1+json' enables API consumers to request version-specific resources. Although flexible, content negotiation requires comprehensive handler support to interpret headers correctly.

Header-based versioning involves using custom headers to indicate the API version, enhancing separation between versioning logic and URL structure. Custom headers such as 'X-API-Version' might be employed, requiring explicit processing on the server to route requests accordingly.

Effective API gateway management in Kong facilitates seamless transitions during API versioning, ensuring that consumers receive the correct service based on their request attributes. The key lies in defining routing rules, implementing migration strategies, and offering version deprecation notifications.

Kong's routing mechanism is pivotal in unifying these versioning approaches. By leveraging Kong's rule-based routing, administrators can facilitate sophisticated request handling. For instance, advanced routes can match payload-specific attributes or headers, directing requests to appropriate service instances based on versions or other differentiators.

Canary releases, a deployment strategy involving progressive rollouts of new API versions, play a crucial role in minimizing disruptions. In a canary release, only a small subset of users is initially exposed to the new API version, providing valuable feedback before full-scale deployment. An element of randomness or systematic criteria (e.g., user type or geographic region) helps determine the canary group.

Kong supports canary releases through plugin configurations, where traffic is intelligently split across different version instances. Consider the following Lua plugin implementation:

```
local BasePlugin = require "kong.plugins.base_plugin"
local random = math.random

local CanaryRelease = BasePlugin:extend()

function CanaryRelease:new()
  CanaryRelease.super.new(self, "canary-release")
end

function CanaryRelease:access(conf)
  CanaryRelease.super.access(self)

  -- Randomly route 10% of traffic to v2
  if random() <= 0.1 then
    kong.service.request.set_header("target-version", "v2")
  else
    kong.service.request.set_header("target-version", "v1")
  end
end

return CanaryRelease
```

This code illustrates a basic canary release strategy, where 10% of the traffic is redirected to the new version, 'v2'. The plugin adjusts the 'target-version' header, subsequently influencing request routing within Kong's service layer.

API version deprecation is an integral element of a healthy versioning policy. Clearly communicated deprecation plans ensure users transition smoothly to newer versions, allowing adequate time to adapt to upcoming changes. The announcement of deprecated versions can occur through multiple channels: headers ('Deprecation' or 'Sunset' headers), public dashboards, or proactive communication through newsletters and other outreach methods.

Additionally, API lifecycle management involves monitoring usage patterns to understand version adoption rates, guiding informed decisions regarding version sunsets. For instance, the following headers can be configured in a Kong plugin to inform consumers about deprecations:

```
local BasePlugin = require "kong.plugins.base_plugin"
```

```
local DeprecationNotice = BasePlugin:extend()

function DeprecationNotice:access(conf)
  DeprecationNotice.super.access(self)

  kong.response.set_header("Deprecation", "Tue, 14 Sep 2027 12:00:00 GMT")
  kong.response.set_header("Link", "<https://api.example.com/docs/v2>; rel=\"
      predecessor\"")
end

return DeprecationNotice
```

This Lua plugin sets headers indicating support discontinuance, providing a timeline for users to migrate to version 'v2'. The inclusion of a 'Link' header educates consumers on the next available API version, thus facilitating smoother transitions.

Kong's dashboard and analytics capabilities significantly assist in API version management by providing insights into version-specific traffic patterns, failure rates, and latency measurements. Administrators can fine-tune deprecation strategies, innovatively leveraging such data to bolster consumer satisfaction and system performance.

Finally, Kong's seamless integration with CI/CD pipelines enhances API version management. By embedding version testing into the CI/CD workflow, organizations can automate the deployment of new versions, alongside conducting rigorous regression testing to ensure backward compatibility. Automated API testing employing tools such as Postman or custom scripts fosters a robust DevOps culture, ensuring that releases maintain rigorous quality benchmarks.

Effective API versioning and gateway management in Kong necessitates a sophisticated interplay between routing practices, strategic version deployments, user communication, and automated infrastructural support. The judicious application of Kong's versatile features ensures that API version management remains fluid, scalable, and consumer-oriented, residing at the heart of modern API ecosystems.

9.3 Kong as a Service Mesh

Kong's foray into service mesh architecture marks a significant advancement in managing microservices, facilitating service-to-service

communications that are secure, reliable, and efficient. Unlike traditional API gateways that focus predominantly on external API management, a service mesh addresses the intricate issues of internal microservice connectivity, including service discovery, load balancing, failure
recovery, metrics, and monitoring. As enterprises increasingly adopt
microservice architectures, the need for effective service mesh solutions becomes paramount.

Kong Mesh, built upon open-source Kuma and powered by Envoy, is
designed to facilitate seamless microservice communication. It supports multi-cloud, hybrid, and multi-cluster environments, offering
a flexible and scalable service mesh solution. Kong Mesh's ability to
provide zero-trust security, traffic management, and observability enhances operational functionalities far beyond traditional API gateways.

At its core, Kong as a service mesh operates through a series of interconnected data planes managed by a central control plane. The control
plane governs the configurations and policies across the mesh, while
the data plane proxies handle the actual service-to-service traffic. This
separation ensures a clean abstraction between policy control and data
flow.

Service Discovery and Load Balancing

Kong's integration of service discovery and dynamic load balancing lies
at the heart of its service mesh capabilities. Service discovery entails
maintaining an updated catalog of services, facilitating seamless routing of requests to the appropriate service instances. This is particularly
crucial in dynamic environments where services frequently scale up or
down.

Envoy, empowered with robust service discovery capabilities,
facilitates automatic detection and updating of available service
instances. Utilizing backends such as Consul or Kubernetes, Kong
Mesh can autonomously propagate changes in the service topology,
ensuring sustained connectivity and traffic distribution. An example
of a Kubernetes-based service discovery configuration in Kong is
depicted below:

```
{
  "kind": "Mesh",
  "metadata": {
    "name": "default"
  },
```

```
"spec": {
  "networking": {
    "serviceDiscovery": {
      "backends": [
        {
          "name": "k8s",
          "type": "Kubernetes",
          "namespace": "default"
        }
      ]
    }
  }
}
```

This configuration instructs Kong to utilize Kubernetes for service discovery within the default namespace, dynamically adjusting traffic routing in response to service scaling events.

Load balancing within Kong Mesh leverages the Envoy data plane, supporting advanced policies such as round-robin, least requests, and ring-hash, among others. The choice of load balancing policy directly influences the efficiency and response latency of the mesh, thus necessitating careful consideration during configuration.

Security and Zero Trust

A vital element of using Kong as a service mesh is its ability to enforce zero-trust security principles. Zero trust assumes that threats could come from both outside and within the network and requires strict verification for every service request. Kong Mesh employs mTLS (mutual Transport Layer Security) to encrypt service-to-service communications and verify identities based on shared certificates.

Configuring mTLS in Kong Mesh involves certifying services, implementing automated certificate renewal, and enforcing role- or tag-based access controls. Below is a YAML configuration to enable mutual TLS in a service mesh:

```
type: MeshTrafficPermission
name: allow-traffic
mesh: default
sources:
  - match:
      kuma.io/service: '*'
destinations:
  - match:
      kuma.io/service: '*'
mtls:
  enabled: true
```

This configuration ensures that all service communications within the mesh are encrypted and authenticated using mTLS, thus safeguarding data integrity and confidentiality.

Kong Mesh's role-based access control (RBAC) implementations allow organizations to specify which services or users have access to particular resources, adhering to the principle of least privilege and minimizing potential lateral movement within the environment.

Traffic Management and Resiliency

Traffic management within a service mesh involves directing, routing, and managing traffic flows according to specified policies and rules. Kong Mesh offers comprehensive traffic management capabilities, including traffic routing, retries, circuit breaking, rate limiting, and fault injection.

Traffic Routing: Kong Mesh's intelligent routing capabilities cater to both simple and complex service mesh topologies. Route rules can be configured based on request attributes such as headers, URL paths, or even payload content. This dynamic routing enables canary deployments, facilitating continuous delivery and reducing risks of system-wide disruptions.

Circuit Breaking: By setting thresholds for timeouts and errors, Kong Mesh empowers services to gracefully degrade under high-load situations, preventing failures from cascading across the network. Circuit breaking configurations can define conditions such as maximum consecutive failures to trigger service halts, effectively curtailing recovery time and maintaining overall system stability.

Retries and Timeouts: Configuring retries ensures failed requests are attempted again, while respected timeouts prevent resources from being unnecessarily held. The amalgamation of these functionalities fosters enhanced user experiences, positively impacting service reliability.

Fault Injection: As a proactive measure, fault injection allows simulated failures to test service resiliency, pinpointing potential weaknesses. These artificial failures prepare services to handle real-world disruptions, supporting robust development methodologies like chaos engineering.

Below is an example configuration for setting up a retry policy in Kong Mesh:

```
{
  "type": "TrafficRoute",
  "name": "retry-policy",
  "spec": {
    "destination": {
      "host": "service-b",
      "port": 8080
    },
    "retries": {
      "attempts": 3,
      "perTryTimeout": "5s"
    }
  }
}
```

This configuration sets a policy to retry requests to service-b up to three times, with a per-try timeout of 5 seconds, ensuring resilience against transient failures.

Observability and Metrics

Observability is an integral feature of service mesh, providing visibility over the microservice interactions within the network. Kong Mesh leverages Envoy's telemetry capabilities to collect and emit granular traffic data. This information is invaluable for monitoring service performance, usage patterns, failure rates, and latency, enhancing decision-making.

Kong integrates seamlessly with monitoring and observability tools such as Prometheus and Grafana, enabling visualization of metrics and insights for actionable intelligence. Administrators can set up alerts and dashboards to monitor applications effectively, quickly identifying performance bottlenecks or abnormal behaviors.

Service mesh observability encompasses key performance indicators (KPIs), distributed tracing, and logging. Distributed tracing, supported by tools like Jaeger or Zipkin, allows end-to-end tracking of requests across services, exposing the service call sequence and highlighting latency hotspots or failure points.

The configuration enabling Prometheus integration with Kong Mesh is illustrated below:

```
{
  "type": "Backend",
```

```
"spec": {
  "metrics": {
    "prometheus": {
      "port": 15090,
      "interval": "30s"
    }
  }
}
}
```

With Prometheus collecting metrics every 30 seconds, organizations leverage precise data to calibrate service performance and architecture commitments, shaping intelligent operational performance strategies.

Utilizing Kong as a service mesh equips enterprises to orchestrate and manage microservices efficiently. From service discovery, load balancing, security enforcement, and traffic management, to comprehensive observability, Kong Mesh presents a holistic solution for modern distributed architectures. By embracing Kong's mesh capabilities, organizations can foster a robust, secure, and resilient microservice ecosystem, poised to meet the dynamic challenges of today's digital landscape.

9.4   Rate Limiting and Quotas

Rate limiting and quota management are fundamental components in API gateway configuration, crucial for both protecting infrastructure and ensuring a fair and optimal allocation of resources. Especially in high-traffic environments, these mechanisms help mitigate risks such as service degradation, denial-of-service (DoS) attacks, and overuse by particular clients. Kong provides a comprehensive suite of strategies for implementing rate limits and quotas, enhancing the security and reliability of API communications within an enterprise framework.

Rate limiting controls the number of requests a client can make to an API within a specified period, thereby safeguarding the backend system's performance integrity. By controlling traffic flow, rate limiting is conducive to maintaining service quality, offering equitable access among clients, and deterring malicious usage patterns.

Kong's rate limiting plugin supports multiple configurations: local (per node), cluster (synchronized across Kong nodes), and Redis-based counters, which store state independently of the gateway nodes. The selected strategy depends on specific requirements regarding consistency, eventual availability, and performance. Below is an example of using Kong Rate Limiting with a local policy:

```
{
  "name": "rate-limiting",
  "config": {
    "minute": 100,
    "hour": 1000,
    "policy": "local"
  }
}
```

This configuration restricts clients to 100 requests per minute and 1000 requests per hour, per Kong node, utilizing a local counter mechanism.

Implementing rate limiting requires choices regarding key identification, which stipulates how individual clients are recognized. Kong supports several consumer-identified key schemes, such as IP address, API key, or custom headers, all of which facilitate tailored rate-limiting applications. Consider an IP address-based approach:

```
{
  "name": "rate-limiting",
  "config": {
    "minute": 50,
    "identifier": "ip"
  }
}
```

Using the IP address as an identifier, client requests are metered based on their originating IP, ensuring isolation between varying consumer hallmarks.

Beyond direct request control through rate limiting, quotas serve as overarching constraints on resource consumption over extended periods (such as daily or monthly usage or computational costs). While rate limiting concerns instantaneous traffic shaping, quota management strategizes long-term resource use, aiding in contractual compliance or cost controls.

A typical quota management scenario involves allowing users access to a predetermined number of requests over a billing cycle, particularly important in tier-based access models and subscription plans. For example, Kong can enforce quotas via plugin configurations integrated with an external storage like Redis:

```
{
  "name": "rate-limiting",
  "config": {
    "day": 1000,
    "month": 30000,
    "policy": "redis",
    "redis_host": "127.0.0.1",
    "redis_port": 6379
  }
}
```

This setup restricts a user to 1000 requests per day and 30,000 requests per month, stored and synchronized using a Redis data store.

In environments where distributed consistency and synchronization across nodes are critical, Kong's cluster policy should be employed. This policy leverages Kong's cluster-wide shared cache, ensuring that all rate limit counters are uniformly updated across all Kong instances. This consistency model is suitable for cloud-native solutions where Kong nodes scale dynamically.

Advanced Features and Customization

Kong's rate limiting and quota features can be extended with custom logic through plugins, adapting to niche business constraints or technical necessities. Consider a scenario where over-limit behaviors involve specific countermeasures like API response slowdowns or client notifications instead of outright request blocking.

Kong supports the development of custom plugins using languages such as Lua, JavaScript, or Go. These plugins can integrate external logics, like sending alerts or adapting rate thresholds based on historical trends or user analytics. Below is a Lua plugin noting request count exceedance:

```
local BasePlugin = require "kong.plugins.base_plugin"
local RateExceedPlugin = BasePlugin:extend()

function RateExceedPlugin:new()
  RateExceedPlugin.super.new(self, "rate-exceed-notifier")
end

function RateExceedPlugin:access(conf)
  RateExceedPlugin.super.access(self)

  local rate_limit_exceeded = false -- Imaginary condition check
```

```
  if rate_limit_exceeded then
    kong.log.crit("Rate limit exceeded for consumer, sending alert")
    -- Code for sending alerts (e.g., email, SMS)
  end
end

return RateExceedPlugin
```

Such a plugin emphasizes intricate monitoring over simple rate limitations, enabling infrastructural awareness and preemptive measures within high-stakes deployments.

Kong's diverse integration ecosystem allows for synergetic coupling with enterprise performance and monitoring tools, enhancing the ways rate limits and quotas are applied. Collaborations with data visualization platforms like Grafana enable real-time insights into traffic trends and patterns, offering administrators foresight into allocation needs and potential bottlenecks.

Design Considerations and Best Practices

Imbuing rate limiting with efficacy necessitates careful design and consideration. Thoughtful integration foregrounds both consumer fairness and systemic feasibility, avoiding penalizing beneficial high-throughput usages while remaining vigilant against misuse. Best practices include:

- Granular Rate Limiting: Stipulating different rate limits based on user tiers or specific APIs (e.g., distinguishing core functionalities and auxiliary services) can cater to varying operational priorities and customer value propositions.

- Strategic Quotas: Crafting quotas in sync with business models (e.g., accommodating upgrades or renewals) buttresses sustaining revenue streams while empowering client development.

- Policy Transparency: Openly communicating enforced limits and quotas in API documentation enhances mutual understanding and consumer trust, incentivizing adherence and participation.

- Dynamic Scaling: Implementing soft-rate limits via elastic modifications, allowing temporary exceedances that require controlled resolutions depending on contextual factors (e.g., notifying stakeholders or renegotiating terms), cultivates resilient infrastructures.

- Incident Logging and Recovery: Systematically capturing instances of rate/limit exceedance aids in retrospective analyses, bolstering client dialogue, and iterating rate-setting strategies aligned with evolving use cases or threats.

By enforcing mindful configurations and implementing reflective practices, Kong's rate limiting and quota management significantly enhance API management operations, maintaining an orchestrated equilibrium between service protection, optimization, and compliance.

Rate limiting and quotas, underpinned by Kong's robust plugin architecture, enable automated, efficient API request management, adeptly defending against excessive use while orchestrating equitable resource distribution. As digital networks evolve, incorporating advanced configurations and analytics allows for enhanced customization suited to dynamic enterprise environments, ensuring sustained performance excellence and fostering scalable API ecosystems.

9.5   Using Kong with GraphQL and gRPC

With the rise of microservices architectures and the need for efficient data retrieval and service communication, modern protocols like GraphQL and gRPC have gained significant traction. Kong, as a versatile API gateway, provides comprehensive support for these protocols, facilitating efficient API management and inter-service communications.

GraphQL and gRPC address limitations inherent in traditional RESTful APIs. While REST is efficient for many scenarios, its rigid nature can lead to over-fetching or under-fetching of data, and complex endpoint management. In contrast, GraphQL provides a flexible query language for APIs, enabling clients to request exactly what they need, thereby optimizing data transfer. On the other hand, gRPC is a high-performance remote procedure call (RPC) framework that utilizes HTTP/2 for transport, protocol buffers for serialization, and supports language-agnostic client-server communication.

GraphQL and Kong

GraphQL, developed by Facebook, allows the client to specify the structure of the response data, thereby reducing the amount of over-fetched data typical of REST API calls. Kong supports GraphQL by providing routes and plugins that facilitate the efficient handling of GraphQL queries and mutations. When integrating GraphQL with Kong, one typically creates a single endpoint to handle queries, reducing endpoint sprawl and fostering backend simplicity.

```
{
  "name": "graphql-service",
  "url": "http://backend.graphql.server/graphql",
  "routes": [
    {
      "paths": ["/graphql"],
      "methods": ["POST"],
      "protocols": ["http", "https"]
    }
  ]
}
```

This configuration directs POST requests sent to '/graphql' on the Kong gateway to the GraphQL server at the specified backend URL.

One of the crucial aspects of managing GraphQL with Kong is its plugin capabilities, which extend the GraphQL server's capabilities in areas such as authentication, rate limiting, and error logging. For instance, one might implement an authentication plugin to check JSON Web Tokens (JWTs) before executing a GraphQL query:

```
{
  "name": "jwt",
  "config": {
    "secret_is_base64": false,
    "key_claim_name": "aud",
    "claims_to_verify": ["exp"],
    "uri_param_names": ["jwt"],
    "maximum_expiration": 3600
  }
}
```

This configuration mandates JWT-based authentication for the GraphQL service, ensuring secure access aligned with backend identity protocols.

Implementing GraphQL with Kong enhances performance by leveraging Kong's built-in caching functionality. By caching GraphQL query

responses, Kong can significantly reduce latency, enhance responsiveness, and conserve backend computational resources. Consider
a scenario where identical complex queries are cached using Kong's
response-transformer or cache plugins.

Efficient caching strategies in GraphQL often involve balancing cache
invalidations and refreshes, ensuring relevancy and data integrity.
Cache management requires careful policy configuration to embody
consistency while optimizing response times.

gRPC and Kong

gRPC, developed by Google, adopts a client-server model where the
client can directly invoke methods on a server application on a different machine as if it were a local object. gRPC's use of HTTP/2 and
protocol buffers makes it particularly suitable for microservices that
require high-throughput, low-latency communication. Kong Gateway
fully supports gRPC and can route gRPC traffic just as effectively as
HTTP traffic.

To work with gRPC in Kong, one must configure services and routes
uniquely suited for gRPC communication. Below is an example configuration for a gRPC service:

```
{
  "name": "grpc-service",
  "url": "grpc://backend.grpc.server:50051",
  "routes": [
    {
      "paths": ["/grpc"],
      "protocols": ["grpc", "grpcs"]
    }
  ]
}
```

Here, Kong intercepts incoming gRPC requests on its '/grpc' path and
forwards them to the specified backend gRPC server using the gRPC
protocol.

gRPC's HTTP/2 protocol offers several advantages: multiplexed
streams, header compression, and bi-directional communication.
These features allow gRPC services to perform efficiently under high
network loads and complex transactional systems. Kong extends
these capabilities by supporting mTLS, authenticating both client
and server connections in gRPC traffic, critical for zero-trust security

models.

```
services:
  - name: grpc-secure-service
    host: backend.grpc.server
    port: 50051
    tls:
      enabled: true
      clientCert: /etc/certs/client-cert.pem
      clientKey: /etc/certs/client-key.pem
```

This configuration mandates the use of mutual TLS, ensuring that both the client and server cryptographic credentials are verified, fortifying security during gRPC communication.

Kong's plugin framework further extends functionality in gRPC communications. Plugins for gRPC traffic can support rate limiting, logging, and traffic control, enhancing operational oversight and system manageability. In conjunction with observability tools such as Prometheus or other APM solutions, Kong facilitates comprehensive gRPC performance monitoring, where key metrics can guide optimizations.

Challenges and Considerations

While Kong efficiently manages these protocols' unique characteristics, developers face challenges such as ensuring adequate support for schema evolution in GraphQL and managing interface definitions in gRPC.

GraphQL API evolution demands stringent schema versioning strategies, ensuring backward compatibility and preserving client contracts. For instance, using deprecation directives in GraphQL can aid in managing schema transitions, ensuring clients remain informed of impending changes without service interruptions.

In gRPC, updating services necessitates maintaining compatibility across protocol buffer versions. Effective use of protobuf encompasses migration strategies where field deprecations or extensions are transparently communicated across versions, balancing innovative evolution while retaining legacy compatibility.

Moreover, integrating these technologies with Kong's lifecycle further requires considering interoperability and performance tuning specifics, frequently aligning with broader organizational API governance practices.

By leveraging Kong's robustness and adaptability, organizations can seamlessly integrate and manage GraphQL and gRPC services, addressing modern communication demands. By abstracting complexity associated with protocol management, Kong enables developers to focus on core application logic while benefiting from enhanced security, performance, and control. As microservice architectures expand and diversify, utilizing Kong's capabilities to orchestrate GraphQL and gRPC infrastructures becomes pivotal, promoting flexibility, scaling, and innovation in today's digital enterprise landscapes.

9.6   Real-time Analytics with Kong

In today's fast-paced digital landscape, capturing, visualizing, and acting upon API data in real-time is a critical capability for organizations aiming to optimize their operations and enhance decision-making. Kong equips enterprises with robust features for real-time analytics, enabling comprehensive insights into API traffic, performance metrics, and user behaviors. This section explores how Kong's analytics capabilities can be harnessed to drive business intelligence and operational efficiency through advanced monitoring and data analysis techniques.

Kong's analytics framework is constructed around a plugin-based model, seamlessly integrating with external systems to gather and process API data. Key metrics such as request counts, response times, error rates, and user engagement are captured and can be visualized to inform strategic decisions and operational adjustments.

Capturing API Analytics Data

Kong captures real-time API analytics data through its logging and monitoring plugins, which can be configured to export data to a variety of external analytics platforms. For comprehensive analytics setups, Kong commonly integrates with systems like Prometheus, Grafana, Elasticsearch, and custom-built dashboards.

The loggly and statsd plugins represent popular solutions for gathering metric and event data from Kong. The loggly plugin directs log events to Loggly's cloud-based logging and analytics platform. Below is an example configuration for the loggly plugin:

```
{
  "name": "loggly",
  "config": {
    "key": "your-loggly-key",
    "host": "logs-01.loggly.com",
    "port": 514
  }
}
```

This configuration enables Kong to stream API request logs to Loggly, where they can be further analyzed and visualized via Loggly's platform tools.

In contrast, the statsd plugin forwards metrics to StatsD, a lightweight daemon intended to aggregate and summarize application statistics. Configuring StatsD with Kong allows metrics like request counts, latency averages, and system throughput to be accessible, as demonstrated below:

```
{
  "name": "statsd",
  "config": {
    "host": "127.0.0.1",
    "port": 8125,
    "metrics": [
      {
        "name": "request_count",
        "stat_type": "counter"
      },
      {
        "name": "latency",
        "stat_type": "gauge"
      }
    ]
  }
}
```

This setup enables application performance data to be monitored and reviewed through tools that support StatsD protocols, enhancing understanding of application efficiency and user patterns.

Visualization and Monitoring

Real-time data is invaluable without suitable visualization tools that transform raw data into actionable intelligence quickly and efficiently. Grafana is a prominent tool that, when integrated with data sources like Prometheus, allows data to be visualized through intuitive dashboards.

```
global:
  scrape_interval: 15s
scrape_configs:
 - job_name: 'kong'
   static_configs:
    - targets: ['kong-server-host:8001']
```

The above Prometheus configuration connects to Kong's endpoint, continuously scraping metrics. Grafana then links to Prometheus data, delivering customizable visual dashboards, able to present real-time traffic patterns, alert statuses, and error trends.

Leveraging Grafana's powerful dashboard capabilities, Kong API performance metrics can be visualized in dynamic ways that enable rapid identification of anomalies and bottlenecks. Visualization tools permit setting thresholds, generating alerts, and conducting sophisticated temporal analyses, enhancing diagnostic speed and depth.

Moreover, custom dashboards furnishing real-time KPI displays for strategic metrics can be pivotal for operational and business users, translating technical data into comprehensible intelligence applicable for decision-making.

Advanced Monitoring Practices

Monitoring practices in Kong transcend basic data visualization, offering integration with comprehensive Application Performance Monitoring (APM) solutions, such as Datadog or New Relic, to further extend monitoring functionality.

Advanced monitoring emphasizes the use of synthetic transaction monitoring, tracing, and end-to-end request visibility across distributed systems. Datadog's APM, for instance, includes features such as:

- Application health scoring based on factors like error rates, request latencies.

- Trace collection for distributed request paths, identifying sluggish components.

- Real-time mapping of service dependencies visualized across the architecture.

The integration with Datadog requires plugin configurations such as

256

the following:

```
{
  "name": "datadog",
  "config": {
    "host": "127.0.0.1",
    "port": 8125,
    "prefix": "kong",
    "metrics": [
      {
        "name": "request_count",
        "stat_type": "counter",
        "sample_rate": 1
      },
      {
        "name": "request_latency",
        "stat_type": "timer"
      }
    ]
  }
}
```

By integrating these comprehensive tools, Kong enables detailed tracing of end-user transactions and internal service hops, enhancing capabilities for identifying system inefficiencies, errors, or latency issues in a distributed service environment.

Alerting and Actionability

For analytics to effectively inform operations and decision-making, data must be actionable. Kong's platform integrates with alerting tools that issue real-time notifications based on defined triggers, thresholds, or anomalies, such as Slack for immediate team communication, PagerDuty for incident response, or directly through SMS and email alerts.

Alerts can emanate from metrics such as elevated response times, error spike detection, or rate limit breaches, facilitating timely intervention to resolve potential disruptions. Configurations for issuing alerts are often specified within visualization and monitoring tools, defining what events should trigger alerts and what actions should occur consequently.

Setting up alerting rules within a Grafana dashboard, for instance, can encompass expressions checked against time series data, triggering alerts when conditions surpass predefined boundaries. These proactive alerts streamline maintenance, enhance reliability, and assist in preventing service downtimes.

Data Security and Privacy

While Kong facilitates comprehensive analytics, ensuring secure and responsible data management practices is paramount. Adhering to data protection regulations such as GDPR necessitates careful handling of user data, anonymizing sensitive information where necessary, and implementing stringent access controls on analytics platforms.

Tools like Elasticsearch offer capabilities for data encryption and secure access protocols to restrict unauthorized data disclosures. Similarly, ensuring logs or streaming data are prudently handled safeguards both user privacy and organizational liabilities.

Kong represents a potent platform for real-time API analytics, empowering organizations to not only visualize access patterns, performance metrics, and operational bottlenecks, but also drive strategic decisions and optimize the digital ecosystem. With integrations to a realm of monitoring and visualization tools, Kong offers adaptability to evolving technical requirements, fostering insights and responsiveness that amplify business agility and performance continuity. As API-driven environments burgeon, leveraging the analytics capabilities of Kong becomes indispensable, turning data into a strategic asset for contemporary digital enterprises.

9.7 Case Studies and Proven Practices

The deployment of Kong in diverse real-world scenarios demonstrates the flexibility and robust capabilities of the API gateway platform, addressing complex challenges across varied industry landscapes. Through examining case studies, organizations can glean insights into best practices and strategic approaches to solving API, service mesh, and microservices-related problems. This section delves into these use cases and sheds light on methodologies that have driven successful implementations.

Case Study 1: E-commerce Platform Transformation

An international e-commerce company sought to streamline its API infrastructure to enhance performance and scalability as its global customer base expanded. Facing latency issues during peak shopping periods, the company aimed to optimize its API gateway solution to manage fluctuating traffic levels and improve reliability.

Challenge: The main challenge was supporting high volumes of concurrent API requests from geographically dispersed users, ensuring seamless user experiences during promotional events and busy seasons.

Solution: The company implemented Kong as a centralized API gateway, replacing a fragmented system of multiple API endpoints with a cohesive solution. By taking advantage of Kong's dynamic load balancing abilities, the company could distribute incoming traffic optimally across available service instances.

The project employed the rate limiting plugin to mitigate excessive load during peak times, preventing infrastructure overstretch. Advanced caching strategies were integrated via the **proxy-cache** plugin, significantly reducing latency by serving cached responses for frequently accessed resources.

```
{
  "name": "proxy-cache",
  "config": {
    "strategy": "memory",
    "content_type": ["application/json"],
    "cache_ttl": 3600
  }
}
```

The above configuration ensures that API responses are cached in memory for an hour, reducing redundant processing and maintaining swift response times.

Result: Post-implementation, the e-commerce platform reported a 30% reduction in latency and improved service stability during high-traffic events. The adoption of Kong facilitated a modular infrastructure that supported effortless scaling, aligning with future business growth projections.

Proven Practice: Robust Caching Strategy

The usage of a granular caching strategy emerges as a best practice in managing response times and offloading backend processing. Implementing cache invalidation logic, particularly for data with high update frequency, ensures cached data remains valid and provides reliable service delivery.

Case Study 2: Banking Industry Compliance

A banking institution required an API gateway ensuring stringent security and compliance while providing seamless access to its services. The organization needed to integrate a service mesh ensuring secure inter-service communications and governed data interactions conforming to industry regulations such as PSD2 and GDPR.

Challenge: The bank's challenge was enabling secure, compliant data exchanges both externally and internally, without compromising on performance.

Solution: Deploying Kong Mesh, the institution adopted mutual TLS throughout service communications, ensuring data encryption and service authentication. Kong's role-based access configurations empowered fine-grained access control over API resources.

This solution featured a custom authentication plugin enforcing OAuth 2.0, monitoring access tokens, and validating scopes, ensuring compliance with data protection directives.

```
{
  "name": "oauth2",
  "config": {
    "provision_key": "secure_key",
    "enable_implicit_grant": true,
    "mandatory_scope": true
  }
}
```

To further safeguard personal data, the Kong logging plugin was customized to redact sensitive PII from logs, aligning with privacy mandates.

Result: Enhanced transparency and security compliance helped the bank optimize its API usage, reduce data exposure risks, and cut down on compliance-related operational costs by 20%.

Proven Practice: Adopting Zero-Trust Principles

Implementing zero-trust architecture principles, exemplified by universal mutual TLS and granular RBAC, is recognized as a vital practice in regulated environments. This establishes strong security postures while ensuring scalable and adaptable service communications.

Case Study 3: Health Tech Streamlining Data Exchanges

A health technology company focused on improving patient outcomes needed to streamline data exchanges between its applications, hospitals, and third-party services. The integration of new data feeds required a robust API management system to oversee service routing and ensure data integrity.

Challenge: Ensuring real-time data availability and low-latency access amidst complex service integrations posed a significant challenge.

Solution: The company utilized Kong to provide a resilient API gateway that could handle various service communication patterns. Leveraging gRPC support in Kong, the organization facilitated low-latency, high-throughput service interactions required for medical data exchanges.

Traffic routing capabilities were enhanced through custom plugins that intelligently prioritized data flows based on urgency and type, which ensured crucial medical information was processed immediately.

Advanced monitoring and analytics integration provided visibility over API interactions, supporting real-time diagnostics and proactive troubleshooting.

```
{
  "name": "datadog",
  "config": {
    "host": "localhost",
    "port": 8125,
    "metrics": [
      {
        "name": "request.latency",
        "stat_type": "gauge"
      },
      {
        "name": "data.exchange.success",
        "stat_type": "counter"
      }
    ]
  }
}
```

This setup facilitates tracking metrics like request latencies and successful data exchanges, which inform operational improvements.

Result: The realignment resulted in an increase in API performance and reliability, reducing data access time by 40%. The proactive analyt-

261

ics approach drove operational intelligence, optimizing data through-put and minimizing downtime.

Proven Practice: Leveraging Protocol Flexibility

Capitalizing on protocol flexibility, such as utilizing gRPC for efficiency, and employing customized traffic routing distinctively align service communication methods, enhancing ecosystem resilience and supporting composite data architectures.

Case Study 4: Retail Chain Digital Integration

A large retail chain sought to unify its digital interfaces spanning mobile, web, and store systems under a single, cohesive API infrastructure. The objective was to synchronize data across various platforms, ensuring consistent and instantaneous access to inventory and customer profiles.

Challenge: The retailer faced synchronization concerns, ensuring data consistency between physical and digital platforms, often challenged by legacy systems.

Solution: Kong was deployed as a central integrative layer, augmented with a GraphQL service that provided unified data access endpoints across channels. By querying specific data fields, applications could minimize redundant data transfers and align customer interactions across touchpoints.

The GraphQL transformers enhanced flexibility by performing on-the-fly data transformations, empowering frontend service customizations tailored to individual user experiences.

The company also integrated a public developer portal using Kong's developer portal capabilities, fostering innovation through third-party partnerships while simplifying service consumption.

Result: Deployment achieved a sophisticated connected retail environment, fostering enhanced customer satisfaction and boosting digital sales conversion rates by 25%.

Proven Practice: Unified Access Interfaces

The use of unified data access interfaces through GraphQL exemplifies a best practice in achieving streamlined data synchronization. The coordination of legacy systems with modern API frameworks provides strategic insights into building adaptable retail environments.

Conclusion: Strategic Approaches

Kong's application across varied industrial cases highlights both fundamental and specialized practices that solidify its eminence in API management. Elevating existing infrastructures with Kong involves adopting flexible, security-oriented designs that adapt to evolving technological and regulatory contexts while maintaining operational continuity and business competitiveness. Adopting the demonstrated best practices furthers stakeholders' capability to exploit Kong's extensibility, directing attention towards transforming complex digital ecosystems into agile, secure, and cohesive architectures that serve diverse strategic objectives.

Chapter 10

Best Practices and Troubleshooting

This chapter outlines essential best practices for deploying and maintaining Kong API Gateway, ensuring optimal performance and security. It covers strategies for effective configuration management, security enhancements, and scalability optimizations. Additionally, the chapter addresses common issues and provides practical solutions for troubleshooting, backed by debugging techniques and tools. It also highlights useful community and support resources, empowering users to navigate challenges efficiently. By adopting these practices, users can achieve a robust, reliable, and well-managed Kong deployment.

10.1   Leveraging Best Practices

In API management, ensuring that resources are used efficiently and that APIs can be managed with maximum effectiveness is a cornerstone of successful deployments. Leveraging industry best practices when deploying Kong API Gateway allows for configurations that optimize both performance and maintainability. This section delves deeply into a structured approach to implementing these best practices, focusing on configuration methodologies, performance tuning, and efficient deployment strategies.

Kong offers a robust platform to manage and scale APIs, but the flexibility inherent in its design also implies that there are multiple approaches to configuring your infrastructure. To achieve a successful deployment, it is essential to incorporate established best practices from the start, minimizing later adjustments and optimizations.

Several key areas deserve focused attention: configuration management, performance tuning, capacity planning, and ongoing maintenance. Each area plays a crucial role in optimizing both the initial deployment and the operational longevity of the system.

Configuration Management

When it comes to configuration management in Kong, it is essential to maintain clarity and simplicity. Overcomplicated configurations can lead to an increase in maintenance burden and make troubleshooting more difficult. Utilizing a structured approach to configuration can mitigate these issues, enhancing traceability and control.

Here, version control systems like Git can provide an excellent foundation by allowing developers to track configuration changes over time. Consistency and repeatability are vital, and adopting Infrastructure as Code (IaC) principles can streamline configuration processes remarkably well. Tools such as Terraform, Ansible, or Puppet can be employed to handle large-scale deployments with precision.

To illustrate a basic approach using Terraform for managing Kong configurations, consider the following example:

```
provider "kong" {
  kong_admin_uri = "http://localhost:8001"
}

resource "kong_service" "example_service" {
  name = "my_example_service"
  url = "http://example.org"
}

resource "kong_route" "example_route" {
  service_id = kong_service.example_service.id
  methods = ["GET", "POST"]
  paths = ["/example"]
}
```

This configuration exemplifies the use of Terraform to deploy a Kong service and route, offering an evident separation of concerns and allowing for incremental updates within the infrastructure.

Performance Tuning

Performance tuning is a continuous process that involves regular assessment and adjustments based on the demands on the system. For Kong, there are several factors to consider: latency, throughput, and the efficient use of resources. Tuning these parameters ensures that the system can handle high volumes of traffic whilst maintaining low latency.

Kong's architecture allows for horizontal scaling, but performance can often be improved by optimizing existing resources before scaling out. Here are some of the best practices in performance tuning for a Kong deployment:

- **Buffer Sizes**: Adjust NGINX buffer sizes for request and response to ensure optimal data flow without overloads.

- **Connection Persistence**: Utilize keep-alive configurations to maintain persistent connections between proxies and backend services.

- **Concurrency Configuration**: Set appropriate worker processes and worker connections to handle the expected concurrency.

Moreover, optimize plugin configurations. Many plugins add processing overhead, so it is crucial to assess their performance impact. Consider the following NGINX configuration snippet as an example for adjusting critical parameters:

```
worker_processes auto;
events {
    worker_connections 1024;
    multi_accept on;
}

http {
    client_max_body_size 16m;
    keepalive_timeout 65;

    server {
```

```
    listen 80;
    server_name kong;

    location / {
        proxy_pass http://example_backend;
        proxy_set_header Host $host;
        proxy_set_header X-Real-IP $remote_addr;
    }
  }
}
```

This configuration ensures that NGINX is optimized for both connection handling and resource allocation, which effectively translates to improved performance of the Kong Gateway.

Capacity Planning

Capacity planning involves predicting future resource needs to ensure that your system meets performance objectives under anticipated demand. This process is crucial in avoiding bottleneck scenarios and maintaining service levels.

To conduct effective capacity planning, it is imperative to consider current usage patterns and projected growth. Tools like Apache JMeter can simulate various loads, providing insights into system behavior under different conditions. By analyzing these results, you can determine if existing resources are sufficient or if additional scaling is needed.

Consider the following sample JMeter test plan configuration, which can be used to simulate HTTP requests to a Kong proxy:

```
<jmeterTestPlan version="1.2" properties="5.0" jmeter="5.3">
  <hashTree>
    <TestPlan guiclass="TestPlanGui" testclass="TestPlan" testname="Test Plan">
      <stringProp name="TestPlan.comments"/>
      <boolProp name="TestPlan.functional_mode">false</boolProp>
      <boolProp name="TestPlan.tearDown_on_shutdown">true</boolProp>
      <boolProp name="TestPlan.serialize_threadgroups">false</boolProp>
      <elementProp name="TestPlan.user_defined_variables" elementType="
          Arguments">
        <collectionProp name="Arguments.arguments"/>
      </elementProp>
      <stringProp name="TestPlan.user_define_classpath"/>
    </TestPlan>
    <hashTree>
      <ThreadGroup guiclass="ThreadGroupGui" testclass="ThreadGroup" testname
          ="Thread Group">
        <stringProp name="ThreadGroup.on_sample_error">continue</stringProp>
        <elementProp name="ThreadGroup.main_controller" elementType="
            LoopController">
          <boolProp name="LoopController.continue_forever">false</boolProp>
          <stringProp name="LoopController.loops">10</stringProp>
```

```
    </elementProp>
    <stringProp name="ThreadGroup.num_threads">50</stringProp>
    <stringProp name="ThreadGroup.ramp_time">60</stringProp>
    <longProp name="ThreadGroup.start_time">1615577804000</longProp>
  <longProp name="ThreadGroup.end_time">1615577804000</longProp>
    <boolProp name="ThreadGroup.scheduler">false</boolProp>
    <stringProp name="ThreadGroup.duration"/>
    <stringProp name="ThreadGroup.delay"/>
  </ThreadGroup>
  <hashTree>
    <HTTPSamplerProxy guiclass="HttpTestSampleGui" testclass="
        HTTPSamplerProxy" testname="HTTP Request">
      <boolProp name="HTTPSampler.postBodyRaw">true</boolProp>
      <elementProp name="HTTPsampler.Arguments" elementType="Arguments
          ">
        <collectionProp name="Arguments.arguments">
          <elementProp name="" elementType="HTTPArgument">
            <boolProp name="HTTPArgument.always_encode">false</boolProp>
            <stringProp name="Argument.value"/>
            <stringProp name="Argument.metadata">=</stringProp>
            <boolProp name="HTTPArgument.use_equals">true</boolProp>
          </elementProp>
        </collectionProp>
      </elementProp>
      <stringProp name="HTTPSampler.domain">localhost</stringProp>
      <stringProp name="HTTPSampler.port">8000</stringProp>
      <stringProp name="HTTPSampler.protocol"/>
      <stringProp name="HTTPSampler.contentEncoding"/>
      <stringProp name="HTTPSampler.path">/my-service</stringProp>
      <stringProp name="HTTPSampler.method">GET</stringProp>
      <boolProp name="HTTPSampler.follow_redirects">true</boolProp>
      <boolProp name="HTTPSampler.auto_redirects">false</boolProp>
      <boolProp name="HTTPSampler.use_keepalive">true</boolProp>
      <boolProp name="HTTPSampler.DO_MULTIPART_POST">false</
          boolProp>
      <stringProp name="HTTPSampler.monitor">false</stringProp>
      <stringProp name="HTTPSampler.embedded_url_re"/>
    </HTTPSamplerProxy>
  </hashTree>
  </hashTree>
  </hashTree>
</jmeterTestPlan>
```

This XML snippet represents a test plan that can be used within JMeter to evaluate how your Kong setup copes with high volumes of traffic, thereby assisting effective capacity planning.

Ongoing Maintenance

Regular maintenance is critical in ensuring that the Kong instance remains stable and performs optimally in the long term. As part of ongoing maintenance, you should incorporate both automated monitoring and manual checks.

Automated monitoring might include utilizing tools like Prometheus to gather metrics that inform performance tuning and identify potential issues before they manifest as significant problems. A basic configuration for Prometheus to scrape Kong metrics might appear as follows:

```
scrape_configs:
  - job_name: 'kong'
    static_configs:
    - targets: ['localhost:8001']
```

This configuration allows Prometheus to collect metrics from Kong's Admin API, providing insights into performance trends and anomaly detection.

Furthermore, applying controlled updates and patches to Kong and its supporting infrastructure is crucial. Implement a rigorous testing process in a staging environment before migrating changes to production. Such due diligence ensures that updates do not inadvertently disrupt service availability or degrade performance.

Finally, adopt a feedback loop mechanism utilizing logs and dashboards to continuously refine configurations and practices based on real-world operational data. This approach not only enhances system robustness but also adaptive capability to evolving business requirements.

Employing these best practices in configuring, tuning, and maintaining Kong results in a strategically sound deployment architecture, designed not only to meet current business needs but also to adapt and scale with future demand.

10.2   Securing Your Kong Deployment

Protecting your Kong deployment against potential vulnerabilities and unauthorized access is a pivotal aspect of managing an API gateway effectively. Drawing upon comprehensive security principles, this section outlines the best practices for securing a Kong environment, ensuring shielded operations from common attacks, maintaining data integrity, and safeguarding access control policies.

The primary objectives in securing your Kong deployment are the following:

- Implement robust identity and access management (IAM).

- Secure data in transit and at rest.

- Ensure API request validation and threat protection.

- Regularly update, audit, and monitor security measures.

Each focal area forms part of a holistic security strategy designed to mitigate risks and fortify your API gateway against evolving threats within the cybersecurity landscape.

Identity and Access Management

The starting point of securing your Kong deployment is establishing strong identity and access management mechanisms. Implementing mechanisms for authentication and authorization ensures that only authenticated users and applications can access your APIs.

Use OAuth 2.0, API keys, or JWT tokens to ensure secure authentication mechanisms. Kong provides plugins that facilitate these mechanisms effectively:

- **OAuth 2.0**: Leveraging the OAuth 2.0 plugin in Kong allows control over access credentials, delegating user authentication to a trusted identity provider.

- **JWT (JSON Web Tokens)**: JWT plugin provides a stateless protocol to transmit claims securely between parties, ensuring the data is encrypted end-to-end.

- **API Keys**: A simple yet effective method to authenticate API consumers, API keys can be easily implemented and managed with Kong's built-in security features.

Below is a sample configuration using Kong's Declarative Config file to enforce API key authentication:

```
_format_version: "2.1"
services:
- name: example-service
```

```
url: http://mockbin.org
plugins:
- name: key-auth

consumers:
- username: consumer1
  keyauth_credentials:
  - key: my_api_key
```

This configuration file demonstrates enabling key authentication for a specific service, granting access to a consumer with a predefined API key.

Securing Data in Transit and at Rest

Ensuring data protection during transmission and storage is vital in maintaining confidentiality and integrity. Utilize Transport Layer Security (TLS) to encrypt data in transit over API communications, preventing exposure to man-in-the-middle attacks.

For securing data at rest, deploy encryption techniques to storage systems and databases supporting your Kong deployment. Encryption services should comply with high standards like AES (Advanced Encryption Standard) to enforce data confidentiality.

A typical NGINX configuration for enforcing HTTPS with Kong is as follows:

```
server {
    listen 443 ssl;
    server_name example.kong.com;

    ssl_certificate /etc/ssl/certs/your_certificate.pem;
    ssl_certificate_key /etc/ssl/private/your_private_key.pem;

    location / {
        proxy_pass http://localhost:8000;
        proxy_set_header Host $host;
        proxy_set_header X-Real-IP $remote_addr;
        proxy_set_header X-Forwarded-For $proxy_add_x_forwarded_for;
    }
}
```

This configuration ensures that connections to Kong API are intercepted over HTTPS, with certificates enforcing secure communications.

API Request Validation and Threat Protection

API request validation is an effective measure to protect your Kong API

Gateway from potentially harmful requests. Implement IP whitelisting, rate limiting, and parameter validation to ensure only legitimate requests are processed. Kong provides several plugins suited for this purpose:

- **Rate Limiting**: The rate-limiting plugin prevents abuse by limiting the number of requests an API consumer can make within a specified period.

- **IP Restriction**: Control access using the IP restriction plugin to permit or deny requests based on the client's IP address.

- **Request Size Limitation**: Limit the size of requests and payloads that can be processed by the gateway to mitigate DoS attacks.

The following snippet shows the configuration for enabling rate limiting in Kong:

```
_format_version: "2.1"

services:
- name: rate-limited-service
  url: http://mockbin.org
  plugins:
  - name: rate-limiting
    config:
      minute: 100
      policy: local
```

Here, the "rate-limiting" plugin is used to ensure that a maximum of 100 requests can be made by a single client every minute, using a 'local' policy for tracking.

Regular Updates, Audits, and Monitoring

Maintaining security involves regular updates and audits of the Kong infrastructure, including plugins and dependent services. Vulnerabilities should be promptly patched with the latest software updates. Adopting a DevSecOps model integrates security measures seamlessly into the deployment pipeline, making continuous integration and continuous delivery (CI/CD) an operational reality.

Implement effective logging and monitoring solutions to keep track of activities in the Kong environment. Use tools like Grafana to visualize metrics captured by Prometheus, facilitating proactive security analysis.

Consider exporting Kong metrics to Prometheus with the following configuration in the Prometheus scrape config:

```
scrape_configs:
  - job_name: 'kong-metrics'
    static_configs:
    - targets: ['localhost:8001']
```

This configuration snippet allows Prometheus to acquire metrics from Kong's Admin API, which can be visualized using Grafana dashboards to monitor your Kong environment in real-time.

Implementing Security Policies

Security policies serve as a framework for enforcing controls and procedures over API operations. Design comprehensive policies addressing data sensitivity, regulatory compliance mandates, and corporate governance frameworks.

A sound approach is incorporating security tools such as WAF (Web Application Firewall) to inspect and filter HTTP requests apart from Kong's native abilities. Further integration with SIEM (Security Information and Event Management) systems strengthens incident response actions, addressing unauthorized activities swiftly.

Utilizing a concerted strategy for securing your Kong deployment addresses API vulnerabilities, validates user authentication mechanisms, and protects both data and reputation. As threats continually evolve, maintaining an adaptive security strategy supported by ongoing education and awareness remains key to shielding against emerging attack vectors.

By incorporating these best practices into your workflow, you maximize your Kong deployment's security while ensuring robust operations with minimal disruptions.

10.3 Optimizing Performance and Scalability

In deploying Kong API Gateway in production environments, ensuring peak performance and scalability is essential to handle variable loads and facilitate seamless operations. This section delves into strategies for optimizing the performance and scalability of your Kong deployment, addressing both architectural considerations and specific configurations essential for efficient request processing and resource utilization.

Kong's inherent design supports extensibility and customization, allowing configuration adjustments that align with specific deployment requirements. Achieving performance optimization and scalability involves fine-tuning various elements such as proxy configurations, caching, and plugin usage while ensuring horizontal and vertical scaling capabilities are effectively utilized.

Performance Optimization Techniques

- **Request Handling Enhancements**: At the core of optimizing Kong performance is the efficient handling of API requests. Configuring NGINX buffer sizes and connection management settings can significantly impact request throughput and latency.

- Increase NGINX worker processes and connections, matching hardware capabilities and expected traffic, ensuring the server can process requests efficiently.

- Implement connection persistency with the 'keepalive' directive to reduce overhead associated with establishing new connections.

- **Efficient Use of Plugins**: Analyze plugin usage critically, as each plugin can introduce processing overhead. Limit usage to essential plugins and configure them to apply only to specific APIs where necessary.

- For instance, tailor authentication and logging plugins precisely by using plugin 'tags' to constrain their scope to critical services.

- **Caching Strategies**: Leverage upstream caching to minimize redundant data fetching from backend services. Adopt APIs that support cache headers, allowing Kong to handle multiple cache types seamlessly.

- Implement content caching in NGINX to store frequently accessed content at the edge, reducing request processing time.

```
proxy_cache_path /data/nginx/cache levels=1:2 keys_zone=my_cache:10m inactive
    =60m;
server {
    location / {
        proxy_pass http://backend;
        proxy_cache my_cache;
        proxy_cache_valid 200 302 10m;
        proxy_cache_use_stale error timeout updating http_500 http_502 http_503
            http_504;
    }
}
```

Here, the NGINX proxy cache is configured to cache successful responses for 10 minutes, aiding performance by reducing repeated backend requests.

- **API Gateway Resource Management**: Fine-tune gateway resources by accurately sizing the memory and CPU resources available to Kong nodes. Use monitoring tools to gather performance metrics, aiding in effective resource allocation decision-making.

Scalability Considerations

- **Horizontal Scaling**: Add additional Kong nodes to handle increased traffic loads, leveraging the platform's flexibility. Use a load balancer to split traffic evenly across the nodes, optimizing resource usage and maximizing throughput.

- Consider deploying Kong in a Kubernetes cluster. Kubernetes simplifies horizontal scaling through features like scaling policies and Service-level load balancing.

- **Vertical Scaling**: While less flexible than horizontal scaling, vertical scaling involves increasing the resources available to existing Kong nodes. This can be useful in handling short-term traffic spikes without the need for additional infrastructure.

- **Dynamic Load Balancing**: Utilize Kong's load balancing capabilities to efficiently distribute incoming requests across diverse backend services, preventing service disruptions or bottlenecks from overloading single points.

- Implement health checks to monitor service endpoints and automatically reroute traffic away from failing instances, preserving availability and service reliability.

```
_format_version: "2.1"
services:
- name: example-service
  host: myservice.internal
  port: 80
  protocol: http
  routes:
  - name: example-route
    paths:
    - /example
  plugins:
  - name: http-log
    config:
        http_endpoint: http://localhost:8181/log
- name: upstream-service
  host: my-upstream-service
  port: 8080

upstreams:
- name: my-upstream
  targets:
  - target: upstream-service:8080
  healthchecks:
    active:
      timeout: 1
      http_path: "/health"
      healthy:
        interval: 5
        successes: 2
      unhealthy:
        interval: 5
        http_failures: 3
```

This configuration enables active health checks, automatically tracking and maintaining the availability of upstream nodes.

- **Database Optimization**: The performance of Kong's data store is critical for operations. Optimize your PostgreSQL or Cassandra configurations for efficient data retrieval and storage.

- For PostgreSQL setups, adjust performance-related settings such as 'shared_buffers', 'work_mem', and 'max_connections' based on traffic patterns and hardware constraints.

- Adopt a replication strategy if using Cassandra to balance read and write operations across nodes, increasing fault-tolerance and throughput.

Monitoring and Continuous Improvement

Performance optimization and scalability are iterative processes that benefit from proactive monitoring and continuous feedback loops. Incorporate these strategies to maintain system excellence:

- **Monitoring Tools**: Utilize monitoring tools like Grafana and Prometheus for real-time insights into Kong's operation. Develop custom dashboards to visualize key performance metrics, identifying potential bottlenecks swiftly.

- **Automated Alerts**: Configure alerts for critical conditions such as high latency, failed health checks, or server overloads, facilitating rapid response to any performance degradation noted.

- **Regular Benchmarking**: Employ benchmarking tools like Apache JMeter to conduct systematic performance tests, calibrating system configurations in response to actual performance data rather than theoretical expectations.

```xml
<jmeterTestPlan version="1.2" properties="5.0" jmeter="5.3">
  <hashTree>
    <TestPlan guiclass="TestPlanGui" testclass="TestPlan" testname="Kong
        Performance Test">
      <boolProp name="TestPlan.functional_mode">false</boolProp>
      <stringProp name="TestPlan.comments"/>
      <boolProp name="TestPlan.tearDown_on_shutdown">true</boolProp>
      <boolProp name="TestPlan.serialize_threadgroups">false</boolProp>
    </TestPlan>
    <hashTree>
      <ThreadGroup guiclass="ThreadGroupGui" testclass="ThreadGroup" testname
          ="Thread Group">
        <stringProp name="ThreadGroup.on_sample_error">continue</stringProp>
        <elementProp name="ThreadGroup.main_controller" elementType="
            LoopController">
          <boolProp name="LoopController.continue_forever">false</boolProp>
          <stringProp name="LoopController.loops">10</stringProp>
        </elementProp>
```

```xml
      <stringProp name="ThreadGroup.num_threads">100</stringProp>
      <stringProp name="ThreadGroup.ramp_time">60</stringProp>
    </ThreadGroup>
    <hashTree>
      <HTTPSamplerProxy guiclass="HttpTestSampleGui" testclass="
          HTTPSamplerProxy" testname="HTTP Request">
        <boolProp name="HTTPSampler.postBodyRaw">true</boolProp>
        <elementProp name="HTTPsampler.Arguments" elementType="Arguments
            ">
          <collectionProp name="Arguments.arguments">
            <elementProp name="" elementType="HTTPArgument">
              <boolProp name="HTTPArgument.always_encode">false</boolProp>
              <stringProp name="Argument.value"/>
              <stringProp name="Argument.metadata">=</stringProp>
              <boolProp name="HTTPArgument.use_equals">true</boolProp>
            </elementProp>
          </collectionProp>
        </elementProp>
        <stringProp name="HTTPSampler.domain">localhost</stringProp>
        <stringProp name="HTTPSampler.port">8000</stringProp>
        <stringProp name="HTTPSampler.path">/api/v1/resource</stringProp>
        <stringProp name="HTTPSampler.method">GET</stringProp>
      </HTTPSamplerProxy>
    </hashTree>
  </hashTree>
  </hashTree>
</jmeterTestPlan>
```

This JMeter configuration allows load testing on a sample API to generate relevant performance insights.

By constantly refining practices and relying on detailed analysis of operational metrics, the handling of traffic can be both dynamically responsive and prepared for any substantial escalation in service demands.

Optimizing performance and achieving scalability are ongoing commitments that require dedicated resources and structured approaches tailored to unique deployment contexts. With effective execution, your Kong ecosystem will remain robust, agile, and capable of sustaining high volumes and demands, thereby driving strategic business value impeccably.

10.4   Kong Configuration Management

Effective configuration management in Kong is crucial for maintaining an organized, efficient, and scalable API gateway environment.

This section delves into best practices for managing and versioning Kong configurations, emphasizing automation tools, policy standardization, and workflow enhancements that facilitate smooth operations and adaptability to changing demands.

Managing configurations inherently involves setting up services, routes, plugins, and consumers in a manner that promotes consistency and decreases the likelihood of human errors. This is particularly important when teams are rapidly deploying numerous microservices, and configurations must be meticulously handled to avoid service disruptions.

Configuration as Code

Adopting the "Configuration as Code" (CaC) approach allows administrators to define Kong configurations using a declarative language stored in version control systems like Git. This method enables version tracking, rollbacks, and collaborative editing, which are essential features in modern DevOps environments.

Utilize Kong's Declarative Configuration format, YAML, to define configurations. The configuration can then be applied using kong config db_import or kong config db_export commands to maintain state and facilitate modifications.

```
_format_version: "2.1"
services:
- name: my_service
  url: http://my-api.internal
  routes:
  - name: my_service_route
    paths:
    - /v1/my-service
  plugins:
  - name: rate-limiting
    config:
      minute: 20
consumers:
- username: joe
  keyauth_credentials:
  - key: abc123
```

The exemplified YAML file outlines a service with an associated route, a rate-limiting plugin, and a consumer authenticated via API keys, demonstrating the pivotal elements of a well-structured configuration file.

Using Automation Tools

Incorporating Infrastructure as Code (IaC) tools like Terraform or Ansible can streamline managing Kong configurations reusable across different deployment stages, from development and testing to production releases.

Terraform Integration

Using Terraform grants not only repeatability but also enriches configuration with modularization capabilities, facilitating the reusability of defined infrastructure. Consider the following example using Terraform to declare a Kong configuration resource:

```
provider "kong" {
  kong_admin_uri = "http://localhost:8001"
}

resource "kong_service" "example_service" {
  name = "example-service"
  url = "http://mockbin.com"
}

resource "kong_route" "example_route" {
  service_id = kong_service.example_service.id
  protocols = ["http", "https"]
  methods = ["GET", "POST"]
  paths = ["/example"]
}

resource "kong_consumer" "example_consumer" {
  username = "john"
}

resource "kong_plugin" "rate_limiting" {
  name = "rate-limiting"
  service_id = kong_service.example_service.id
  config_json = jsonencode({
      minute = 100
  })
}
```

This script sets up a service, route, consumer, and rate-limiting plugin, encapsulated within a reusable Terraform module, thereby promoting configuration portability.

Employing Ansible Playbooks

Ansible playbooks can automate complex, multi-step processes required to bring a Kong deployment to the desired state. Below is a sample Ansible playbook tasked with configuring a Kong service and route:

```
---
- name: Configure Kong API Gateway
  hosts: localhost
  tasks:
    - name: Configure service
      kong_service:
        name: 'my_service'
        url: 'http://mockbin.com'

    - name: Configure route
      kong_route:
        service: 'my_service'
        hosts: ['example.com']
        paths: ['/v2']
        protocols: ['http', 'https']
```

The playbook facilitates provisioning services and routes through declarative task definitions, enhancing automation of deployment workflows.

Version Control and CI/CD Pipeline Integration

Managing configurations with a version control system like Git enables traceability of changes, facilitating teamwork and ensuring configurations are appropriately documented. Every configuration change or improvement should follow a formal review process before integration to the branch responsible for deployment, leveraging pull requests to verify code quality and accuracy.

Integrating configuration management within a CI/CD pipeline supports continuous deployment and testing of configuration changes. When configurations are modified, automated testing ensures correctness and validates the impact of any adjustments in isolated environments before transitioning to production.

Sample GitLab CI configuration for Kong configuration management:

```
stages:
  - test
  - deploy

test_configuration:
  stage: test
  script:
    - echo "Testing Kong configuration..."
    - kong config db_export config.yml

deploy_configuration:
  stage: deploy
```

```
script:
  - if [[ "$CI_COMMIT_BRANCH" == "main" ]]; then
      kong config db_import config.yml;
    fi
only:
  - main
```

This pipeline ensures that configuration is tested prior to deployment, and only merged code from the main branch can be imported, preserving environment state integrity.

Establishing Configuration Policies

Standardizing configurations through policies defines a predictable, scalable infrastructure, reducing complexity as Kong scales. These policies should enforce naming conventions, resource quotas, and service-level security settings.

- **Naming Conventions**: Establish clear and consistent naming conventions for services, routes, and plugins to increase clarity and cohesive communication within teams.

- **Resource Quotas and Limits**: Apply resource quotas to prevent configurations from inadvertently consuming more than allocated, ensuring equitable resource distribution among API consumers.

- **Security Policies**: Secure configurations should adhere strictly to established standards, such as ensuring transport security through TLS or enforcing authentication boundaries.

- **Documentation Standards**: All configurations must be accompanied by consistent documentation, detailing services, consumers, and dependencies, serving as a reference for future iterations and team onboarding.

Monitoring Configuration Changes

To actively manage configuration drift, implement continuous monitoring solutions that detect unauthorized changes. Automation tools such as Ansible Tower or HashiCorp Sentinel can enforce policies and validate configurations against defined states.

283

- **Automated Alerts**: Set up alerts for unauthorized modifications or drifts. Tools like Prometheus and Grafana can be configured to include Kong Admin API metrics, ensuring real-time visibility into operational states.

```
scrape_configs:
 - job_name: 'kong-config-monitor'
   static_configs:
   - targets: ['localhost:8001']
```

This configuration provides insights into changes made within the Kong deployment, ensuring timely awareness and response to shifts from intended configurations.

Effective configuration management in Kong hinges on a blend of code-driven strategies, automation tools, and robust policies that collectively ensure an agile and resilient API gateway. By leveraging best practices outlined herein, organizations can establish a repeatable, scalable framework that supports evolving business needs while minimizing misconfigurations and potential service disruptions.

10.5 Common Issues and Solutions

Deploying and maintaining the Kong API Gateway in production environments can present several challenges. In this section, we will explore common issues encountered during Kong deployment and operation, offering detailed solutions and preventive measures to ensure a stable and efficient API management ecosystem.

Addressing these issues involves recognizing patterns in error logs, performance bottlenecks, and misconfigurations. By systematically analyzing the root causes and implementing targeted solutions, administrators can maintain an optimal configuration that enhances Kong's robustness and reliability.

Issue 1: High Latency on API Requests

Cause: High latency in API requests can often be attributed to suboptimal resource configurations or overloaded upstream services that delay response times. Additionally, misconfigured rate limiting or request processing plugins may contribute to delays.

Solution:

- **Optimize Resource Allocation**: Verify that the worker_processes and worker_connections in your NGINX configuration match the server's capacity and expected load.

```
worker_processes auto;
events {
    worker_connections 1024;
}
```

- **Review Plugin Configuration**: Ensure that plugins, especially those involving authentication or rate limiting, are applied only where necessary and are properly configured to balance performance with security.

```
_format_version: "2.1"
routes:
- name: restricted-route
  paths:
  - /vip
  plugins:
  - name: rate-limiting
    config:
      second: 5
```

- **Monitoring and Scaling**: Implement monitoring solutions like Prometheus paired with Grafana dashboards to visualize latency trends. Where physical resources fall short, consider horizontal scaling by adding additional nodes.

Issue 2: Error 502 Bad Gateway

Cause: A 502 Bad Gateway error typically arises due to communication failures between Kong and the configured upstream services. Such breakdowns could result from incorrect DNS settings, upstream service outages, or network partitioning.

Solution:

- **Verify Upstream Service Status**: Ensure all upstream services are responsive and properly configured within Kong. Use tools like curl or Postman to check upstream endpoints directly.

```
curl -I http://upstream-service.domain/status
```

- **Check DNS Resolution**: Validate DNS entries for upstream hosts and ensure they resolve correctly within the network settings configured with Kong.

- **Audit Kong Configuration**: Inspect service and route definitions in Kong for typos or misconfigurations which might redirect requests incorrectly.

```
_format_version: "2.1"
services:
- name: correct-service
  url: http://upstream-service
```

Issue 3: Plugin Execution Failures

Cause: Plugin execution failures are typically due to incorrect configurations, conflict with other plugins, or missing dependencies the plugin relies upon for execution.

Solution:

- **Validate Plugin Configuration**: Begin by reviewing the specific plugin's configuration through the Admin API endpoints to identify any discrepancies.

```
curl -X GET http://localhost:8001/plugins/<plugin-id>
```

- **Ensure Plugin Compatibility**: Confirm the plugin version is compatible with your version of Kong, as API changes in newer releases might necessitate different configurations.

- **Check for Conflicting Plugins**: Identify and resolve any conflicts between active plugins, ensuring they do not interfere with each other's operations.

Issue 4: Security Vault Misconfigurations

Cause: Configuration missteps in security vault integrations within Kong may lead to credential retrieval failures or access control inconsistencies.

Solution:

286

- **Verify Vault Connection Parameters**: Ensure correct connectivity parameters, such as URL, authentication tokens, and namespaces, are configured within Kong.

```
_format_version: "2.1"
vaults:
- name: my-vault
  config:
    url: "http://vault-server.domain"
    token: "s.xxxxxxx"
```

- **Audit Access Policies**: Examine policies in Kong and the associated Vault to confirm that credential access permissions align and do not restrict necessary operations.

- **Test Secret Retrieval**: Test secret retrieval directly using vault CLI tools or HTTP requests, ensuring secrets used by Kong components are both available and correctly stored.

Issue 5: Configuration Drift

Cause: Over time, unmanaged changes in configurations lead to drift, where the actual state deviates from recorded configurations, reducing predictability and increasing errors.

Solution:

- **Implement GitOps Practices**: Enforce "Configuration as Code" practices, storing all configurations in version control and reconciling current states against desired states defined within repositories.

- **Utilize Infrastructure as Code Tools**: Integrate tools like Terraform for declarative configuration management, applied across diversified environments.

- **Automate Compliance Checks**: Regularly automate checks using configuration management tools to ensure alignment with predefined configurations.

```
resource "kong_route" "consistent_route" {
  service_id = kong_service.some_service.id
  paths = ["/consistent"]
}
```

Issue 6: Debugging and Monitoring Challenges

Cause: Effective diagnosis of issues can be hindered by inadequate logging or inefficient monitoring setups. These limitations obscure visibility into operations, making it challenging to identify root causes.

Solution:

- **Enhance Logging**: Activate comprehensive logging at both the Kong and NGINX levels, capturing detailed request and error logs. For brevity, ensure logs are structured and stored where they can be easily accessed and analyzed.

```
http {
    log_format main '$remote_addr - $remote_user [$time_local] "$request" '

                    '$status $body_bytes_sent "$http_referer" '
                    '"$http_user_agent" "$http_x_forwarded_for"';
    access_log /var/log/nginx/access.log main;
}
```

- **Deploy APM Tools**: Utilize Application Performance Monitoring (APM) tools offering deep insights into performance metrics and API behavior. Integrate tools compatible with Prometheus or ELK for a comprehensive monitoring stack.

- **Construct Dashboards**: Build Grafana dashboards featuring real-time metrics and triggers for alert conditions, empowering teams to remain proactive in resolving issues before impacting service availability.

In providing personnel with detailed resolutions and preventative measures for these issues, your Kong deployment will be better situated to operate smoothly, responding adeptly to the dynamic demands modern API-based environments present. These practices not only simplify resolving recurring errors but further champion a standard of excellence in operational management for Kong infrastructures.

10.6   Debugging Tools and Techniques

In managing a Kong API Gateway, efficiently diagnosing and resolving issues is critical to maintaining high availability and performance standards. Debugging is an indispensable skill that allows developers and administrators to explore and fix errors in real-time operations of their Kong deployments. This section highlights various tools and techniques that can enhance your debugging capabilities when dealing with Kong, providing you with insights necessary to troubleshoot effectively.

A systematic approach to debugging involves identifying symptoms, isolating the root cause, testing hypotheses, and implementing solutions. The application of appropriate tools during each of these steps can streamline the resolution process significantly. We will examine both built-in and third-party tools that complement Kong's architecture and aid in thorough diagnosis and rectification of issues.

Utilizing Kong's Built-in Debugging Features

1. Kong Admin API:

Kong's Admin API is a powerful tool for inspecting configurations and gathering metrics essential for debugging. It provides endpoints that allow you to access detailed information about services, routes, and database entities. Using simple HTTP requests, you can interactively query the state of the gateway.

Example: Listing all services configured in Kong.

```
curl -X GET http://localhost:8001/services
```

This command returns a JSON object containing metadata for all services, allowing you to verify configurations or detect missing services.

2. Debug Mode:

Kong can be started in debug mode by setting the KONG_LOG_-LEVEL to debug. This will increase verbosity, providing detailed logs about program execution, HTTP transactions, and plugin operations. This is invaluable for identifying unexpected behaviors during plugin execution or request handling.

Example: Starting Kong in debug mode for increased logging.

```
export KONG_LOG_LEVEL=debug
kong start
```

Leveraging External Debugging Tools

289

1. Log Analysis with ELK Stack:

The Elastic Stack (ELK) comprises Elasticsearch, Logstash, and Kibana and is ideal for managing and analyzing large volumes of log data. By shipping Kong logs to ELK, you can visualize traffic patterns, identify anomalies, and diagnose issues through comprehensive searches and structured analysis.

Example: Configuring Logstash to receive Kong logs.

```
input {
  file {
    path => "/var/log/kong/access.log"
    start_position => "beginning"
  }
}
output {
  elasticsearch {
    hosts => ["localhost:9200"]
  }
}
```

By centralizing logs in Elasticsearch, the processed data can be visualized with Kibana dashboards, enabling efficient pinpointing of error occurrences and patterns.

2. Network Analysis with Wireshark:

Wireshark is an open-source network protocol analyzer used to capture and interactively browse traffic running on a computer network. When experiencing unexpected latency or request failures, Wireshark can be particularly useful to analyze the details of HTTP requests and responses over the network interfaces used by Kong.

Example: Capturing network packets on the default HTTP port.

```
tshark -i eth0 -Y "http" -w captured_http_traffic.pcap
```

Analyzing the captured packet data helps identify anomalies, misrouted requests, or potential SSL handshake issues that could impair API responsiveness.

3. Scripted Connectivity Tests with cURL and Postman:

Basic connectivity issues can thwart communication between Kong and upstream services. Tools such as cURL and Postman can be used to manually test routes, ensuring correct connectivity, header transaction, and payload processing.

Example: Using cURL to mimic a client request through Kong to an upstream service.

```
curl -X GET http://localhost:8000/service-api/v1/resource
```

Performance Monitoring and Profiling

1. Prometheus and Grafana:

Prometheus is a metric-based alerting and monitoring toolkit. It captures real-time analytics about operational states and can be employed to identify latency, request throughput, and error rates.

Grafana serves as the visualization tool, offering aesthetically informative dashboards.

Example: Prometheus scrape configuration for Kong metrics.

```
scrape_configs:
 - job_name: 'kong'
   metrics_path: /metrics
   static_configs:
     - targets: ['localhost:8001']
```

Visualizing the data in Grafana can highlight areas requiring attention such as rising error counts or performance bottlenecks.

2. API Performance Testing with Apache JMeter:

JMeter supports load testing and provides a means to execute stress tests on Kong, simulating traffic peaks and evaluating scalability under pressure. Understanding the limits and identifying potential points of failure can guide tuning and scaling efforts.

Example: Configuring JMeter to perform performance testing on a Kong route.

```
<jmeterTestPlan version="1.2" properties="5.0" jmeter="5.3">
  <hashTree>
   <TestPlan>
    ...
   </TestPlan>
   <hashTree>
    <ThreadGroup>
      <stringProp name="ThreadGroup.num_threads">200</stringProp>
      <stringProp name="ThreadGroup.ramp_time">60</stringProp>
    </ThreadGroup>
    <hashTree>
     <HTTPSamplerProxy>
       <stringProp name="HTTPSampler.domain">localhost</stringProp>
       <stringProp name="HTTPSampler.port">8000</stringProp>
```

```
    <stringProp name="HTTPSampler.path">/stress-test/service</stringProp>
    </HTTPSamplerProxy>
  </hashTree>
  </hashTree>
 </hashTree>
</jmeterTestPlan>
```

Executing this plan evaluates how well the gateway handles high traffic volumes and assesses response times throughout stressful conditions.

Ensuring a Successful Debugging Process

To achieve efficient and effective debugging, consider adopting a well-structured plan:

- **Thoroughly Define the Problem**: Start by precisely articulating the symptoms and error messages. Review relevant logs and metrics beforehand to understand the extent and nature of the problem.

- **Isolate Components**: Isolate components to deduce if the problem resides within Kong, the upstream services, or the client-side.

- **Iterate and Test Assumptions**: Formulate hypotheses based on gathered information, implement changes one at a time, and validate their impact through repeated testing.

- **Document Findings**: Accurately document any discovery processes and solutions, fostering a repository of knowledge for future reference.

- **Prevent Recurrence**: Integrate solutions and create checks in the deployment pipeline to prevent similar issues from resurfacing.

Through robust debugging techniques and the proficient use of suitable tools, managing and resolving problems in Kong deployments becomes a more controlled and predictable process. This facilitates operational consistency and reliability essential to managing API gateways efficiently in dynamic environments.

10.7 Community and Support Resources

Engaging with community and support resources is invaluable for maximizing the benefits of using Kong API Gateway, both from a technical and practical perspective. This section explores the extensive array of community-driven platforms, official resources, and professional networks dedicated to supporting Kong users. By leveraging these resources, users can enhance their problem-solving capabilities, stay informed about evolving features, and gain access to expert knowledge.

Official Documentation and Tutorials

The foundation of any operational strategy with Kong is understanding the platform thoroughly. The official documentation provided by Kong is a robust resource that covers all aspects of usage and offers detailed guides on API gateway management.

- **Kong Documentation Website:**

  - The documentation found at https://docs.konghq.com provides comprehensive resources on getting started with Kong, utilizing its plugins, and deploying complex architectures.

  - It is structured into sections including installation guides, usage policies, plugin configurations, and system architecture best practices.

- **Kong Tutorials:**

  - Beyond standard documentation, Kong offers tutorials and how-to guides focused on implementing specific features or solving common use cases. Available on the Kong website and the Kong Nation community, these tutorials serve as hands-on resources for practical learning.

Example: Setting up a simple authentication plugin using a tutorial.

```
curl -i -X POST http://localhost:8001/services/my-service/plugins \
  --data "name=basic-auth" \
  --data "config.hide_credentials=true"
```

Online Community Forums and Platforms

Engaging with online communities enables users to connect with other Kong practitioners, sharing insights and troubleshooting advice. Several forums and platforms act as gathering spots for discussion and collaboration.

- **Kong Nation:**

  - Kong Nation is an official community forum that connects developers, engineers, and business users of Kong around the world.

  - This forum supports discussions related to API gateway operations, plugin development, and performance tuning. Users can ask questions, provide answers, and engage in web-based events.

- **Reddit and Stack Overflow:**

  - The Reddit channel r/Kong is an informal venue for users to share their experiences with the API Gateway, offer advice, or share recent developments in the Kong ecosystem.

  - Stack Overflow, with its large developer community, includes questions tagged with 'kong' for technical problem-solving, code examples, and scripts.

Social Media Connectivity and YouTube Channels

Social media further enhances connectivity by offering real-time announcements, best practice sharing, and community highlights.

- **Twitter and LinkedIn:**

  - Follow Kong Inc (@thekonginc) on Twitter for official updates, releases, and event announcements. LinkedIn groups related to Kong provide networking and professional interaction spaces.

- **YouTube:**

- Kong's YouTube channel features webinars, training sessions, and recorded talks from conferences. Content here extends from general introductions to specific technical deep dives.

Enterprise Support and Professional Services

For enterprises seeking assured performance guarantees and response times, engaging directly with Kong through enterprise support services offers significant advantages.

- **Enterprise Subscriptions:**

  - Enterprise subscriptions with Kong include advanced features not available in the community edition, along with formal support channels, professional consultations, and SLA-backed support.

- **Professional Services:**

  - Expert-led training sessions, on-site implementations, and managed services provide organizations with access to top-tier knowledge and direct assistance in configuring or optimizing deployments.

Kong Summit and Conferences

Attending conferences and summits not only provides educational insights but also opportunities for networking and collaboration with industry professionals.

- **Kong Summit:**

  - An annual event where Kong users and contributors gather to learn, share, and collaborate on advancements in API management. Participants can attend workshops, panels, and innovation showcases organized by Kong experts.

- **Tech Conferences:**

  - Speaking engagements, workshops, and participation in broader technology gatherings provide not only

Kong-specific insights but also enrich knowledge sharing across related domains like cloud-native technologies and microservices architecture.

Contribution to the Open-Source Community

The Kong project invites contributions from developers to enhance its codebase, provide plugin extensions, or document improvements, driving a collaborative evolution of the platform.

- **Kontributors:**

    - Developers are encouraged to contribute code, report bugs, and merge pull requests, aiding the open-source development cycle. Standards for contributions are documented on Kong's GitHub repos.

- **Writing Plugins:**

    - Develop and contribute custom plugins tailored to specific organizational needs. Through Lua or other languages supported by Kong, developers can build plugins handling security, analytics, or authentication.

Best Practices in Engaging with the Community

1. **Proactive Participation**:

    - Actively participating in forums and discussions enriches understanding and offers diversified viewpoints. Collaborative problem-solving raises one's knowledge ceiling substantially.

2. **Continuous Learning**:

    - Regularly updating skills and knowledge helps keep pace with technological advancements. Use available resources continuously to explore, experiment, and innovate.

3. **Networking and Collaboration**:

- Building a network in the community assists in accessing diverse expertise. Networking cultivates shared learning experiences and supports career development.

Success Story: Implementing a Kong Platform Upgrade

Let's illustrate how utilizing community resources can assist with a Kong platform upgrade. A mid-sized organization planning to upgrade from an earlier version of Kong intended to integrate new features, such as service mesh capabilities.

- By accessing Kong Nation, they gathered preliminary assessments and potential impacts shared by other organizations who underwent a similar upgrade.

- Through engaging with professional services, the organization partook in an architected design session to align their needs with best practices.

- Training materials and videos from Kong's repository and YouTube channel expanded team knowledge, facilitating smoother transitional workflows.

- Attending a Kong Summit post-upgrade allowed them to cross-reference their approaches, validating assumptions and gaining constructive insights from industry peers.

By engaging thoroughly with Kong's community and support resources, organizations and individuals alike can navigate the complexities of API gateway management with confidence and competence, leading to strategic benefits and enhanced technical prowess.

www.ingramcontent.com/pod-product-compliance
Lightning Source LLC
La Vergne TN
LVHW051434050326
832903LV00030BD/3083